PRAISE FOR *PANCAKES IN PARIS*

"The author demonstrates that no idea is too crazy if one has the determination to pursue it to its fruition. A light, entertaining story of how a man turned his pipe dream into a profitable, highly respected business."

—*Kirkus Reviews*

"Craig's book is as cheerful as his diners and as satisfying as his pancake breakfasts."
—Stephen Clarke, author of *A Year in the Merde* and *Paris Revealed*

"A hearty and delicious serving of adventures about starting the first American breakfast joint in Paris."
—Jennifer Coburn, author of *We'll Always Have Paris*

"Anyone who fantasizes about selling everything and moving to France should read this refreshingly honest memoir about what it really takes to operate a successful business in Paris. The real takeaway is how Craig's love for his adopted city and its people is stronger than ever despite—or perhaps because of—the Kafkaesque ordeal he went through to make his dreams come true here."
—Heather Stimmler-Hall, editor of *Secrets of Paris* newsletter

"I loved reading this book. Craig Carlson tells his story with an openness and ironic sense of humor. *Pancakes in Paris* is a great success story and will inspire readers to never stop trying to achieve their goals."
—Roger S. Christiansen, Director of *Friends* and *Hannah Montana*

"*Pancakes in Paris* is a tall stack of only-in-Paris adventure, told with a delicious blend of sweet wit and salty charm."
—Amy Thomas, author of *Paris, My Sweet*

Happy Birthday
Susan -
2020 - the
year that nothing
happened!

Love,
Barb C

LIVING THE AMERICAN DREAM IN FRANCE

PANCAKES
IN
Paris

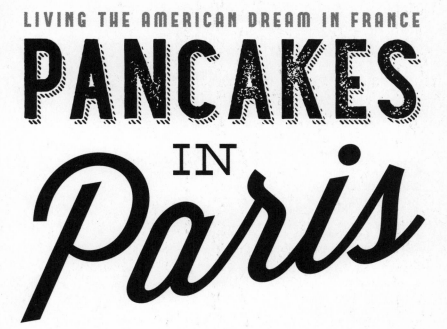

CRAIG CARLSON
OWNER OF THE BREAKFAST IN AMERICA RESTAURANT CHAIN

 sourcebooks

Published by Sourcebooks, Inc.
P.O. Box 4410, Naperville, Illinois 60567-4410
(630) 961-3900
Fax: (630) 961-2168
www.sourcebooks.com

Library of Congress Cataloging-in-Publication Data

Names: Carlson, Craig, author.
Title: Pancakes in Paris : living the American dream in France / Craig
    Carlson, owner of the Breakfast in America restaurant chain.
Description: Naperville, Illinois : Sourcebooks, [2016]
Identifiers: LCCN 2016008292 | (pbk. : alk. paper)
Subjects: LCSH: Carlson, Craig. | Restaurateurs--United States--Biography. |
    Breakfast in America (Restaurant chain) | Diners
    (Restaurants)--France--Paris.
Classification: LCC TX910.5.C296 A3 2016 | DDC 647.95092 [B]--dc23 LC record
available at https://lccn.loc.gov/2016008292

Printed and bound in the United States of America.
VP 10 9 8 7 6 5 4 3 2 1

In loving memory of my grandma Lizzy
and her delicious scrambled eggs.

Breakfast in America, Paris.

"I don't think I knew happiness until I
opened the Breakfast in America menu."

—Stephanie, a homesick American customer

MENU

Dessert
Love Among the Milkshakes

Digestif
La Grande Disillusion

Notre Dame as viewed from the pont de la Tournelle.

PROLOGUE

I HAVE THE BEST COMMUTE IN THE WORLD. MY SCENIC WALK TO WORK begins on the Left Bank of Paris, where the original Breakfast in America (BIA) restaurant is located, and continues on to the Right Bank—home of the second BIA. Along the way, I get to cross the lovely Seine not once, but twice, thanks to one of my favorite places in Paris, an island located smack in the middle of my route—Île Saint-Louis. With its narrow streets full of quaint shops and restaurants, this tiny island paradise always makes me feel as if I've been transported back in time—from the hustle and bustle of a modern city to a sleepy, medieval village somewhere in the French countryside.

But by far the best part of my commute is the view of the Notre Dame Cathedral from the first bridge I cross, the pont de la Tournelle. In my humble opinion, Notre Dame looks best from this angle. With its majestic spire reaching toward the heavens—in sharp contrast with its flying buttresses keeping the heavy stone walls from collapsing to the ground—Notre Dame always reminds me of that mysterious interplay between heaven and earth, between the seen and the unseen.

No matter how much of a hurry I'm in or how bad my day has been, I always take a moment to stop and gaze at this architectural wonder. There's something about staring at a structure from the twelfth century—still standing strong—that puts things into perspective.

I'm reminded, once again, of what it is that I've always loved about Paris. And what brought me here in the first place...

How many people have imagined running off to the City of Light, opening their own café, and starting a whole new life in the most beautiful city in the world? Well, I actually did it. Me, a former Hollywood screenwriter who used to read scripts where the main character dreamed of doing what I did—no small feat considering that I had never owned a business before, let alone a restaurant, with their notoriously high failure rates.

And if that weren't crazy enough, I decided to open my restaurant in a foreign country with a foreign language *and* in a city that just happens to be the culinary capital of the world—Paris. But my restaurant wasn't just any restaurant; it was an American diner, the first of its kind in the city. Yet despite all the odds against me, my little dive, my greasy spoon, became a great success, with lines of customers stretching down the block.

Before I knew it, my diner, Breakfast in America, started appearing all over the national and international press, including CNN, the *New York Times*, BBC, French television, and more. Here's just a sample of what they were saying about us. NBC's *Today Show* raved on its website, "Breakfast in America is *the* American place in France." Frommer's called us "Paris's most famous American diner."

T: *The New York Times Style Magazine* said, "The early trendsetter was Connecticut-bred Craig Carlson." (Imagine that—*me*, a trendsetter!) And last but not least, *Let's Go Paris* proclaimed, "It doesn't get more American than this."

No, it doesn't. And neither does my story. After all I've been through, I could practically be the poster child for the American Dream—except for one *petit* detail:

In order to live the American Dream, I had to move to France.

Whenever people hear about Breakfast in America for the first time, they always ask me the same questions: How did you come up with the idea? Had you ever owned a restaurant before? Do you speak French? Is doing business in France complicated? Are most of your customers French or American?

On the political side of things, a lot of people want to know if I've experienced any anti-Americanism. Or if I'm a socialist. My favorite questions come from those who harbor dreams of moving to France and opening an establishment of their own. Questions like: Is it hard to find the right ingredients? What's the most popular item on the menu? Do you have to adapt your food for French tastes? Do you miss the States? And the biggie: Are you going to live in France *forever?*

The more I pondered these questions, the more I realized that I'd never answered the biggest questions of all: my own. How did I get here? What were the chances? One in a million? A billion? In fact, the more I put the pieces of my crazy life together, the more I realize how far I've come—and how much I've had to *overcome*—to be who I am today: a successful restaurateur in France.

"Remember, Craig," my first investor, Todd, once said to me

when he saw me with dark circles under my eyes, picking French fries off the diner floor like a zombie, "you're living your dream. Tell yourself that whenever you feel like you can't go on: 'I'm living my dream... I'm living my dream.'"

Over the course of my unconventional restaurant career, there would be many occasions for me to repeat that mantra, especially on that fateful day when, overwhelmed by the stress of doing business in France, I collapsed, unconscious, while jogging along the lovely *quais* of the Seine.

I was living my dream, all right. And it almost killed me.

Apéritif

The Road to the Crazy Dream

Me at age four and a half. Now used on a promotional label for BIA.

Chapter 1

THE FRENCH CONNECTION: HOW I ENDED UP IN FRANCE

"Every man [should have] two countries: his own and France."

—Thomas Jefferson, paraphrasing
Henri de Bornier's *La Fille de Roland*

IF YOU HAD MET ME AS A KID AND SEEN WHERE I CAME FROM, YOU would have never in a million years imagined that one day I would end up living in France. I hardly could have imagined it myself. First of all, nothing about me is French. *Rien, nada,* zilch. I grew up in upstate Connecticut in a poor immigrant family, one side Polish, the other side Finnish. My three older siblings and I were bounced back and forth between grandparents more than a dozen times before I was nine years old.

The reason? Neither of my parents, who had been divorced for as long as I could remember, were capable of being…well, parents.

My father wouldn't let a little thing like parental responsibility get in the way of his drinking and gambling. And my bipolar mom had trouble staying in one place; every few months or so, she would be hauled off to a mental hospital by burly male orderlies. Each time it happened, no one bothered to explain to me why my mom kept leaving like that, but eventually I figured it out: it was *my* fault whenever I became "too demanding"—meaning, whenever I craved love or attention—my mom would suddenly disappear to a place called Norwich, a town two hours south of us, that had the biggest asylum in the state.

Because my grandma Mary didn't drive, our kindly but kooky neighbor, Mrs. Martin, would sometimes take us kids down to Norwich to visit my mom. Racing down Highway 91 in her massive green '68 Chevy Impala, Mrs. Martin, a Jehovah's Witness, would tell us fantastical stories about how God and Satan were at war—but not to worry. "One day, God will win," she'd say, "and the earth will be a paradise again, just like Eden, where we'll all be able to pet snakes and spiders—and they won't even bite!"

Eew, I'd think. *Some paradise. Can I just have my mom back?*

When my mom finally *did* come back, the family was so tired of taking care of us kids they decided it was *our* turn to be sent away. Again, with no explanation, we were dropped off for an entire year at a children's home—or the more sexy Dickensian term, an orphanage. I tried to run away with my older brother, Eddie, but my little legs weren't quick enough. Eddie did escape, but he got hungry fast and was back at the orphanage in time for his gruel.

Despite all evidence to the contrary, I always felt loved as a kid—just never *wanted*. My grandma Lizzy, on the Finnish side of the family, was particularly loving—as long as you didn't ask for anything or overstay your welcome. I was especially fond of her delicious scrambled eggs, the taste of which I've never been able to duplicate, not even at Breakfast in America.

As for my Polish grandma Mary, her favorite breakfast was fish sticks and prune juice—there's a reason why my diner is *not* called Breakfast in Poland.

Oh, and here's another reason:

Grandma Mary's Recipe for
Old World Chicken à la Polonaise

1 chicken (any size you can get your grubby hands on)

Salt (if available)

Boil water. Add chicken. Salt.

Serves a Polish family of 12.

Having emigrated from the United States to France, I often think about my grandma Lizzy, who was a first-generation American herself. She loved telling me stories about how her parents had left Finland with nothing more than big dreams of a better life. In fact, the main thing on their minds was how they were going to spend the fortune that awaited them in the New World.

"Everyone in Finland used to say that the sidewalks in America were covered with silver dollars!" my grandma Lizzy loved telling me. "All you had to do was bend over and scoop up as many as you wanted!"

I wish my grandma Lizzy were still alive today. I would give anything to hear her wonderful stories again. And just think of all the stories I could tell *her*. Stories about how there's another place where dreams come true, a faraway place, across the sea, in the Old World. A magical place with castles and health care...cafés and free college...demonstrations and endless vacations. Where the sidewalks are covered with silver euros, yours for the taking. All you have to do is bend over and scoop them up—assuming you can find them buried deep beneath a pile of dog shit.

Of course, France wasn't even on my radar back when I was a kid growing up in small-town Connecticut, and it certainly wasn't a potential travel destination. But thanks to a twist of fate (or two), all that was about to change.

My first French memory took place in a swirl of suffocating cigarette smoke. It was Sunday morning, and my dad had just picked up my sisters and me from my grandma Mary's place. Forced to spend quality time with his kids, my dad dragged us along with him to his favorite pub, the Rustic Bar & Grill. Divorced and digging his new lifestyle as a swinging bachelor, "Fast Eddie" (as the ladies called him) had just painted his rusty, old station wagon a vibrant Van Gogh blue with a bright yellow racing stripe running down the side.

As we drove through town in Fast Eddie's slick, two-toned chick-mobile, my older twin sisters, Colleen and Cathy, slouched in the backseat, hoping none of their friends would see them. Like most teenage girls at the time, they wore their long, blond hair parted in the middle *à la* Ali MacGraw in *Love Story,* their faces locked into adolescent sneers. I sat in the front seat and could barely breathe as my dad chain-smoked his way through another pack of More cigarettes.

Up ahead, my dad spotted two of my sisters' friends walking along the sidewalk. He glanced in the rearview mirror. Seeing how embarrassed my sisters were only brought out the devil in Fast Eddie.

He slowed the station wagon down, pulling up beside my sisters' friends. Then with a big, shit-eating grin, he started waving and honking his horn. My sisters sank down even lower in their seats, shooting death glares at my dad.

That's when I heard *le français* for the very first time.

Not wanting anyone to understand what they were saying, my sisters turned to each other and began conversing in their newly acquired, seventh-grade pidgin French.

"*La famille est...*" Colleen struggled for just the right French word. Then it hit her: "*Stupide!*" (pronounced *stoo-peed*).

Cathy nodded enthusiastically. "*Ah, oui! Très stupide!*"

"*Oui, oui! Beaucoup stupide!*"

"*Oui, oui! Très beaucoup stupide!*"

"*Oui, oui, oui! Stupide, stupide, stupide!*"

As if watching a tennis match, my eyes followed my sisters back and forth. With each "*oui*" and "*stoo-peed*," I nodded in wholehearted agreement. Not to brag or anything, but at barely seven years old, I could totally understand what they were saying. And I hadn't even taken a single French lesson yet. I guess you could say I had a gift for languages right from the start.

Fast Eddie, on the other hand, had no clue. "Whatever you dingbats are babbling on about," he said, "enough already!"

The girls snickered. "*Oh là là! Papa pas content!*"

Non, Papa was not content at all. In fact, he was furious because he wanted my sisters to take Spanish, so they could tell him what the Puerto Rican neighbors were saying about him.

As the cacophony of "*ouis*" drifted into the air and joined in a dance with the swirling cigarette smoke, my dad turned to me and said with a stern look, "Don't you *ever* take that useless language, *comprende?*"

After such an inauspicious start with the French language, it certainly looked like France just wasn't going to be in my stars. But then, for some reason, events in my life began pushing me toward France again and again, as if I always belonged there—as if there were something more at work than mere coincidence. Whether one believes in destiny or not, my life certainly makes a strong argument for it.

Case in point, by the time I was nine, one by one, my restless family members got out of town—and as fast as possible. The first to leave were my sisters, who quit high school and joined the Air Force. My brother followed suit. The last to go was my mom, who eloped to Florida with her boyfriend, the charmless Monsieur Ducharme (a second-generation French Canadian). Still too young to run away, I suddenly found myself living alone with my dad in the bad part of town—the curiously named Frenchtown.

Seriously. The most formative years of my life occurred in a place called Frenchtown. Adding to the irony, not a single French person lived in Frenchtown, and no one there could tell me where the name had even come from.

Located in the shadows of a massive, abandoned carpet factory, the once-elegant neighborhood had slowly transformed into a crumbling wasteland, teeming with poverty and crime. Although it was no Harlem or East LA, Frenchtown *was* a tough neighborhood. Of course, one doesn't usually associate the word "French" with the word "tough," but Frenchtown had it all, including its very own gang. By the time I moved there, stories about badass rumbles with its crosstown rival, the Green Valley gang, had become legendary.

I tried to imagine what the rumbles between these two wimpy-sounding gangs must've been like. In my mind, I see the Frenchtown gang, staring at their enemies with Gallic contempt, threatening to mime them to death; on the other side, the Green Valley gang, getting ready to pelt the Frenchtown gang with cans of peas.

Most of the kids I knew back then ended up becoming druggies, high school dropouts, or deadbeat dads by the age of sixteen. But I didn't go down that route. Why?

One reason most certainly had to do with my dad, Fast Eddie. Living with him forced me to develop strong survival and entrepreneurial skills, all of which helped set the stage for my future business endeavors. I don't think I've ever met anyone cheaper than my dad, but the way he taught me to marry ketchup in order to get every last drop out of the bottle definitely came in handy later on.

I also learned a strong work ethic living with Fast Eddie. But not from him, because he had none. Instead, I had to develop one on my own, quickly learning that if I wanted anything at all—including little things like food or clothing—I would have to buy it myself. Hence, at the age of twelve, I landed my very first job as a paperboy. But not satisfied with just one paper route, I had two—one in the morning and one in the afternoon. I also earned money shoveling snow in the winter and selling cans of cola in the summer—to people stuck in their cars during the long gas lines of the seventies. RC Cola, to be exact, because it had a better profit margin.

When my dad saw that I was making some money, he told me it was time for me to start paying him room and board, just like he'd done during the Depression (a lie, as I later found out). And if that weren't character-building enough, Fast Eddie also made me work for free on *his* paper route; he was the guy who dropped off the newspapers for us paperboys to deliver, one of the many odd jobs he held throughout his lifetime.

Ah oui, life rolled merrily along like this, and it may have stayed like that forever—if it weren't for a pair of pimple-faced twelve-year-olds who hated my guts.

"What's it going to be, Craig?" my teacher Miss Jessup asked, starting to lose her patience.

As was often the case back then, my mind had drifted off to some faraway place. I was no longer in my sixth-grade classroom, surrounded by kids with better clothes than me—and even better social skills. I was, instead, lost in the world of my favorite book, *My Side of the Mountain*, which was about a boy who runs away from home and lives in a hollowed-out tree in the woods, along with his best friend, a pet falcon.

Miss Jessup cleared her throat. "*Uh-hum.*"

I looked up from my book to see Miss Jessup standing there holding a clipboard. "Craig, have you even heard a single word I've said?"

"Yes," I replied, not having heard a single word she'd said.

It turned out Miss Jessup had been going around the room asking each student which foreign language they wanted to take for their seventh-grade language requirement.

"So what's it going to be, Craig?" she repeated. "French or Spanish?"

Here it was. My life had come to its first major fork in the road. I would no longer be just a pinball, bounced about by forces beyond my control. This time, I would actually play an active role in my own destiny. Or so I thought.

As I considered which language to take, my mind flashed back to the smoky episode with my twin sisters in my dad's station wagon all those years ago, and in particular, to Fast Eddie's disdain for the French language.

"Spanish!" I said, as if I were a game-show contestant about to win a fabulous new prize.

"Okeydokey," Miss Jessup said, marking it on her clipboard.

Two of the most popular kids in class, Ann and Dan, who'd been dating since, like, the fifth grade, looked at me with disgust. "Oh, nooo!" they whined. "Don't take Spanish! *We're* taking Spanish!"

Ouch. I looked at Ann and Dan with Gallic contempt, then turned to Miss Jessup and said, "Okay. French then."

"Okeydokey." Miss Jessup turned her pencil upside down, erased the word *Spanish*, and replaced it with that other glorious word.

From that moment on, *mon destin* was set in motion.

I loved the French language right from the start, especially the way it made me think completely differently from how my family thought. It was as if a switch had been turned on inside my head, lighting up a whole new realm of possibilities. From that point on, my whole world changed.

I practiced my new language every day. On my paper route, I would count—*en français*—the number of times I pedaled my bike or how many steps it took me to get to the stoops of my customers' apartments to lay the paper down. I even had imaginary conversations with people on the street.

"Garçon, combien pour le journal?" ("Young man, how much for the newspaper?")

"Quinze centimes, monsieur!" ("Fifteen cents, sir!")

There was one downside, however. Except for my imaginary friends, there was no one in Frenchtown I could speak French with. This concerned me because I had heard that language classes were notorious for not preparing you for the real spoken language once you're in the actual country. When I asked my French teacher if this rumor was true, she replied, "What are you talking about? Why would I ever wanna go to France?"

Fortunately for me, I didn't have that problem. Thanks to my new language, I was starting to develop a strong case of wanderlust, with dreams of getting out of my small town and seeing the world. It didn't take long before I figured out that the only way out of *ma vie misérable* in Frenchtown was going to be, well...*French.*

By the time I was in high school, I was taking advanced-level French classes that would allow me to get free college credit at the University of Connecticut—if I opted to go there and *if* I got accepted. That's when I first toyed with the idea of going to college.

My dad had trouble wrapping his brain around the concept of higher education, convinced that I would end up joining the Air Force—just like he and my siblings had before me. He'd been stationed on the tiny island of Guam. "Trust me," he'd say. "It's the only way you'll ever get to see the world."

As for my grandma Mary, when I told her about my college plans, she just laughed and said in her thick Polish accent, "Bullshit college! Who's going to drive bus?"

No offense, but it wasn't going to be me.

With my new goal in mind, I realized that if I were ever going to get into UConn, I would have to buckle down and study hard. And that's exactly what I did, eventually getting inducted into the National Honor Society. But I felt like a misfit, because most of the other members were rich kids who would never dare step foot in Frenchtown.

Realizing it was time for me to work on my lagging social skills, I joined just about every club that existed—and even some that didn't. Since my high school didn't have a newspaper, I started one. It ended up winning a prestigious regional award, which gave me the confidence to run for senior-class president (after a disastrous junior year bid) and—get this—I won by a landslide.

Incroyable! If only Ann and Dan could see me now. (Actually, they could; Ann was now my *vice* president.)

Ironically, one of the reasons I started excelling at school was because of my dad. Living with him was the longest I'd ever stayed in one place; it gave my life much-needed stability. That is, until halfway through my senior year, when Fast Eddie sat me down in the living room and gave me some game-changing news: he was moving to Massachusetts with his blond-wigged girlfriend.

"You're gonna have to find a new place to live," Fast Eddie said as he sucked on a More cigarette.

"Where?" I asked in shock.

"I don't know. Why don't you ask the Bakers?"

The Bakers were a big Irish family who lived down the street and always welcomed me into their home as if I were one of their own.

"You can't be serious," I said. "The Bakers?"

"Why the hell not?" Fast Eddie said, exhaling a thick plume of smoke. "They already got six boys. Probably won't even notice a seventh."

Fortunately, my grandma Mary was kind enough let me stay with her. At nearly seventy years old and living by herself, the last thing she needed was to take care of one of her grandkids again. But I told her not to worry; I was now completely self-sufficient, which pleased her to no end.

Able to focus on school again, I received some great news: UConn had accepted me! But then, barely two weeks into my college career, I almost had to drop out. The reason: in order to get a tax deduction, my father had claimed me as a dependent living with him and his girlfriend in Massachusetts. As a result, the university switched my status to out of state, which caused the price of my tuition to skyrocket. Even with my student loans and the small journalism scholarship I'd won, there was no way I could afford to pay for school, which would have literally left me homeless.

After a long, *long* battle with the university, I was finally able to convince them that I had never lived in Massachusetts. They switched me back to the in-state tuition rate, and I was able to stay in school. *Whew. That was close.*

Sitting alone in my dorm room late one night during my sophomore year, I heard a swooshing sound behind me. I turned and saw that an envelope had been slipped under my door. *Strange*, I thought. *I never get mail that way.* I went over and picked it up. It was an invitation to a meeting for the Junior Year in France study abroad program. *How weird.* I was studying journalism, not French. In fact, I hadn't taken French in years, having fulfilled my college language requirement through my advanced classes in high school.

As I stared at the invitation, it conjured up all the fond feelings I'd always had for *le français,* and it made me think about how the language had saved me. It's difficult to describe, but even though studying abroad had never been part of my plan, I felt compelled to go to the meeting.

When I entered the small auditorium, there were about thirty other students sitting there, listening to a professor, Dr. Perry, as he explained the details of the program: how we'd be living with a French family; how we'd get to study at a real French *université*; and how the program would look great on our résumés. I was intrigued but still on the fence.

What sealed the deal for me wasn't the lovely slideshow of Paris, with its breathtaking photos of Notre Dame and the Eiffel Tower. No, what pushed me over the edge was when I saw an alumnus from the program talking with his French friend. I couldn't believe how passionately they spoke to each other, *en français*, as if they were the only two people in the room. They leaned in close—unabashedly invading each other's personal space—speaking with an intimacy I had never seen before.

At that moment, I had an epiphany that would take me years to fully comprehend: *I want that kind of human connection!*

I signed up for the program immediately.

On the morning I was to head off on my big French adventure, I bummed a ride to JFK airport with a fellow student from the study abroad program. At the airport, I was surprised to see all the other students lost in the throes of tearful farewells with their families. Watching from the sidelines, feeling awkward and alone, I started to crave that ol' forbidden fruit—love and attention. Even though the voice inside me said, *"Don't do it. Don't do it,"* I did it. I stepped over to a pay phone and called my mom in Florida.

The charmless Monsieur Ducharme answered. "Hello?"

"I have a collect call from Craig in New York," the operator said. "Will you accept the charges?"

"No!" Monsieur Ducharme said, slamming down the phone.

I stared at the receiver, devastated. The dial tone switched over to that obnoxious beeping noise, indicating that the phone was off the hook.

Just then, the PA system announced: "Last call. Final boarding for flight 44 to Paris." As tears welled up in my eyes, I hung up the phone, then made my way toward the gate, passing by the other students who were still struggling to pull themselves away from their sobbing parents. At the gate, I stopped and took one last look around; it would be the last time I would see America for an entire year.

I smiled, despite myself, then took a deep breath and stepped on the plane.

Next destination: Paris, France. In every sense, there'd be no turning back now.

Rouen, France.

Chapter 2

PARIS AND ROUEN: A MOVABLE FEAST

"If you are lucky enough to have lived in Paris as a young man, then wherever you go for the rest of your life, it stays with you, for Paris is a movable feast."

—Ernest Hemingway

PERHAPS THE HAPPIEST MOMENT OF MY LIFE WAS WHEN I ARRIVED IN Paris for the first time. To give you a sense of what it felt like, imagine the following scene: The airport shuttle pulls up to the curb and the door opens. I step out onto the sunny Parisian streets, beaming like Mary Tyler Moore in the opening credits of her TV show, overcome by such unbridled joy that I can't help but spin around and toss my beret into the air.

Now imagine one montage moment after another, shots of me taking in all that is Paris: I'm strolling down an empty cobblestoned street, munching on a scrumptious baguette. I'm surrounded by a bunch of adorable French kids in the Tuileries Garden, laughing hysterically at a marionette show. I'm cruising down the Seine on a Bateaux Mouche tour boat, with a bottle of wine and a lovely *chérie* by my side. The montage ends with a close-up of me atop the Eiffel Tower, then zooms out to reveal a breathtaking view of the city below.

Okay, so maybe the reality was somewhat different. According to my journal from that time, our bus pulled into Paris in the middle of a torrential downpour, the driver cursing and screaming because he couldn't get his enormous vehicle down the tiny Parisian side streets. Instead, he pulled the bus to a screeching halt on a dangerously busy boulevard, jacked open the door, and kicked us all out. We then had to drag our suitcases through the pouring rain for several blocks, until we reached the drafty, overcrowded youth hostel where we'd be staying for the next five weeks.

Ah, welcome to France!

I can still remember my first thought as I walked down the lovely streets, observing elegantly dressed Parisians lost in the throes of passionate conversation: "*Sacré merde!* What freakin' language are these people speaking?"

Just as I had feared, it was definitely *not* the textbook French I'd learned in school. Fortunately, though, I was a fast learner. For instance, I quickly learned that nobody in France says "*sacré*" anything when they want to curse (*putain de* is more like it). Or wears a beret. Or is fat. And I also learned that the trip was going to be a lot of myth-busting, including letting go of French stereotypes. And letting go of me.

The group in my study abroad program was made up of thirty-eight students, thirty girls and eight guys. The plan was to spend the first five weeks in Paris totally immersed in the French language and culture. After that, we'd head off to Rouen, in the northern region of Normandy, to live with a host family and study at the *université* there for the rest of the year. However, by the second week of the program, two girls bailed, catching the next plane back to the States because they were homesick—a malady I was not at all familiar with. *Au contraire.* I had a different disease. I was lovestruck!

Ah, France, how do I love thee? Let me count the ways. Here's just one: in France, one doesn't have to be constantly up and bouncy like an American cheerleader. One can be dark and moody too, which translates to deep and interesting. And if you're going to be blue, there's no better place than Paris. In the States, whenever I got depressed and wanted to stuff my face, I had to settle for Ding Dongs and Ho Hos. But Paris had *pâtisseries!* *Éclairs au chocolat, chocolat aux amandes, fondant au chocolat.* And one of my favorites, delicious *petit* cinnamon rolls called *pets de nonnes*—nun's farts. ("So light they're heavenly!")

In short, life in France meshed perfectly with my personality. So much so that I wanted to totally blend in and be seen as a *real* Frenchman. However, as a blond six-foot-three Scando-Slav with a thick Yankee accent, somehow I had trouble passing as *un vrai français.* Undaunted, I kept trying anyway, believing that it would only be a matter of time before I was babbling on like Molière.

Every morning, our group met downstairs in the dimly lit, sixteenth-century *cave* (cellar) of our youth hostel for an intensive French grammar class. Our professor was a small, unassuming woman who would suddenly spring to life whenever the subject turned to her favorite passion—complex French verb conjugation. We nicknamed her "the Petit Dragon" because of the way she waddled around the room, one short step at a time, hunched over like a Gallic Godzilla.

Madame (Mme) Dragon would rub her hands together, survey the room, then suddenly point her finger at an unsuspecting student.

"*Vous!* Give me the imperfect subjunctive imperative of the verb 'to fear'!"

"Ah!" The chosen student would recoil in actual fear before spitting out the wrong answer.

"*Non!*" the Petit Dragon would shout, flames shooting out her nose. Then she'd spin around again before abruptly coming to a stop, pointing her finger at her next victim. "*Vous!* Answer!"

"Ah!"

It was like a sadistic form of linguistic Russian roulette. But damn if I didn't learn how to conjugate. Now if I could only learn how to *communicate*.

The Petit Dragon's class was followed by my favorite class of all—French culture. There, the fashionable madame taught us all about the "French attitude," including many valuable tips for living in France, like how to hold a cigarette in the proper French way (i.e., nonchalantly, beside your waist).

With both classes wrapped up by lunchtime, we had the rest of the day to do as we pleased. I spent my afternoons visiting museums and cultural landmarks, depending on which days had free admission. I also took great pleasure in simply getting lost down Paris's many hidden streets and alleyways.

And then there was the country's national pastime—*le vin!* Naturally, I had to partake, since the French believed I was responsible enough to drink at twenty years old. On the practical side, I found that after consuming a nice glass of red, my French would start to roll effortlessly off my tongue, and, amazingly, Parisians could completely understand what I was saying. Or at least that's how I saw things through my blurred vision.

Actually, I soon learned that one *real* indication that you were making progress with the language was if you had a dream in French.

As time went by, one student after another would boast over breakfast about having had their first dream *en français*. And, as often happens in group situations, it soon turned into a competition, with me, sadly, coming in dead last; everybody was having their *rêve en français* but me.

And that wasn't the only way that I couldn't keep up with my classmates. I hadn't realized until we were all in France together that, financially speaking, all the other students were in a completely different league than me, way beyond what I'd thought was rich back in Frenchtown. But unlike the French, who prefer to be discreet about such matters, my fellow students had no problem showing off their silver spoons. In fact, some actually admitted that the main reason they had come to France was to shop.

There was a good reason for that; 1984 was a record year for the exchange rate, at more than ten francs to the dollar! As a result, Europe was being transformed into a shopping mecca. As the other students shopped until they dropped—buying up as many Ray-Bans and Lacoste "alligator" shirts as they could stuff into their suitcases—I counted my *centimes*, having come to France with just $300 in my pocket to last the whole year. And the only cash that I had coming in—a small *per* diem provided by the university to cover meals— barely kept my stomach full.

Desperate times called for desperate measures. I needed to find a job ASAP. But being in a foreign country without a work visa, what could I do? It was time to put on my entrepreneurial hat once again. It took some fast-talking on my part, but eventually I was able to convince the director of the program, Dr. Perry, to give me a work-study job as "official photographer." My pitch? The slideshow used to lure future students into the program needed updating.

"Uh, ok," Dr. Perry said.

And with that, every two weeks, I received a check from UConn—in good ol' American dollars. Perfect for exchanging into a thing called *francs*.

With camera in hand, I got right to work doing the best job in the world—roaming the streets of Paris as a shutterbug. Hemingway himself would've been proud, as image after image of Paris's movable feast was forever seared into my young, impressionable brain: the beautiful stained glass windows of Sainte-Chapelle; the grotesque gargoyles perched atop Notre Dame, spitting out water during a rainstorm; the topless Frenchwomen sunbathing on the riverbanks of Île Saint-Louis; and the steamy PDAs (public displays of affection) that were everywhere, making it abundantly clear why Paris was considered the most romantic city in the world.

Perhaps before the year is over, I thought, *I'll have a* chérie *of my own.*

It was unbelievable how fast our five-week immersion in Paris flew by. It was now onto Normandy and Rouen for ten more months of study. Even though Rouen was only an hour away from the city, from the way our group was grumbling, it might as well have been on Mars. That's because we all wanted to stay in chic and cosmopolitan Paris, the city where all the action was—not *en province*, anywhere outside of Paris, from which that icky word "provincial" originated.

Dr. Perry told us to look on the bright side. Rouen would be great for improving our French because, unlike in Paris, nobody in Rouen spoke English. Nor did they want to. And Rouen was beautiful, with all its medieval, half-timber buildings and its famous gothic cathedral, which Monet had captured beautifully in several of his paintings. "In all kinds of different lighting conditions!" Dr. Perry said excitedly. "Sunny! Rainy! Cloudy!" Unimpressed, we grumbled even more.

The morale did not improve when our bus pulled up to the *université* and we saw the "campus" for the first time. Turns out the concept of a college campus didn't exist in France. There was no quad, no dorms, no student union. As I gazed at the surroundings—a collection of cold, concrete buildings designed in the absolute worst style from the sixties—I thought, *Wow, for a socialist country, it doesn't have any place to socialize.*

On the plus side, all of our classes were taught only *en français*. UConn had even hired a bunch of local professors who were instructed to speak slowly and to articulate every word. That lasted for about a minute. First, the French are incapable of speaking slowly. And second, the notion of "articulation" in the French language is absurd. Hell, half the letters in French aren't even *pronounced*, so how are you supposed to articulate silence?

In any case, I was surprised that Dr. Perry placed me in the intermediate group. I had been convinced that all the other students spoke French much better than me, especially since I was the only person in the group who still hadn't had his *sacré*, er, I mean, *putain de "rêve en français"* yet.

One of the best selling points for the study abroad program was getting the opportunity to live with a real French family. French or not, I was excited just to have my first *real* family experience. I imagined the whole works: a mom, a dad, siblings, a dog (or cat, I loved them both), a picket fence, keeping up with the Joneses, midlife crises, disillusionment…

But when the host families came to greet us, they didn't exactly represent the socialist/egalitarian model that I'd hoped for. The families varied greatly from rich blue bloods to average *bourgeois* to…mine.

I was assigned to Mme Yvart, *une vieille fille* (an old maid) who was half mad genius, half schoolmarm. A devout Catholic, Mme

Yvart lived alone with her piano and crucifixes. She reminded me a lot of my grandma Mary—only my gram's Polish chicken recipe would've put Mme Yvart's cooking to shame.

Mme Yvart lived in a narrow, four-story town house not far from the city center. The location was the best thing her place had going for it. Actually, it was the *only* thing it had going for it. Her home had definitely seen better days. Paint was peeling off the walls, the hardwood floors were creaky and warped, and there was a constant, bone-chilling draft coming from God knows where. Perhaps her soul.

At least I didn't have to live there alone. I had a roommate, Richard, a fellow student in the program. The moment we arrived at her house, Mme Yvart gave us a lightning-fast tour, racing from one room to the next, chattering a mile a minute *en français*. Richard nodded the whole time, "*Ah, oui, oui, oui! Bien sûr, madame, oui, oui, oui!*"

I turned to Richard and whispered, "What's she saying?"

Richard shrugged. "Hell if I know."

Mme Yvart stopped in her tracks and looked at us sternly. *Busted.*

"Leesten!" she said in her heavily accented English. "Except for zee kitchen—wherrre you may take your brrreakfast in zee morning—zee rest of zee house is off lee-meets. Is that clearrr?"

Richard and I nodded.

"Now!" Mme Yvart said. "Follow me!"

Mme Yvart exited out the back door without waiting for us. We caught up to her in the courtyard as she trotted along a pathway running through a small, weed-infested garden. On the other side was a large structure that looked remarkably like a toolshed.

"*Voilà*," she said, pointing at the structure. "Your sleeping quarters."

Richard and I exchanged looks. It actually wasn't that bad—for a converted toolshed, that is. It was about the size of a small camper, kind of cute and cozy. Plus it was chock-full of amenities: a bunk bed, a closet, a shower, a small fridge, and a space heater, which, we later learned, had only one setting—boiling. Finally, thrown in at no extra charge were some friendly garden slugs, which had undoubtedly slithered in to warm themselves from the cold, incessant Normandy rain outside.

"*Bon!*" Mme Yvart said, satisfied with herself. "*À ce soir!*" ("See you tonight.") Mme Yvart spun around on her heels and headed back into the house. Richard and I looked at each other again, then broke out into hysterical laughter, lest we break out into tears.

Due to some unfortunate incidents in the past, UConn required host families to sign a detailed contract before paying them to take care of us. Mme Yvart's obligations were simple: to house and feed us, but only breakfast and dinner, Monday through Friday; lunches and weekends, we were on our own.

By our third or fourth dinner, I began to long for my grandma Mary's Polish "cooking." Every night the menu at Chez Yvart was the same, consisting of such World War II–style rations as a bowl of soup and a hard-boiled egg (sometimes two), which sat on a bed of wilted lettuce tossed with an intense, nasal-cleansing vinaigrette. The "meal" usually ended with a dry hunk of Camembert and/or an economy-size variety pack of biscuits.

I noticed that Mme Yvart would leave the pot of soup sitting on the stove for days on end. Whenever it got low, she would simply open a new can and add it to the mix. She didn't seem to pay atten- tion—or care—if the flavor of the new can was the same as the flavor that had been there previously. By the time Friday rolled around, the mélange of lumpy soup would have mutated into a strange and unappetizing brown color.

In contrast, my fellow student Gail was having a very different experience with her host family. "Oh my God," she said one day before class. "I think *ma mère française* is trying to kill me! I've gained, like, fifteen pounds in a month."

"Really?" I said as the faint sound of hunger pangs rumbled in my stomach. "Tell me more."

"Well, every evening starts off with an aperitif, usually a kir or a kir royale, accompanied by an amuse-bouche, like foie gras or salmon on toast."

I could feel my mouth starting to water.

"Next, we have a starter, maybe a salad like *frisée aux lardons* or something like that. Then it's on to the main course, like *confit de canard* or whatever. Madame tries to mix it up so that we don't have the same meal twice over a two-week period."

I wiped the drool from my chin. "Go on."

"After *le plat principal*, we take a short break, change wines, you know, the usual." Gail then put her hand on her stomach. "By now, I'm so stuffed, I can hardly move. By the time Madame rolls out the cheese cart, I—"

"Stop!" I said, holding up my hand. "I don't want to hear any more!"

A cheese cart? Aw, for crying out loud! I wanted a cheese cart!

Thanks to Mme Yvart, I came dangerously close to spending an entire year in France without ever having had the most important cultural experience of all—*la vraie cuisine française*.

Of course, when it came to food, my family had not set the bar very high. That's why, when I first went to France, even the simplest of French breakfasts seemed exotic to me—even though they consisted of the same thing every morning: a demi baguette (or *tartine* in French) with jam and *pur beurre*. I was especially impressed by how coffee and hot chocolate were served—in big bowls that you grabbed with both hands and lifted up to your mouth, slurping to your heart's content.

But it wasn't long before I began craving a good ol' American breakfast with fluffy pancakes, Eggo waffles, or, especially, my grandma Lizzy's scrambled eggs. But I tried to put my cravings aside, telling myself, "*When in Rome...*"

Thanks to the strong exchange rate, Dr. Perry would sometimes take us out to eat in fancy French restaurants. Although I enjoyed the experience, I have to admit, having never been properly educated about food, I was much more concerned with quantity over quality, meaning, the more the better. For me, food was sustenance; haute cuisine was something reserved for the rich. That is, until one weekend in Dijon—"the Mustard Capital of the World." After that, everything changed.

I'd been invited to go on a three-day excursion to Burgundy with some friends from the *université*, including Cédric, a debonair French student who was dating a girl in our group. With six of us crammed into a rickety old van, we drove all night to the city of Dijon to take part in the annual Foire Gastronomique (the Gastronomic Fair).[1]

Forget Ferris wheels, cotton candy, and pony rides; this fair was about one thing and one thing only: the celebration of fine wine, cheese, and world-renowned *cuisine*. When I stepped into the huge convention center for the first time, I couldn't believe my eyes. I'd never seen so many stinky, moldy cheeses gathered in one place. Hundreds and hundreds of them sat side by side with every Burgundy delicacy you could think of: garlicky *escargots* (with *pur beurre*), foie gras, *terrine de canard*, *bœuf bourguignon*...the list went on and on. A true visual—and culinary—feast!

---

1   When I originally attended the fair in 1985, this was its official name. It has since been changed to the Foire Internationale et Gastronomique.

If it hadn't been for Cédric, however, I probably would've spent the whole weekend gorging myself—sated and satisfied, but still completely uneducated about the art of food and wine.

"Hold the glass up to the light," Cédric said as he swirled a glass of sauvignon blanc at eye level, the wine's golden color glistening like a diamond. "Now compare it to this Sancerre," he said, holding up a second glass. "What do you see?"

See? Since when did you *see* wine? Wasn't it something you just drank?

After carefully observing the wine, Cédric put the glass to his nose. Took a sniff. *"Le premier nez."* I had never heard that term before—nor had I heard a slew of other words that began to flow from Cédric's lips as he described the wine he was tasting. Words like *la robe* (the color), *le deuxième nez* (the second sniff), *le tanin* (the tannin), *le bouquet* (the aroma), *l'équilibre* (the balance), and *l'acidité* (the acidity).

Slow down, mon ami! I thought. I barely understood regular French. Now all of a sudden I was finding out that wine had a whole vocabulary of its own.

Cédric moved on to the next table, this one full of a variety of red wine. Each bottle was paired with a different cheese or amuse-bouche, depending on the vintage. *Now we're talking!* I thought. Famished, I began to stuff my face.

"Oh là là!" Cédric said, motioning for me to slow down. *"Doucement!"*

With incredible patience, Cédric began walking me through everything that I needed to learn. First, he explained that although wine could be delicious all by itself, it served another purpose as well. When paired with the right cuisine, it could raise the taste experience to a whole new level. Cédric then proceeded to guide me through that experience, moving from one delicious table to the next, from *coq au vin* to chardonnay, from pinot noir to comté.

I could feel my senses starting to stir. It reminded me of trying

to start a fire when you're camping. You can see the embers beginning to glow, but there's still no spark. You give it some air. Poke it
with a stick. Then, all of a sudden, it comes to life. As I stood there
at the fair, that's exactly what happened to me. I could feel the lightbulb turning on inside my head. It was exhilarating...transcenden-
tal...*and* delicious! The awakening of my palate.

So this is what all the fuss is about! I thought. Food was more than
just sustenance—more than just something that kept us alive. It *was*
alive. Even more, it was something that connected us to the earth, to
our physical selves, and most importantly, to each other.

Along with this new awareness came something else—a kind of
daring fearlessness. If food were alive, well then, I wanted to live! I
couldn't wait to try *everything* after that. Tripe? Bring it on. Foie gras?
Cut me a chunk.

And the best thing of all was that the Foire Gastronomique had
shown me that fine cuisine wasn't something reserved for the rich;
it was a completely democratic experience, part of the very fabric of
French society. Everyone was welcome at the fair, from the posh to
the peasant, from the *bourgeois* to the blue collar.

By the end of my amazing weekend in Dijon, it was clear to
me that not only did France mesh perfectly with my personality, but
it also meshed perfectly with my budget. Here, you didn't have to
be *money* rich to enjoy life; you could be *quality-of-life* rich instead.

After my incredible experience at the Foire Gastronomique, one
expression—*en français*—became my motto: "*Il faut en profiter.*"
Literally it means, "it's necessary to profit or take advantage (of the
situation)." But to the French, it means much more than that. More
like, "Live life to the fullest" or "Carpe diem!"

As the last few months of my year abroad flew by, I tried to *profiter* as much as I could. During school breaks, I bought a train pass and backpacked all over Europe. I also got involved in as many extracurricular activities as I could, including playing the role of the Major General (Stanley) in a university production of *The Pirates of Penzance*. We played to sold-out crowds and even took the show on the road!

One big fan of the show was Isabelle, a French student studying English at the *université*. Pretty and skinny, with long, dark hair, Isabelle reminded me of the singer Crystal Gayle. And *dieu merci*, unlike every other person in France, she did not smoke! Before I even knew what had hit me, Isabelle became my very first romance *à la française*.

It was all quite innocent. I would meet Isabelle at Printemps, a moderately upscale department store where she worked in the perfume department. After her shift, we'd go to a café and talk. And laugh. And talk some more. Maybe hold hands a little. Feeling brave, I even had my very first espresso with her.

But unfortunately, I wasn't brave enough for much more.

One time Isabelle and I were all alone outside the theater where I had performed as the Major General. Before I knew it, things got all gauzy and romantic. As Isabelle moved in for a *bisou*, her eyes started to glaze over. Suddenly, I began to panic. It's hard to explain, but what I felt was an intense, primal panic. It was the *exact* same feeling I'd get every time my mom would get that strange look in her eyes—right before they'd drag her away to the asylum.

I started hyperventilating. Poor Isabelle was confused. All she wanted was a *petit bisou*. Instead, I smiled nervously, shook her hand—then turned around and ran off to the nearest bakery as fast as I could so I could stuff my face with delicious *pâtisseries*.

Alas, as far as romance was concerned, *il faut en profiter* would have to wait until another time.

With only a couple of weeks to go before the end of the program, I stepped into the *université* lounge area, where my fellow students were congregated, and proudly proclaimed for all to hear, "Last night, it finally happened!" I could barely hold in my excitement. "I had my first dream *en français!*"

The group cheered and applauded. "It's about time!" someone said. Indeed, my *rêve en français* could not have happened more in the nick of time. Unfortunately, I couldn't remember what my dream was about. But I *did* know that it was in French, because I only understood about three-quarters of it—much more than if I'd had it at the beginning of the year.

For our final week in Rouen, Dr. Perry organized a big farewell dinner. Everyone was invited, including our professors, host families, and friends. It was an amazing party. As the wine flowed and our hearts opened up, I was surprised to learn how many myths my fellow students and I held about each other. For example, from the beginning, I had been convinced that everybody spoke French better than I did. It turned out that nearly everybody in the group shared the same secret fear.

Another assumption I'd made was that big ol' chip on my shoulder. Although I was certainly the poorest kid in the group, not everybody there was rich either. Far from it. More importantly, it really didn't matter anymore. I had different priorities now. Simple pleasures like having a delicious six-course meal with friends and family, where you stayed at the table for hours on end, *that's* what became important.

Il faut en profiter.

With the program officially over, it was time to head back to Connecticut. But I wasn't finished with France yet. I still wanted to have the full *real-world* Parisian experience. As my fellow students rushed back to the States, I stayed behind and found a great studio apartment to sublet in the heart of the Latin Quarter. And the best part was that it only cost me 1,500 *francs* a month—or just 150 American dollars, thanks to that record exchange rate. It was a bargain even back then.

Next, I found a job working under the table at an English language school run by an American expat, Mr. MacD. Like me, Mr. MacD had been an exchange student in France, but he never left. As he described it, "I woke up one morning with a French wife and three kids, wondering, 'How in the hell did that happen?'"

Interestingly enough, during this time, I received a lot of letters from my fellow students saying that they wished they'd stayed in France like me. Of course, I was glad I'd stayed behind, but truth be told, I was feeling a bit lonely, especially on my twenty-first birthday that July.

To commemorate my special day, my dad sent me the longest letter he had ever written to me. Although you'd never expect it, Fast Eddie had the most beautiful penmanship I'd ever seen, full of curly flourishes that reminded me of a girly love letter. All the more disturbing given the subject matter of his missive: How to Seduce a Woman.

Craig, here are a few tips about women I've learned over the years. Women live in a romantic fantasy world. This is a fact. That's why a great lover is always a great talker. A woman wants to know she's different, that she's spectacular, that she's wanted. Remember, very shortly you will be leaving France, maybe never to go back. Now is the time to be aggressive and bold! Let Isabelle know that the distance you travel to see her is no inconvenience at all because of the reward of seeing her, being with her, etc., etc., etc.

I wished my dad hadn't mentioned Isabelle. Truth be told, I'd gotten so tired of him asking me since high school if I'd gotten laid yet, I caved and said that Isabelle was my girlfriend. I didn't have the heart to tell him what had *really* happened—how I'd had a panic attack when she tried to kiss me.

Why did I have such a problem with intimacy? I couldn't afford a therapist at the time, but I figured it might have something to do with the fact that, as a kid, whenever I craved love or attention, my mom would suddenly disappear. Whatever the reason might be, I tried not to think about it too much. If I did, I'd get depressed and end up eating a whole bag of nun's farts.

As the summer came to an end, I still had one more year to go at UConn. But there was just one *petit problème*: I still didn't know what I wanted to do with my life. I thought I wanted to be a journalist, but from the moment I became a reporter for the campus newspaper, I clashed with the editor. He said I was too nice to be a journalist, because I cared too much about people to smear them. He was right. I had to confess, what I loved most about my high school newspaper was *starting* it, not reporting for it.

In any case, I'd been leaning toward a new career path, but I wasn't 100 percent sure about it. But, as often happens in life, I found my answer that summer when I wasn't looking for it.

I'd always known that Paris was famous for its world-class

museums, its beautiful architecture, and its fascinating history. But until that summer, I had no idea that it was also known for its amazing *cinémas*. Growing up, I'd always loved going to the movies, but it wasn't until my sojourn in Paris that I became a full-fledged film buff. In any given week, more than two hundred different films from all over the world would screen in the city, including classic films, contemporary films, and foreign films—and all in their original languages. At one theater, I saw a poster that perfectly summed up how I felt: "*Quand on aime la vie, on va au cinéma!*" ("When one loves life, one goes to the movies!").

Of course, I loved life…and *especially* romance—as long as it was safely up there on the big screen and not causing me to have panic attacks. Of all the films I saw that summer, one in particular changed my life forever: François Truffaut's masterpiece, *Les quatre cents coups* (*The 400 Blows*). I couldn't believe how Truffaut, who grew up in postwar France, was able to capture the exact same feelings of isolation and pain that I'd experienced as a kid growing up in Connecticut.

Thanks in large part to that film, I now knew what I wanted to do next with my life—*le cinéma!*

As I packed my bags to return to America, my feelings were decidedly mixed. I felt very melancholy leaving France—a magical, mystical place that had forever changed my life. But I also felt unbridled hope for the future and what lay ahead.

As I shut off the lights of my tiny Parisian apartment for the last time, I didn't know if I would ever return to France again. But if I did, I was sure it would be to the Cannes Film Festival as an award-winning filmmaker.

But, of course, the universe had other plans.

The perfect breakfast.

Chapter 3

THE CRAZY DREAM

"I truly believe that one day your life is going to make sense."

—Deb, a dear friend

AFTER MY INCREDIBLE YEAR IN FRANCE, I REALLY DID THINK I WAS going to make it big in Hollywood, since, in so many ways, that year had helped send me down the path toward success. First, it helped me get accepted into the best film school in the world—the University of Southern California—which, according to the school's marketing materials, was harder to get into than Harvard. How did France help me get in? In my application, I quoted the line from the poster I'd seen in Paris: "*Quand on aime la vie, on va au cinéma!*" A professor later told me that he'd been so moved by the quote that he recommended that USC accept me.

Second, my experience in France helped me to connect with

all those *trust funders*—a.k.a. the super rich. Before going to USC, I'd never even heard of a trust fund, let alone a trust funder. But the school was so full of them, I realized I'd better get used to it, especially if I wanted to make friends (or "connections"), which was crucial for me if I expected to work in Hollywood. Fortunately, I was no longer intimidated by rich people. Thanks to my time in France, I was now worldly—*and* bilingual. And financially speaking, it was always great to have a trust funder as a friend. They always seemed to have privileged, insider information, which proved to be super helpful when dealing with important things like USC's extraordinarily expensive tuition.

"Hey, Craig," my new trust-funder friend Dave said to me one day. "Did you know that if you pay all four years of tuition up front—in cash—USC will give you a huge discount?"

"Well, no, Dave, I did not know that. Thanks for the tip!"

Since I was unable to pay my tuition in cash like Dave was, I decided to try out as a contestant on the game show *Wheel of Fortune*. During my audition, I told the female producer, "If I win, I'll return to France and see Isabelle, the girl who stole my heart." (Okay, so maybe I embellished it a little). When I saw the producer's eyes watering up, I knew I was in! Even Pat Sajak mentioned France when he presented me as a contestant for all of America.

I was the big winner that day. I solved all the puzzles and won a ton of prizes, including a brand-new convertible. But then all hell broke loose. First, I didn't receive the same prizes that I'd won. For example, my sky-blue convertible was replaced by a family station wagon that sat seven. Next, I had to sell all my prizes in order to pay the taxes on them. My nightmare continued when I was audited by the IRS.

I ended up making a short thesis film about my experience. I called it *Wheel of Torture*. The tagline: "The other side of the American Dream once the TV is shut off." Shortly after I finished my film, it started getting a lot of buzz around town, especially since it was about to be screened at the Academy of Motion Picture Arts and Sciences—a.k.a. the Oscar people.

This was huge. My fellow students and I had spent an entire year organizing the big event. On the night before my screening, I stood in the Academy lobby, staring at the long list of VIPs who had RSVP'd. I couldn't believe my eyes. Everybody who was anybody was planning to attend, including A-list Hollywood agents, producers, and directors, all of whom were just itching to sign on new talent.

My heart raced as I imagined myself finally buying that plane ticket to Cannes after all. I looked back at the VIP list. *Everything* was riding on my screening the next day: four-and-a-half years of graduate school; $64,000 in student loan debt; and so many maxed-out credit cards that I'd lost count. *But no need to worry*, I reassured myself. *In less than twenty-four hours, all my hard work is going to pay off.*

That night, as I drove home from the Academy, LA burned.

As fate would have it, that Wednesday, April 29, 1992, was the day the Rodney King verdict was announced. The historic LA riots followed. As I headed home along Sunset Boulevard, pillars of smoke and flames shot up into the night sky as far as the eye could see, while a fleet of helicopters circled overhead.

The riots reached their peak the following day, Thursday, which happened to be my big day. I walked around my neighborhood in a daze, past smoldering ruins, sirens blaring in the distance, bullets whizzing overhead, and helicopters…everywhere, helicopters…a war zone.

I stared off into space, mumbling to myself like a selfish idiot, "They can't cancel the screening. Please…don't cancel the screening."

They canceled the screening. It was rescheduled for six months later. But by then, the buzz was gone. Nobody who was anybody came.

Sadly, my ticket to Cannes would have to be put on hold. Indefinitely.

Times were tough after that. Even though my film won some awards at festivals, and even though every producer I met with said they couldn't wait to read my scripts, there was just one *grand problème*: nobody would *pay* me to write any of them. Not a problem if you're a trust funder. But if you gotta pay the rent...

Fortunately, I found a cheap place to live in a former servant's quarters in the back of a massive hillside duplex. It reminded me a lot of the toolshed...*er*...guesthouse where I'd lived in Rouen. My friends nicknamed it the Hobbit Hole. While I lived there, I worked for several long years as a struggling screenwriter, *almost* getting my big break several times.

To survive, I scraped by as a temp—just like so many other writer/director/actors in Hollywood. For some reason, the temp agency loved sending me to Disney's studios in Burbank. But unfortunately, the meager wages I earned barely covered the *interest* on my student loans, let alone the payments on all my maxed-out credit cards. Now in my midthirties, living alone in the Hobbit Hole, with my career going nowhere—I hit the lowest point in my life.

"Craig, I know things are confusing right now," my friend Deb said to me. "But I truly believe that one day your life is going to make sense. That all the twists and turns, all the ups and downs...they happened for a reason."

I wanted to believe her. But it seemed like every day my faith was being tested, over and over again, especially on the day I received a phone call from my sister back East. My dad had passed away after a long battle with leukemia.

I thought about the last time I'd seen my dad, six months earlier, when he was at the VA hospital, receiving a blood transfusion. When I arrived, my dad was sitting in a chair, slumped forward, his face pale, his mouth hanging open. My heart sank, afraid that I'd arrived too late. But then I noticed my dad's shrunken stomach (where his beer belly used to be) was slowly rising up and down. I breathed a sigh of relief, realizing that he'd only been asleep.

Just then, a nurse stepped up and whispered, "Are you Craig?" I nodded. "Oh, I've heard so much about you!" she said. The nurse went on to tell me how my dad couldn't stop talking about me...how he'd gone on and on about how I'd lived in France and now I was a big screenwriter in Hollywood...and how I knew famous people like Cheryl Ladd.

"You're a lucky guy," the nurse said, smiling. "I've never seen a father more proud of his son."

The nurse turned and left. I stood there, numb. Who knew my dad was so proud of me? How come he never told me himself? But then I realized that it didn't really matter. What was more important was how lucky I was to have met that nurse. Otherwise I might never have known how my dad truly felt about me.

Back in the Hobbit Hole, reeling from my dad's death, I decided to call some old friends, just to hear some friendly voices, to boost my morale. My first call was to my old friend Dave from film school.

"It's so funny you should call," Dave said. "I literally just turned down a job working on a TV show in France."

"No way," I said.

"Yeah," he laughed. "What a coincidence, right?"

Hearing the word "coincidence" sent a shiver down my spine. After a long silence, Dave said exactly what I was thinking: "Hey, wait. You speak French, right? Would you be interested in the job?"

"Are you kidding?" I said. *Mais, bien sûr!*

I applied for the job right away, but I didn't get an answer before my flight back East for my dad's funeral. I decided to pack for six months—just in case.

Back in Connecticut, after the funeral service, my brother and I went to get an extra-large pizza in my dad's honor, since pizza was his favorite food. In the deserted parking lot outside the pizza parlor, I made a long-distance call to Paris from a pay phone. The producer from the TV show answered.

"Congratulations, Craig!" he said. "You got the job! Get packed. You're coming to Paris!"

"I'm already packed!" I said. I turned to my brother, who was waiting in the car, and gave him a big thumbs-up. I couldn't believe it. I was going back to Paris. But this time it was different. This time I was going back as a *professionnel*!

What a difference a day makes. Just one week earlier, I'd been living in the Hobbit Hole with debt collectors pounding down my door, and now all of a sudden there was a chauffeur waiting for me at the airport in Paris, holding up a card with "Monsieur Crag" written on it. (Nobody in France could *ever* get my name right). There was even a chocolate on my pillow at the four-star hotel where the show was putting me up.

As I strolled down the familiar streets of Paris, observing elegantly dressed people lost in the throes of passionate conversation, I thought, *Ah, it's good to be home.*

My official job title was postproduction supervisor on a *Xena* rip-off called *The New Adventures of Robin Hood*, an international co-production. In theory, because I had directed a film, I was qualified for the job. But technically, the position was way out of my league.

But I told myself that even if the job didn't work out, at least I had gotten a free trip to Paris. Fortunately, it did work out.

As post-production supervisor, I managed a team of about a dozen people, mostly French. I quickly learned that the American way of doing business was very different from the French way. For example, the American producer of the show, Fred G., a Hollywood bigwig who had produced many classic kung-fu films, believed that you should squeeze as much work out of employees as possible, making them come in on weekends—even if there was no work to do.

This did *not* fly well with the French.

Furthermore, Fred couldn't understand why the French took everything so personally. "It's just business," he said. What I knew—and he failed to see—was that for the French, there were more important things in life than making money. Like, for example, vacations. In fact, before *Robin Hood*, I, like many Americans, suffered from workaholism; I truly believed that if you took more than a week off, you were lazy and irresponsible. France quickly cured me of that disease.

Given Fred's attitude, another important part of my job involved playing the referee between him and the French crew. As a zero-tolerance former smoker, Fred would literally grab cigarettes out of French people's mouths and snuff them out.

"These things'll kill ya," he would growl.

On the other end of the spectrum, the French producer of the show, Chantal, adhered to a completely different business model. In her long, slinky tube dress, perpetually holding a cigarette in her hand, Chantal reminded me of a dark-haired Sharon Stone from *Basic Instinct*.

"Kraaag," Chantal would purr, exhaling a stream of smoke. "Your work here is…*comme ci comme ça* (not bad). But I must give you some advice: you need to flirt more to get what you want."

Naturally, there were no sexual harassment laws in France. Yet.

Working on *Robin Hood* turned out to be an amazing experience. Not only did I become lifelong friends with many of my colleagues, but my French improved to a whole new level. I was now able to speak the language of *business*. In the end, the experience rivaled that of my junior year abroad, especially considering what happened the day I was about to leave my favorite city and head back to LA.

It was a beautiful Sunday morning as I stepped out into the courtyard of the nineteenth-century apartment building where I was staying. I could hear a piano playing softly in the distance, its lovely melody echoing in the courtyard. I looked up to see the Eiffel Tower peeking over the rooftops, its spire reaching up to the sky so blue. Suddenly, a thought came to me as clear as day: *I do not want to grow old in LA.*

It's hard to explain, but in that instant I knew that *here* was where I belonged—in Paris. But doing what?

Back in LA, I returned to my life as a struggling screenwriter. As before, I had a few close calls, but no big breaks. A couple of my USC friends who had hit the Hollywood big time told me there was a reason my career wasn't taking off like theirs had. "You're too nice a guy," they said. "You've got to be more ruthless!"

That wasn't the first time I'd heard that. Who knows, maybe they were right. Maybe I wasn't ruthless enough. Or maybe I just didn't have the talent to be a successful screenwriter. But to be honest, after my big aha moment in Paris, my heart just wasn't into Hollywood like it had been. All I could think about was France—and how to get back there.

Then, one bustling Saturday morning, I joined some friends

downtown at my old haunt, the Original Pantry Café, a famous LA diner where, legend has it, all the waiters are former felons. After a year in France, I was dying for a good ol' American breakfast. With great anticipation, I ordered a ham steak, scrambled eggs, home-fried potatoes, and buckwheat pancakes. When my breakfast feast arrived, I stared at it wide-eyed and said, "Oh my God, this is the one thing I missed when I was in Paris!"

At that instant—just like a flashback in a movie—a year's worth of eating French breakfasts replayed before my eyes. But the problem was that every breakfast was exactly the same—croissants and *pains au chocolat*, croissants and *pains au chocolat*.

Back at the Pantry, I stared down at my pancakes…my heart racing as I repeated the phrase, "The one thing…I missed…in Paris."

Suddenly, I could see everything so clearly. It was as if my life were a connect-the-dots game and every important moment were a numbered dot, and I had just drawn the last line revealing a perfectly clear picture. Suddenly, I realized that all those twists and turns, all those ups and downs… They really had happened for a reason.

And at that moment, I knew exactly what I wanted to do—no, *had* to do next: open an American diner in Paris! I even knew what I was going to call it—Breakfast in America.

There are few moments in life that are so lucid. This was one of those moments. But how to realize this vision (as in, make it *real*) was something else entirely. It would require a whole new set of twists and turns before my crazy dream could become a reality.

And I would barely survive to tell the tale.

Starter

If You Build It, They Will Come

*Researching breakfast at the Dinerama
tour in Pittsburgh, Pennsylvania.*

Chapter 4

THE BUSINESS PLAN AND
THE BEST KIND OF R & D

"Paris has it all. The Louvre. The Eiffel Tower. Romance and fine cuisine. But
one thing it doesn't have is an authentic American breakfast."

—BIA's original business plan

FLUSH WITH MY CRAZY IDEA OF OPENING THE FIRST AMERICAN DINER
in Paris, I rushed to the nearest Barnes & Noble and bought a book
on how to open a restaurant. Since I had never owned a business
before—let alone a restaurant in France—I literally had to start from
square one.

Pas de problème. I was used to that.

I don't recall the title of the book I bought, but it might as
well have been *Oh, So You Really Wanna Do This, Huh?* The author
did not mince words when it came to describing the risky business

I was about to get myself into. Sure, I had heard all about how 60 percent of restaurants fail in the first year and 80 percent by the fifth year...blah, blah, blah. But when you're obsessed with an idea, the last thing you want to hear are pesky little words like "obstacles" or "risks" or "utter failure."

But the author went beyond the usual scare tactics, hitting hard with a reality check I wasn't expecting. Let's say your restaurant was a success—meaning you had enough customers to *not* go bankrupt. Between all the expenses, including rent, wages, and taxes—not to mention the inevitable *unexpected* costs—you'd be lucky if you ended up with a profit of $5,000 by the end of the first year.

Talk about a buzzkill. It was as if the author were saying, "Are you *that* passionate about your dream to slave away for years on end and have *next to nothing* to show for it—except maybe self-satisfaction?"

Are you kidding? That's exactly what it was like being a screen-writer in Hollywood—except for the self-satisfaction part.

In any case, I had an easy solution for all the warnings the book was giving me: I simply put my fingers in my ears and sang "la-la-la-la" as I continued on to the software section of the store, where I bought a program called Business Plan Pro.

Even though I had developed solid entrepreneurial skills over the years, putting together a business plan was very intimidating for me. There was so much I needed to learn, including the company structure; start-up budget; fixed costs; employee costs; the break-even point; advertising and publicity strategies; projected sales; risk factors; return on investment; shares and dividends; the one-, three-, and five-year plans; and, finally, the exit strategy.

Merde! This stuff was complicated. Didn't you need a degree for this? Wasn't that what MBAs were for?

Of course, with my crushing student loan debt, there was no way I could afford to go back to school. Nor did I want to. Instead,

I opted for the self-taught, crash-course method. I figured that once I'd learned as much as I could on my own, I could seek out professional advice as needed.

Feeling a little overwhelmed, I realized that the best way to take on such a monumental task would have to be in baby steps. Thus my "journey of a thousand miles" began with my first step: research. Luckily for me, my business of choice was not rocket science or a dot-com startup. It was a diner. Which meant doing research would be both fun *and* delicious.

Because I wanted Breakfast in America to be as authentic as possible, I began looking into exactly what it was that makes diners so special. I was surprised to discover that there was an American Diner Museum in Rhode Island. I contacted them and told them about BIA. Intrigued by my idea, the head of the museum asked if I wanted to join the Diner Rescue Fund, a nonprofit organization whose mission was to preserve historic, old diners.

Mais, bien sûr!

As a proud card-carrying member of the "diner club," I was invited to attend a special event being held in Pittsburgh, Pennsylvania, called Dinerama 2001. Before I knew it, I found myself in the Steel City on a bus full of eccentric diner aficionados, taking part in a whirlwind tour of all things greasy spoon.

Over the course of a weekend, we visited one perfectly preserved diner after another, beginning with a delicious breakfast in a dinette, or lunch car, that dated back to the 1920s. Next, we had a hearty lunch in a late 1930s Sterling Streamliner diner, which had been converted into a redneck hangout for bikers and muscle car lovers with a sign on the wall boasting, "There is *no* 'Nonsmoking' section." We then had a *second* lunch in a classic 1950s-style diner, which had been inspired by the space age—all shiny, sleek, and aerodynamic.

And the best part of all was, included in the price of the tour, we were given carte blanche to order whatever artery-clogging fare we wanted. By the end of the weekend, we were all so full and happy we could barely move.

Of course, I hadn't come all the way to Pittsburgh just to stuff my face with comfort food (although, believe me, that was certainly reason enough). I'd also come to meet with diner décor suppliers. But sadly, what had once been a thriving industry had dwindled down to only a handful of small family businesses. I met with one of them who still made authentic boomerang laminate, the iconic colorful boomerang patterns that can be found on the countertops of many vintage diners. I desperately wanted the same laminate in BIA. When I told the supplier that my diner would be in Paris, he joked about stowing away inside the shipment so that he could get a chance to see the Eiffel Tower.

Interestingly enough, it wasn't until I took part in the Dinerama tour that I learned that diners had originated in the Northeast. In fact, the very first "diner" was a horse-pulled wagon built in 1872 in Rhode Island, right next to my home state of Connecticut. I wasn't aware of this history because, sadly, there were no diners anywhere near Frenchtown, just a Denny's and a Friendly's. Of the two, I preferred Friendly's, especially for my favorite meal—breakfast. But, of course, that's because I wasn't familiar with the *real deal*.

It wasn't until I moved to LA that my love affair with diners—or "coffee shops" as they're known out West—really started. In film school, because I pulled a lot of all-nighters, I practically lived in twenty-four-hour coffee shops, my favorites being the mom-and-pop joints. I loved getting to know all the waitresses by name. And I especially loved how they always seemed to know what I wanted to order, even before I did.

"C'mon, Craig, you had the Santa Fe scramble yesterday," Peggy, a sassy waitress, would berate me. "You want the biscuits and gravy. They just came out of the oven—hot and fresh."

No matter what time of day or night, if I was in a coffee shop, I always ordered breakfast. Always. Compared to the chains back home, breakfasts in LA were Michelin-star delicious. On top of that, for a penniless student like me, you couldn't ask for a better deal. In no time flat, I figured out which places had the best early-bird specials. For example, at Astro's Family Restaurant in Silver Lake, I could get their "Hotcake Sandwich" (flapjacks with eggs, sausage, or bacon)—plus a bottomless mug of joe—all for under five bucks! Other favorites of mine included the Pantry (*bien sûr!*), Norms, Jan's, Johnie's, and Canter's, which was more a deli than a coffee shop. But who cares? Their matzo brei omelet was to die for!

Of course, nobody had to twist my arm to go back to my old haunts. However, this time, because I was wearing my business cap, I saw things differently. I noticed that each coffee shop had its own distinct character and personality. As a result, each one inspired me to bring something unique to Breakfast in America. For example, thanks to Ships (a coffee shop which, sadly, has since closed down), I came up with the idea of putting toasters at every table. At Du-par's, I paid extra-close attention to the way they made their world-famous pancakes.

But perhaps the one place that inspired me the most was the Hollywood Hills Coffee Shop (now the 101), where the film *Swingers* was shot. I spent hours and hours chatting with Janet, its gracious owner, absorbing whatever advice she was willing to give me. It turned out to be volumes.

"Diners and coffee shops have evolved over the years," she told me once. "In the fifties, they used to serve frozen vegetables. Now you could never serve frozen vegetables. They have to be fresh!"

"That will *not* be a problem in France!" I said.

Janet agreed, having been to France a couple of times herself. And, like me, she lamented the fact that the French had a bad impression of American cuisine. "It pains me to see that diners have been overshadowed by McDonald's and Domino's," she said.

"That's exactly what I've been saying," I said. "The French need to know there's more to American cuisine than fast food."

"So that's your mission, huh?"

"Yeah." I smiled. "That's my mission."

Thanks to chatting with people like Janet, I was able to define what it was that I loved about diners so much, which I summed up in my business plan this way:

> An American diner conjures up images of the open road and Route 66...of boundless space and limitless possibilities. It's a place where you can stop in at any hour of the day or night...where you're always guaranteed a good, hearty meal at a reasonable price...where you can pass the hours away, chatting with friends...and where everyone—young and old, local and foreigner—is always welcome.

Of course, running a restaurant is not all fun and games, *n'est-ce pas?* It's also serious business. Hence the next *big* baby step for my business plan: the cold, hard numbers. When it came to complex graphs and spreadsheets, however, I was entering territory that was way beyond my pay grade.

Needing some professional guidance, I decided to pay a visit to USC's business school. I'd heard that many of the professors there had their own consulting firms on the side. As an alum, I was sure I'd find at least one professor willing to give a fellow Trojan some free advice.

After pounding on several doors, that's exactly what I found— just *one* professor willing to take time out of his busy schedule to talk with me. In the hallway outside his office, the professor flipped through my business plan, giving it a quick once-over, then closed it and said, "There's absolutely no way you can afford me."

On to Plan B: USC's archrival, UCLA. There I found Carlos, an ambitious young MBA student from South America. As a future business tycoon, Carlos saw great potential in my idea—but not quite in the same way I did. After crunching the numbers, he came up with a very ambitious plan. According to his projections, by the fifth year, there would be dozens of BIAs everywhere, with sales in the tens of millions. And not just in France, but in the Netherlands, Germany, and Spain. And if all went well—Asia, Australia, and South America too.

And why not a "Breakfast on the Moon" while you're at it? I thought.

"Carlos," I said. "I'm fine being ambitious and all, but aren't these numbers just a tad unrealistic?"

"Who's going to business school, huh? Me or you?" Carlos replied. Then with a wry smile he added, "Don't worry, bro. I ran all the numbers by my professor. And believe it or not, he thinks I'm being too conservative."

"That may be true," I said. "But right now I just need to figure out how much it'll cost for just *one* BIA."

"One BIA? No way, man. It's gotta be a chain! Nobody's gonna invest in just one."

Investors? A chain? ¡Tranquilo, *Carlos!* I thought. *Baby steps, remember?*

"Ok," I said, taking a deep breath. "But first things first. Did you get a chance to look at my budget for BIA number one?"

"Yeah, yeah, it's here," Carlos said, pointing at one lowly figure buried among many.

When I saw Carlos's budget, I nearly had a heart attack. I had calculated $250,000 for the first BIA. But Carlos had calculated almost twice as much—nearly half a million dollars! And that was just for start-up costs alone.

"How am I ever going to come up with half a million bucks?" I said.

"Exactly," Carlos said. "See, that's why you're gonna have to find investors."

MBAs suck. Especially when they're right.

However, before I could even consider looking for investors, I had to find a lawyer to set up the holding company to issue shares. Since my business would be in France, I figured a good place to start was the French-American Chamber of Commerce (FACC).

I had trouble finding the FACC offices, which were located in the trendy part of Hollywood, on the second floor of an art deco building above a furniture shop. There were only two people in the office, one of whom, the president, was away on vacation, which left an intern in charge. When I told her I was looking for a lawyer, she handed me a short list of firms that had offices in both Los Angeles and Paris. One firm in particular stood out: Coudert Brothers. From the folksy sound of their name, I figured they might be a small family firm. *Maybe they'd be willing to help me out, in exchange for some free BIA mugs and T-shirts*, I thought, half in jest.

After making an appointment, I drove downtown to the Coudert Brothers offices with my new and improved (or rather, MBA-approved) business plan in hand. I was surprised to see that the firm was housed in a gleaming new high rise. After signing in at the front security desk, I crammed my way into an elevator full of suits. In sharp contrast to them, I wore a rumpled dress shirt and chinos. The higher the elevator climbed, the more I became concerned that perhaps I was in the wrong place.

My concerns were quickly put to rest the moment I met Adam, a young lawyer at the firm. After a friendly handshake, Adam invited me into his office, which had a magnificent view of LA from on high. Knowing that lawyers—like therapists—charged by the hour, I wasted no time getting down to business, telling Adam about BIA and my limited funds. He admitted that normally Coudert Brothers wouldn't take on a project like mine. But he loved my idea so much—and especially my passion for it—that he was willing to work for a small fee to help me get started.

I knew Adam and I were a good fit the moment he looked at Carlos's numbers and said, "Very ambitious. But why don't we start off with just *one* diner first, okay?"

I nodded and smiled. *Yep, this was definitely a French firm.*

Next, Adam explained that we would need to set up a limited liability company (LLC) for the holding company and to house the start-up capital, which would later be wired to France. Lastly, along with the LLC, Adam said he would need to draft up an operating and subscription agreement for future investors.

"How much will all that cost?" I said, afraid of the answer.

"I'll need to get back to you on that," Adam said. "It's a little complicated, since your diner will be operating in France, but your investors will own shares here in California."

To get started, Adam said he would need a $1,000 retainer. I pulled out my checkbook, knowing that the balance in my account would barely cover the check I was about to write.

"I have one last question," I said. "About the name of my diner…"

I explained that when I first came up with the idea for Breakfast in America, it never crossed my mind that the British rock group Supertramp had an album with the same name. A friend pointed it out to me, concerned because Jimmy Buffett had successfully sued a restaurant in Arizona that called itself Margaritaville, the name of one of Buffett's most famous songs.

"If you think it'll be a problem for Breakfast in America, I can always try to talk to Supertramp about it," I said.

"You know them?" Adam asked.

"No. But my friend lives next door to their drummer. Crazy coincidence, huh?"

"Yeah," Adam said. "But I wouldn't worry about it. Your diner is a completely different entity than an album. We call it a 'noncompete.'"

"Okay, you're the expert," I said with a smile, even though I wasn't sure why the noncompete thing hadn't applied to Margaritaville as well.

As Adam prepared the paperwork—and the price tag that went along with it—I continued working on other things for BIA, including the company logo and business cards. My good friend Cecilia, an artist, writer, and cookbook author, offered to design BIA's logo for free. Featuring an iconic frying pan and two sunny-side up eggs in the middle, it's the same logo we still use today. I also got help from another good friend from USC, Will, who set up BIA's website for free as well.

The more I worked on developing the idea for BIA, the more obsessed I became with it. But I wasn't the only one who was becoming obsessed. My friends were too. And their friends. Before I knew it, total strangers wanted to introduce me to people they thought might be able to help me.

"You've got to meet Eric!" a friend of a friend said. "He owns a popular French restaurant called Cafe Beaujolais in Eagle Rock. You heard of it?"

I hadn't, but I was anxious to meet its French owner, Eric, so I could pick his brain. Up until that point, I'd only met with American restaurant owners.

Eric loved the idea for BIA but laughed when I told him it would be in Paris. "I had a restaurant in France once," he said. "Never again."

"Why not?"

"You'll find out," he said. Then, with a smile, he added, "Forget what I just said, okay? I don't want to discourage you." When I pressed Eric for more information, he would only say, "The French don't like it when you're successful. If you are, they'll make your life hell."

"I should be so lucky," I said. "I mean, to be that successful, that is."

"You will be," Eric smiled. "You have a great idea. So go for it!"

Perhaps it was the screenwriter in me, but when I spoke with restaurant owners like Eric, what got me most excited were their personal stories—how they'd gotten close to their staff and customers, helping them out with their problems, attending their weddings and baby showers, and, in one case, even coming together to care for a terminally ill waiter. These stories stirred my heart. I realized that by creating BIA, I was creating something more than just a restaurant; I was creating the home I had always wanted.

One afternoon, I returned home from my temp job to find my answering machine flashing. Maybe it was just my active imagination, but I could've sworn that the red light was more intense than usual. I played the message.

"Craig, it's Adam. Your lawyer. Call me back. It's urgent!"

Oh merde, I thought. *Sounds serious.* I called Adam right away.

"You're going to have to change the name of your diner!" he said.

"What? Why? I thought you said it was a noncompete."

"I know, I know," he said. "Let me explain."

Adam went on to tell me that earlier that day, he was making copies of some documents for me when a colleague noticed that "Breakfast in America" was written on them.

"Oh, I love Supertramp!" she said.

"You've heard of them?" he asked.

"Of course," she said. "I had all their albums back in the eighties."

From his colleague's reaction, Adam began to suspect that perhaps there was more to this Supertramp thing than he'd realized. He decided to do a quick survey around the office and discovered that everyone over the age of thirty was familiar with the band. Anyone younger, like him, had never heard of them. Digging deeper, Adam was shocked to discover that in their heyday, Supertramp had sold nearly thirty million albums worldwide.

"I'm sorry, Craig," Adam said. "But when you first told me about Supertramp, I thought they were just a local band. I didn't realize they were so famous."

"Why would you think they were a local band?"

"Because you said your friend lived next door to the drummer."

"It's LA! Everybody lives next door to somebody famous!"

After a long pause, Adam said, "I'm sorry, Craig, but the rules are different for the bigwigs. That's why you'll never see a 'Coca-Cola Rent-A-Car.'"

I knew what Adam was trying to say before he said it: "The bottom line is, unless you can get Supertramp's blessing, you're going to have to change the name of your diner."

The next day, my friend went to see the drummer from Supertramp. He refused to talk to her. Instead, he gave her his manager's phone number and said, "Call Max."

When Max answered the phone with his gruff Brooklyn accent, I pictured a classic old-school manager dressed in polyester from head to toe, sitting in a wood-paneled office. At first, Max thought I wanted money.

"No, Max, I don't want money," I said. "I'm calling about a little diner I'm opening in Paris. I want to call it Breakfast in America and was hoping I could get Supertramp's blessing."

"I don't know," he said suspiciously. "A diner, huh? Let me check with the boys. I'll give you a holler next week."

True to his word, Max called me back the following week. "The boys don't want to do it," he said.

"Why not?"

"They're worried it'll hurt their image."

"How? It's just a little diner."

"You gotta understand something. The boys are *huge* in France. They don't want their fans to think they sold out."

"But...I'll make sure the French don't think that," I said, desperately trying to think of something quick. "Like...I don't know, I could put a big mural on the wall—dedicated to Supertramp—thanking them for not being money-grubbing capitalists who would sue a tiny little diner just because it happens to have the same name as an album they recorded twenty years ago!"

"Nah," Max said. "Nice try, kid. But it ain't gonna happen."

"But—"

"And just so there's no funny stuff, I'm letting you know right now, the boys own the copyright to Breakfast in America. And not just in France. But the whole goddamn world! Same with a live album they recorded in Paris—called *Paris*. I'm pretty sure they own that word too. But I gotta check."

Merde alors.

After I hung up with Max, I called Adam to tell him the news. Adam was sorry to hear it, but he said he had some good news that might cheer me up: he had figured out the price tag for setting up Breakfast in America...er...the to-be-named American diner in...some French city.

The next day, I met with Adam in his office. "Five thousand for everything," he said with a smile. "That includes setting up the LLC, as well as the operating and subscription agreements."

"That's great news, Adam," I said. I'd been worried that it might cost twice that much. "But, um...is that before or after the retainer?"

"After."

I didn't have the heart to tell Adam that I didn't have $5,000 to fork over to him just yet. As if reading my mind, he said, "Don't worry, Craig, there's no hurry. You can pay us once we've drafted up the documents."

"That's very kind of you, Adam," I said. "I can't thank you enough."

"Hey, we're all behind you on this, Craig. Everybody in the firm can't wait to go to Paris and have some pancakes!"

"You and me both." I smiled.

Wow, what a week! Not only did I have to come up with a new name for my diner, but I also had to come up with $5,000. As the obstacles kept piling up, I had no idea how I would ever be able to overcome them.

My official Disney name tag.

Chapter 5

MERCI TO THE MOUSE

"You may not realize it when it happens, but a kick
in the teeth may be the best thing in the world for you."

—Walt Disney

AFTER MY MEETING WITH ADAM, I REALIZED THAT MY FINANCIAL situation was far worse than I had thought. In reality, I wasn't just $5,000 short for the LLC. It was more like $25,000, due to my maxed-out credit card debt. Actually, if you counted my student loans, the total was closer to $100,000.

Since I was so far in the hole, I would need to find investors as soon as possible. That's when I found myself in the perfect catch-22: in order to get money from investors, I needed to set up the LLC; but in order to set up the LLC, I needed money from investors. It was time to face a hard reality: I would have to find a full-time job.

And where did I end up? *Chez* Disney, thanks to my friend Susan, who worked in the marketing department, where an assistant position was available.

"But here's the thing," Susan said. "You'll have to start off as a temp. Are you okay with that?"

"A temp? Sure! I'm used to it."

Of course, I had a long history with the Mouse House; after all, it was the number-one place that temp agencies used to send me to when I was a struggling screenwriter. Back then, the work was so much fun, I entertained thoughts of slitting my wrists on a daily basis. Until, that is, a very special assignment came my way. Because I spoke French, the temp agency assigned me to the animation department, where a group of French artists had just arrived from Paris. They were in Burbank to learn the "Disney Way," and I was called on to be their *attaché culturel*, if you will. My job included such things as showing them the sites of Los Angeles and playing *pétanque* (a game similar to bocce ball), a glass of Ricard in hand, *bien sûr*. Nice work if you can get it!

I became very close with the French gang during that time, especially Sylvain and Catpou, both of whom would end up playing important roles in the creation of BIA. Furthermore, my new French friends and I bonded over what it meant to do things the Disney Way. For them, as animators, it meant homogenizing their individual artistic talents into a generic, mass-produced package—much like fast food. For me, it somehow meant selling a piece of my soul. That's why when this new job came along, I was fine being just a temp—and not a cast member (which is what Disney actually calls all of their employees). In any case, it didn't really matter what Disney called me, because I wasn't planning on sticking around for very long anyway.

From my first day back at Disney, I never tried to hide the fact that my ultimate goal was to one day open an American diner in Paris. In fact, all of my colleagues knew that as soon as I had saved up enough money for the LLC, I'd be punching out my last time card and boarding the next plane for the City of Light.

I was amazed by how supportive my colleagues at Disney were. I could see the longing in their eyes whenever I spoke of my favorite city and how beautiful it was...how all it needed was an American breakfast joint, and then it would be perfect! From their enthusiastic reactions, I got the feeling that some of my coworkers were vicariously living their dreams through me. For instance, one day a woman who worked down the hall came by my cubicle and said rather shyly, "*Bonjour, je m'appelle* Fiona."

"*Enchanté*," I said.

A look of panic crossed her face. "That's it for my *fran-say!*" she said. Then her eyes lit up. "I hear you're opening a diner in France! I just *love* France, and I think it's a great idea! So if you're ever looking for a waitress"—she raised her hand—"I've got experience, and I'm available!"

Fiona was the only person on the entire floor who had a coffee machine. Every morning I would pass by her office, empty mug in hand. With a big, warm smile, Fiona would fill up my mug, inviting me to come back anytime for as much coffee as I wanted.

As time passed, I began to realize that even though I was getting a steady paycheck, it would be nearly impossible for me to save the $5,000 I needed for the LLC. Between rent and minimum payments on my maxed-out credit cards, plus my student loans, I was barely able to squeak by month to month.

As Paris seemed to slip further away, I began to fear that I would end up like Manny, the guy downstairs in consumer products who proudly wore his twenty-five-year-anniversary pin. Manny was such a dedicated employee, he barely left his cubicle. At one point, he had accumulated so many vacation days that the company *made* him take time off. (Tell this story to a French person and their eyes will bug out in horror: "Forced to take *vacances*? *C'est pas possible!*") So imagine how I felt the day my boss, Lance, called me into his office.

"Craig, I've got some good news," he said. "Since you've been with us for a couple of months now, and you're doing a great job..."

Oh no, I thought. *Please, no.*

"I want to make it official." Lance smiled. "I want to make you a *cast member!*"

Aw, not that corporate-speak again! At Disney, you couldn't just be an employee. You had to be a cast member, as if you were touring in a goddamn Broadway musical. I took a deep breath and kept my composure.

"Wow, Lance, I don't know what to say."

"Look, Craig, you're working here already, right? Why not get benefits too?"

Hmm...benefits. Now he was talking. At thirty-seven years old, I had never had benefits in my life. The more I thought about Lance's offer, the more appealing it seemed. Disney was known for its great medical plan, which included dental coverage. I hadn't had a checkup in years—not to mention I was battling a stubborn case of plaque buildup.

Just then, like in those old cartoons where there's a little devil on one shoulder and an angel on the other, the devil's voice chimed in: "Don't do it, Craig! Don't sell your soul! You've held off for this long! *Résiste!*"

"Aw, that's bunk!" the voice of the angel countered. "Selling your soul is a small price to pay for good oral hygiene."

Lance looked at me long and hard. "Craig, you seem torn."

"No need to feel torn," the angel said to me. "Mental health coverage is in the Disney plan. You can get therapy to deal with your conflicting feelings."

Oooh, therapy. The angel and the devil looked at each other a second, nodded, then said in unison: "Do it!"

"I'll do it!" I said, shaking Lance's hand.

And with that, I was one step closer to becoming an official Disney cast member—and one giant leap closer to making Breakfast in America a reality.

I'm sure that someday anthropologists will be able to trace the roots of the Disney indoctrination ceremony back to the rituals of early man. The tribal mentality is pretty much the same, but instead of grunts and chest thumping, the modern-day version is done in a high, squeaky voice, accompanied by reams and reams of paperwork from the legal department.

For half a day, I was holed up in a conference room with a couple dozen ecstatic game-show contestants, er...I mean, *cast members*, who stared in rapt attention at the orientation leader, Paula. Every time she told a corny joke or flashed an image of a furry, animated character, the crowd reacted with the appropriate giggle or childlike "aaahhh."

After warming up the crowd, Paula went around the room to ask each cast member who their favorite Disney character was—as if it were a given that you actually had one. Like cliques in high school, the ass-kissers picked Mickey or Minnie. The cutups went with Goofy or Grumpy. And the gays and lesbians—Cruella de Vil.

Somehow I ended up being the last one called upon. "Tell us, Craig." Paula smiled. "Who's your favorite Disney character?"

All eyes stared at me in eager anticipation. I strained to think of which group I belonged to. The nerds? The loners? The friends of

Dorothy? After a moment, I looked at Paula and said, "Gosh, there are sooo many. How can I choose just one?"

With that, the crowd erupted in laughter and applause, a chorus of, "How true!" and, "Ah, there's the rub!"

Paula smiled. "Okay, everybody, we're going to take a short break. When we come back, we will have your official cast member name tags ready for you!"

Whoops and hollers erupted from the crowd. All except for me—I sank deep down in my seat.

During our break a table was set up outside the conference room on which name tags were spread out alphabetically and in perfect rows. One by one, enthusiastic cast members plucked up their newly minted identities (replete with smiling Mickeys) and pinned them onto their lapels. After a congratulatory hand-shake, they pivoted and strutted off like good soldiers back to their posts.

As I got closer to the table, I tried to make out where my name tag was. Very few remained, none of which contained five letters beginning with a C. I stepped up to the table, where a lady with a pasted-on smile sat like an automaton, unblinking.

"Wow! Looks like you're the last one!" she said cheerfully. "Name please?"

"Craig," I said.

The lady began fingering through the few name tags that remained... Robbie. Gail. Miguel. But no Craig. Realizing my name tag wasn't there, her body began to freeze up. There was a glitch in the perfectly oiled Disney machine!

Just then, a frantic middle-aged woman burst through an unmarked door in the hallway, her arms flailing as she ran toward me. "Oh my goodness! Oh my goodness!" she said as she tried to catch her breath. "Are you Craig?"

I nodded.

"I've been doing this for more than twenty years, and nothing like this has ever happened before."

With immense shame, the woman opened her hand to reveal my name tag. But instead of my name, there was what looked like the beginnings of the letter *C*, but it quickly deteriorated into a long scraggly line, like a needle scratch across a vinyl record.

"I don't know what happened!" she moaned. "It's like the machine wouldn't do it! We tried and tried, but it just wouldn't do it!" She was near tears now. "I'm so sorry, Craig. We'll make you another one as soon as possible. I promise."

I shook my head and said softly, reassuringly, "No, no. It's okay." I then gently pried open her clenched hand and retrieved my bastard name tag. "It's perfect."

I couldn't help but smile. Poor Walt. After what had just happened, he must've been spinning in his cryonic grave.

As my dream seemed to get pushed further and further down the road, I tried to make the best of my situation. I took full advantage of my cast-member benefits, including getting a long-overdue medical exam, a thorough dental *détartrage*, and, most importantly, weekly sessions with a shrink, Dr. Emily.

The main topic of our discussions involved Fiona, who I was now dating. I was hoping Dr. Emily could help me get a better understanding of my problems with intimacy, including the panic attack I'd had years earlier with Isabelle. Although we were making some progress, Dr. Emily and I soon discovered that there was one *petit problème* getting in the way of my having a serious relationship: I didn't like to be touched.

Dr. Emily suspected that it might have had something to do

with a story my grandma Lizzy used to tell me. Back when I was a baby and my parents were still together, my gram decided to stop by the house one day and check up on me. She was concerned because right after I was brought home from the hospital, my mom started acting very strangely.

When my gram rang the doorbell, there was no answer. She rang it again and again. Nothing. After a few minutes, my mom finally opened the door, but she just stood there without saying a word, a dishrag in her hand, staring off into space. My gram could hear me crying upstairs.

"Louise, do you mind if I check on Craigie?" she asked.

After a long pause, my mom mumbled something unintelligible, then stepped aside. My gram rushed upstairs to my crib, where she found me kicking and screaming, my face beet red and covered with dried tears. My gram said she had no idea how many times—or for how long—I'd been left alone like that. She picked me up and began rocking me in her arms. She said it took forever to calm me down.

Back in Dr. Emily's office, I tried to make light of the situation. "Okay, I think I get it now," I said. "As long as Fiona doesn't touch me or stare into my eyes with that crazy lovestruck look, then she and I will get along just fine."

Just when I thought I'd be stuck at Disney forever, my ship finally came in. It happened on a lovely April day on the Burbank lot, as squirrels chased each other down Dopey Drive, birds welcomed spring with a song, and CEO Michael Eisner sat in his office calculating how the value of his stocks and bonuses would soar pursuant to a decision he'd just made.

As I walked back from lunch at the commissary, I could sense that something was in the air. It wasn't until I got back to my cubicle that it became clear that indeed something was *very* wrong. Instead of displaying their usual hustle and bustle, cast members stood at their desks in stunned silence, their eyes glued to letters that they'd found waiting for them upon their return from their lunch break.

I went over to my cubicle and picked up my copy of the letter. It was from Disney CEOs Michael Eisner and Bob Iger. It began with the usual corporate-speak, informing cast members of all the "strategic initiatives" Disney had undertaken in order to achieve "long term-growth and profitability." *Blah, blah, blah.*

Just when I was about to fall asleep from the snooze-inducing letter, it suddenly took a sharp turn and began talking about the "softening economic environment" as well as the challenge of operating in "the most efficient way possible." Right near the end, the letter got down to the nitty-gritty, declaring that Disney had made "the difficult but necessary decision" to cut down the company's global workforce by a whopping *four thousand full-time employees.*

As I read those words, I felt as if I could hear a collective gasp coming from thousands of cast members all across the Disney empire. This was historic. In its company history, Disney had never made such a drastic move. It was so extreme that it evoked the ire of Roy Disney himself, Walt's nephew. Sometimes referred to as Disney's "conscience," Roy was not afraid to let his feelings be known. He saw the decision as another nail in the coffin of the once-humane business that his uncle had built. He even went so far as to suggest that instead of giving pink slips to four thousand employees, Eisner should cut part of his $72 million in bonuses and stock options.

But this was *not* a typical corporate downsizing. Reading the letter further, it became clear that *Messieurs* Eisner and Iger had something else up their sleeves. Instead of *them* having to make the "difficult but necessary decision" of who to fire, Mike and Bob hoped that cast members would step up and volunteer to leave the company themselves. To encourage them, Disney was offering something called the *Voluntary Separation Program* (VSP), ensuring that cast members would receive special severance incentives if they left on their own. But if enough cast members did *not* volunteer to jump ship, Disney warned that "mandatory workforce reductions" would have to take place instead—but with much *lower* severance benefits.

Wait a second. Were they saying what I thought they were saying? Leave voluntarily and get paid more, or risk being axed *involuntarily* and get paid less?

I read the letter again, this time much more carefully—it seemed too good to be true. Was Disney really willing to pay me a bonus to leave? And all because I wasn't a temp, but a cast member, something I never wanted to be in the first place? *How ironic was that? Or is a better word serendipitous?*

As the realization began to sink in that this could be the golden ticket I needed to get myself to Paris, I found myself doing a little jig right there in the hallway. I really started getting into it, tapping my feet and doing the hippy hippy shake. That is, until I looked up and saw a bunch of stone-faced cast members staring at me. I stopped dancing, smiled sheepishly, then crumpled up the letter. "Damn corporate overlords!" I growled.

"I'm not surprised that you decided to take the VSP package," Fiona said to me over breakfast the next morning. The two of us had been getting together a lot lately to explore new breakfast joints, hoping to discover delicious new recipes for my diner. Today's selection was Marston's in Pasadena. The popular coffee shop was known for its "Fantastic French Toast" dish, which was made with two thick slices of sourdough bread dipped in egg batter and rolled in cornflakes.

"Hey, what could I do?" I said as I took a big, crunchy bite of my French toast. "Disney made me an offer I couldn't refuse!"

Fiona laughed. She then took a sip of her coffee and looked down at her plate for a long moment, swirling her maple syrup with her fork.

"I'm going to miss you coming by my office every morning for coffee," she said, taking my hand.

"Me too," I said.

As Fiona held my hand, I could feel a slight panic attack coming on. Truth be told, Fiona and I had been taking things very slowly. In fact, we hadn't even kissed yet, which was probably for the best, since I wasn't going to be sticking around LA much longer anyway. But when I spoke to Dr. Emily about this, she wondered if perhaps I was using my leaving as an excuse to avoid intimacy—to kick the can farther down the road.

Perhaps. But I had so much going on with BIA, I didn't have time to think about it. Sensing my unease, Fiona let go of my hand and returned to her French toast. "This is delicious, don't you think?" she said. "You have to have it on the menu at Breakfast in America."

"Absolutely," I said. "As long as they have cornflakes in France."

After bidding my colleagues in the marketing department *adieu*, I made my way over to the HR department. According to the VSP agreement, I would receive one lump sum of ten weeks' severance pay—just two weeks less than what employees who'd been working at Disney for up to four years would get paid. And I'd only been there for a few *months*.

With armed security guards watching me from the sidelines, I readied myself to sign the pile of legal paperwork stacked in front of me. But first, the HR rep wanted to make sure that I understood that this was my own decision, that I was in no way forced into it, and that I was at peace with my decision.

I assured her I was.

Once I had signed everything, she pulled out a crisp paper sleeve from her desk drawer and opened it, revealing my last cast member paycheck. But before handing it over, she said, "Oh, almost forgot: I'll need your parking badge, parking pass, and name tag."

I handed her each item, one by one, ending with my squiggly, nameless name tag. She stared at it a long moment, not sure what to think. I raised an eyebrow as if to say, "long story." She examined my nameless name tag one last time, then waved her hand and said, "I don't need that."

Then, at long last, she handed me my big fat paycheck—for almost $6,000. As fast as my clunky old '64 Chevy could get me there, I raced over to Coudert Brothers and happily forked over the funds to pay for the creation of BIA Investments, LLC.

Whoo-hoo! BIA was on its way—thanks to *Mickey la Souris!*

In the end, three thousand cast members took the VSP package, and one thousand were involuntarily let go. As for the employees of Disney's operations in that faraway magical kingdom of France, where I'd soon be living? According to an article in the *Los Angeles Times*, "Disney's European operations survived relatively unscathed because of restrictive labor laws abroad." I didn't know it yet, but the term "restrictive labor laws" would turn out to be a *major* understatement.

A fabulous gift for potential investors: a mug with BIA's new name on it.

Chapter 6

SHOW ME THE MONEY!

"Investing in a restaurant is a risky labor of love."

—Paul Sullivan, the *New York Times*

NOW THAT I HAD THE LLC SET UP, I COULD MOVE ON TO THE next step: finding investors for American Breakfast Diner. *Nope, that's not a mistake.* "American Breakfast Diner" was now the new and *temporary* name for BIA. (Or at least I *hoped* it would be temporary).

But before I could begin my search for investors, I needed to meet with Adam to go over the final drafts of the operating and subscription agreements, both of which were required for investors to be able to purchase shares in the company. I was surprised to see that Adam had added two lines under the "Return on Investment" (ROI) section of the documents:

> All our projections and future plans are based solely
> on our expectations. The possibility exists that no
> funds will ever be distributed and all investment will
> be lost.

"What's this?" I asked.

"Just standard legal jargon. To protect yourself should...things not go as planned."

"The wording's kind of strong, don't you think? Won't it deter investors?"

"No. Not if they're *real* investors."

I nodded. But still, it didn't sit well with me. I reread the line:

> All our projections and future plans are based solely
> on our expectations...

Solely? Wasn't my dream more than just my imagination? Or was I living in some kind of Hollywood fantasy land?

Adam brought my attention back to the next subject at hand: the start-up budget for BIA #1. Fortunately, I was able to bring it back down to my original amount of $250,000. In Carlos's version, he had calculated building the diner from the ground up. I, on the other hand, discovered ways to save money, including looking for an existing restaurant space that could be converted into a diner.

Carlos *was* right about one thing, though: if I wanted to attract serious investors, I would have to show them that they had the potential to earn serious dividends. But instead of the multinational megachain that he'd envisioned, I trusted my gut and went with a more conservative projection: three diners in Paris by the end of the fifth year.

However, in order to finance the first restaurant, I would need a loan from a French bank. It's hard enough for a *French* person to get a loan from a French bank, but if you're a foreigner like me with a risky business venture that's never been tested, well… In short, I would need to come up with a much larger down payment than I had originally anticipated—roughly 40 percent, or a minimum of $100,000!

Adam advised me to keep it simple: one investor—two at the most—willing to go in at $50,000 each. *Easier said than done*, I thought. I'd had enough trouble finding $5,000 to set up the LLC. How was I ever going to find twenty times that amount?

Adam had a suggestion. Since my little Parisian diner was an unconventional business, he recommended that I look for someone unconventional to invest in it. That is to say, I should try to find an angel investor, a wealthy individual who was willing to take a risk on what's called a "passion investment," meaning someone who was motivated more by love than money.

As logical as that sounded, I could tell it wasn't going to be easy; I had never even heard of angel investors before, nor did I have any idea where to find them. And as the name implies, angels were *not* easy to find. I decided to go back to the French-American Chamber of Commerce, figuring that if ever there were a place to find investors passionate about France, that would be it. The president was *still* on vacation, but his intern gave me a list of weekly mixers, or symposiums, where venture capitalists met. I signed up for as many as I could.

Things got off to a promising start. Every person I met loved my idea and couldn't wait to have pancakes in Paris once BIA was open. But when the subject of investing came up, they all said the same thing: "Do you have anything more high-tech?"

After attending several of these events, I ended up with only two bites. The first came from a Russian oligarch who loved France, and especially French women. I had no idea how he'd made his fortune, but that didn't matter to me. I just wanted him to stop leading me on and write a goddamn check already! Instead, I found myself following him around, from one swanky party to the next, acting as his translator whenever he wanted to impress a French *femme fatale* who didn't speak English. It was a total waste of my time.

The only other potential angel was a wealthy California-based surgeon who was also a passionate Francophile. The surgeon told me that he would invest on two conditions: (1) BIA would have to be completely nonsmoking, and (2) it would have to be located in Marseille, his favorite city.

It's important to note that, in 2001, California was the only place on the planet that had banned smoking in restaurants, thanks in large part to this surgeon, who had helped champion the law. However, as much as I loved the idea of a smoke-free restaurant, I was pretty sure that the chances of the French banning smoking in my lifetime were about...*zéro*. Still, I told the surgeon that I would think about it. I even added Marseille to our business plan as a possible location for a future BIA.

Despite jumping through hoops for him, the surgeon turned out to be all talk and no action, much like most of the people I met at these symposiums—especially consultants. These guys had such high opinions of themselves, they would charge clients an arm and a leg just to hear their "secrets" of success. (An example: "If you're going to meet with investors," a consultant told me, "be sure to iron your shirt.")

I can only speak for myself, but I soon came to the conclusion that, "Those who can't do, consult."

Case in point, at one of these mixers, I ran into the same professor from USC's business school who I'd met with before—the one who said I could never afford him. Let's call him "Professor Windbag." He asked me where I was on my project. When I told him I was having a little trouble raising the funds, he offered to make a deal with me: if I presented my project to his class, he would give me a free consultation—and perhaps introduce me to some investment angels!

Of course, I accepted. I couldn't wait to pitch my idea to his students. Not only was my business plan in great shape, but I also had an impressive PowerPoint presentation, having taken a free course on the software when I worked at Disney. I was sure that once the class heard my idea for BIA, they would go gaga over it.

Au contraire. Throughout my entire presentation, the students sat there stone-faced, looking at me as if I were a hick who had just fallen off his tractor. Professor Windbag was even less gracious. He sat there the whole time, shaking his head and tsk-tsking, just like my grandma Lizzy used to do whenever she disapproved of something I'd done.

"It never ceases to amaze me," he said, "but no matter who comes here to present their 'brilliant' idea, they always forget... *What,* class?"

"A management plan!"

"And what else?"

"An exit strategy!"

A management plan? An exit strategy? Yeah, yeah, but what about my idea? You have to admit it's original! Brilliant! Ground-breaking even!

Nope. No love from this crowd.

As for my free consultation? Professor Windbag said, "I'll give you the time it takes to walk to my car to ask me whatever you want."

After episodes like this, I was starting to lose hope that I would ever find an investment angel. And then a funny thing happened. My friend Will was looking for funding for a dot-com when he unexpectedly found himself in a meeting with my old trust-funder pal from film school, Dave. Frustrated with Hollywood, Dave had decided to go back to school to get his MBA and was now a billion-aire venture capitalist living in Silicon Valley.

Now, I'm no MBA, but if there was one thing I'd learned from putting my business plan together, it was that a billion dollars was a *lot* of money.

Amazingly, not only had Dave remembered Will from our film-school days, but during their meeting, Dave had also asked about me and how I was doing. When Will told him about my restaurant venture, Dave handed him his personal email address and told Will to have me drop him a line.

Incroyable! I thought. Perhaps my expensive stint at USC was going to pay off after all.

I immediately wrote Dave an email, telling him all about my crazy dream of opening the first American diner in Paris and won-dering if he knew of anyone who might be interested in invest-ing. Dave wrote right back with perhaps the nicest email I've ever received. In it, he fondly recalled our days living in the same dorm, playing guitar, and singing James Taylor tunes. Then he recounted how he had made his fortune. In one deal alone, Dave had made a good chunk of his billions by getting in on the ground floor of a risky little Internet start-up called Yahoo.

I stared at my computer screen. This was so unreal. How easy it would be for Dave to invest a piddling sum like $100,000 in my diner. He probably wouldn't even notice a blip in his bank account. At that moment, it suddenly clicked. *Of course*, I thought, *that's why they're called* angel *investors*. With one stroke of his pen, Dave could perform a miracle!

My heart raced as I skimmed through several more paragraphs of Dave describing his amazing success story, looking to see if he'd mentioned my diner anywhere. He had. Right near the end. First, he wanted to let me know how much he loved my idea. Having been to France, he was sure it would work. Next, he wanted to give me a vote of confidence, saying that he was sure I had the chops to pull it off, even though I'd never owned a business before. And lastly, Dave wished me luck finding investors.

Wait, wait. Back up.

I reread Dave's email at least a hundred times, especially the last paragraph. I was sure I had missed something. Nope. Dave made it quite clear that when it came to investing, his forte was high-tech. The same was true of his millionaire/billionaire friends. Try as he might, Dave said he could not think of a single person he knew who would want to invest in a restaurant. Although he didn't come out and say it, I could read between the lines: "I may be a billionaire risk-taker, but I'm not crazy!"

I learned two important things from my experience with Dave. First, even though I'd developed important entrepreneurial skills growing up, I still had my fair share of mental blocks too, which had the potential of stopping me dead in my tracks. Of all the challenges I faced in creating my diner, asking for money was the *hardest* thing for me to do.

Dr. Emily said the reason for that was simple: as a result of never being allowed to ask for anything when I was growing up, I'd never actually learned *how* to ask for anything. When speaking with dozens of potential investors, not once had I been able to come out and ask the simple, direct question: "Would you like to invest in my diner?" Instead, I would beat around the bush and say, "Hey, I have this great idea! Wanna hear it? Gosh, I sure hope that other people will be as excited about it as I am!"

It's a miracle that I was ever able to raise a dime.

The second thing I learned from Dave was that no investor in his or her right mind would invest in my diner out of love instead of money. It was time to accept the fact that no angel investor was ever going to come along and save me.

It was time for a new strategy. *Okay, no takers at $50,000? How about $25,000—and you'll get your very own booth with a plaque that has your name on it! Still no takers? Do I hear $15,000? $10,000? $7,500?*

Cue the sound of crickets.

Seeing the difficulty I was having finding investors, some of my friends who weren't trust funders stepped up and offered to help. The only problem was that the maximum they could afford to invest was $5,000 each. Was I okay with that?

It's funny how some things never change. When I was a paperboy, my poorest customers always gave me the best tips. And when it came to investors, those who had the least gave the most.

"Sure!" I told my friends. At this point, I was willing to take anything.

Adam cautioned me about the complications that could arise from having too many investors. For example, it could make it very difficult for my exit strategy, if one day I wanted to buy back all the shares and sell the company.

Not a problem, I thought, *since I didn't have an exit strategy anyway.*

My very first investors were my friends Todd and Tiffany, a young newlywed couple who were struggling to make ends meet. For them, $5,000 was a lot of money. I felt extremely guilty and wanted to make sure they understood the risk they'd be taking. I pointed to the fine print at the bottom of the subscription agreement:

> The possibility exists that no funds will ever be distributed and all investment will be lost.

"Do you know what that means?" I asked. "This is not your normal investment. It's a labor of love."

Todd and Tiffany looked at me, smiled warmly, and said, "Where do we sign?"

Getting my first investor helped me immensely in convincing others to hop on board. Before I knew it, I had a total of seven investors! Although it took much longer than I'd anticipated—almost a year—I was able to raise a total of $35,000.

That was the good news. The bad news: after raising the initial $35,000, I hit a brick wall, falling $65,000 short of my goal. No matter how hard I tried, I was unable to raise another penny. I needed to come up with something quick—or else risk losing my dream forever.

The French Chamber of Commerce, Paris.

Chapter 7

BIA VF (*VERSION FRANÇAISE*)

"The problem with the French is they don't have a word for 'entrepreneur.'"

—President George W. Bush[2]

I HAD NO CHOICE BUT TO KEEP MOVING FORWARD. I WAS SURE THAT the reason I had hit a brick wall with investors was because Breakfast in America was still just an idea on paper, "based solely on my expectations," as Adam had so eloquently put it. If there was one thing I learned from my adventures with consultants and venture capitalists, it was that smart investors preferred to put their money into something *real*.

With that in mind, I decided it was time to find a location, an honest-to-goodness physical space. That way my idea would be

....

2   This famous quote was reported by the British press but was never substantiated.

more than just air. I was sure that once I had secured the restaurant space, *beaucoup de* moola would start gushing in.

That meant I *had* to go back to Paris. (Go ahead. Twist my arm.) But paying for a plane ticket was not going to be easy. I didn't feel comfortable using any of the $35,000 I'd raised from investors. Instead, I did the credit-card shuffle, transferring my outstanding balances to new credit cards that inexplicably kept arriving in the mail faster than I could amass debt. *But no need to worry*, I told myself. Once the business was up and running, I could reimburse myself for the travel expense. The first thing on my to-do list when I got to Paris was to set up the French company. After that, I could put a down payment on a location—assuming I found one. However, just as I was about to leave, the tragic events of 9/11 occurred. All flights were canceled. The nation was in shock, as was the rest of the world. France, our closest ally, showed its undying support when President Jacques Chirac became the first foreign leader to visit the White House after the tragedy. And, in a touching tribute, the French newspaper *Le Monde* famously declared on the front page of its September 13 edition: "*Nous sommes tous Américains*" ("We are all Americans").

Once flights resumed, the mood was very somber. The tension on board the plane that October, so soon after the tragedy, was palpable. All the passengers were completely silent, and I noticed a lot of small changes that had been implemented in a rushed manner. For example, the metal knives and forks for the in-flight meal had been replaced by a tiny plastic spork.

When I arrived in Paris, the amount of goodwill that I received from my French friends was overwhelming. Not only did they let me crash on their couches, but they also offered to help me with BIA in any way they could, especially Jérôme, a friend from *Robin Hood*. He and his father, Jean-François, who was a business consultant of the *best* kind, graciously offered to help me adapt my business plan into VF—or *version française*.

Jérôme was the perfect person for me to bounce my ideas off of. Having lived and studied in Pennsylvania, he was part of a new generation of *français* that was very open to American culture—especially the noncorporate kind.

"You have to have Philly cheesesteaks!" he said excitedly. "And crispy bacon and bagels and carrot cake and pancakes!"

"You got it, Jérôme," I said. "Anything for my best customers!"

Jérôme fit my target market to a tee: Parisians between the ages of twenty-five and thirty-five. When I showed him the pie chart from my business plan, he said it looked spot-on.

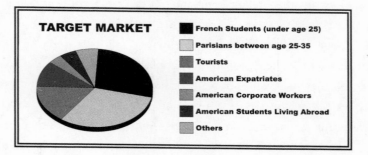

From BIA's original business plan.

The one thing Jérôme was not crazy about was the new name for BIA—"American Breakfast Diner," which, of course, I'd had to come up with because of the Supertramp debacle.

"I'm worried it might be a little confusing," he said. "Seeing those three words together—American Breakfast Diner—what if your customers think that you only serve two meals: American breakfast and dinner?"

Of course, I already knew that the word "diner" had the potential to be a problem, since *dîner* means both "dinner" and "to dine" in French. But I was convinced that once our French customers got to know us, they would find the American meaning of the word cool and *branché* (hip).

"Besides," I said to Jérôme, "the French already know what a diner is—even if they don't know it yet."

"What do you mean?"

I explained that, thanks to the saturation of American culture in France, all I had to say was "*Happy Days*" or "*Pulp Fiction,*" and a French person's eyes would light up: "*Ah… C'est ça un 'diner'!*" ("So *that's* a diner!" which the French would pronounce *daïneur,* or "da-i-neur").

"Maybe so," Jérôme said. "But still… I liked the name 'Breakfast in America' much better."

"I know, I know. Me too," I said. "That's actually one of the reasons I came to Paris this time. I'm hoping there's still a chance to get that name back."

The National Institute of Intellectual Property (INPI) was tucked away on a small street, not far from the Gare Saint-Lazare, the station where I used to catch the train to Rouen. Inside the INPI building, I sat at a tiny cubicle across from an agitated *fonctionnaire* (civil servant) who kept glancing at her pack of cigarettes on her desk, as if she couldn't wait to go on her smoke break.

"Can you spell that again?" the woman asked *en français.*

"B-R-E-A-K-F-A-S-T…as in *petit-déjeuner,*" I said. "Then, 'in,' as in *dans.* And lastly, 'America'…like the country."

"And what activity would this be for?"

"A diner."

"*Un dîner?*"

"*Non, daïneur.* A kind of restaurant."

"That serves only dinner?"

"No. Lunch, too. And particularly breakfast—all day long."

The *fonctionnaire* looked confused. "So then it's…*American* cuisine?"

"*Oui!*"

"I do not like 'amburgers," she sniffed.

"*Oui, madame,*" I said. "But you have to know, there is more to American cuisine than '*amburgers.*"

The *fonctionnaire* was not buying it. She turned back to her computer and entered the last bit of information.

"You are in luck, *monsieur,*" she said, looking at her computer screen. "'Brreck-fass een Amer-ee-ca' is available."

"Really? Are you sure?"

"But of course. We are in France. We do not use this word, 'Brreck-fass.'"

I knew it! The trademark *and* the copyright for "Breakfast in America" were still available—despite the lofty claims of Supertramp's manager. I quickly registered the name in every category I could think of that was related to food, including restaurant service (dine-in, takeout, catering, and food trucks), as well as all product lines (BIA pancake mix, maple syrup, jam, etc.), and finally merchandising, such as T-shirts, mugs, and other swag. I even registered the logo.

"Anything else?" she asked.

"Yes. Can you please look up 'Paris'?"

"*Oh là là!*" she said, giving me a look as if to say, *You Americans think you can buy everything!* "I am sorry, *monsieur,* but 'Par-ee' is not for sale!"

Et voilà. Take that Supertramp!

With my original diner name secured, I could now set up my French company and call it Breakfast in America, LLC. Or more precisely: CC's Breakfast in America, SAS (short for *société par actions simplifiée*)—the French version of an LLC.

However, when I tried to set up the SAS, I found myself in

yet another debacle, just like when I'd tried to set up the LLC in the States—only this time, my catch-22 was *à la française*. I couldn't create the SAS until I had a commercial visa, but I couldn't get a commercial visa until I had the SAS.

That's when I had my first inkling of how complicated and *slow-moving* everything was going to be in France. In the States, as long as you had the money to pay for it, you could set up a company in just a few days. But in France, it could take months.

I won't get into all the grisly details, but here's just one example of what it was like setting up a business in France. After I filled out reams of paperwork for the SAS, my application was rejected. If that weren't bad enough, the French government charged me a "rejection fee," on top of which was a "value-added tax." The way I saw it, a rejection had no value, so how could you possibly add a tax to it? *Absurde.*

Anyway, seeing how complicated everything was going to be, I decided that perhaps it might be a good idea to partner up with an actual French person—a native who could help me navigate all the crazy French bureaucracy. And, if possible, someone with restaurant experience.

This reasoning led me to André, a successful restaurateur who I'd met through yet another friend from *Robin Hood*. André owned a classic French bistro, the kind that, sadly, was becoming a rarity in Paris. With its beautiful polished brass decor and plush, burgundy-colored banquettes, André's restaurant was very popular with the old-school crowd—and in particular, the political set, which included government ministers and other bigwigs. Even more impressive, André's restaurant once had a Michelin star—a very high distinction in the culinary world. Even though his restaurant had since lost its star, the press still came to his place in droves. In fact, André had scrapbooks full of articles from nearly every French newspaper and magazine. He had even appeared on TV multiple times.

Since André was a bit of a celebrity in the culinary world, I was surprised—and grateful—that he was willing to work with a newbie like me. Although he never came out and said it, I got the impression that André saw BIA as a fun project, something that was in sharp contrast to the high-pressure, often snooty world of *haute cuisine*.

"I want to be clear about one thing, though," André said. "I will not put any of my own money into the business. But I am happy to offer my expertise."

In exchange for said expertise, André said he was willing to take shares (or sweat equity) in the company. It sounded fair to me, but when I told Jérôme and his father about the deal, they warned me to be very careful. What kind of business partner would expect to benefit from the success of a company without incurring any financial risk in it?

A very smart one, it turns out.

Despite my friends' concerns, I agreed to work with André anyway. To me, he was a really nice guy who had nothing but good intentions. For example, he *really* wanted to help me set up the French company, but since he had inherited his restaurant from his father, he didn't really know how to do so. His expertise was owning and operating a famous restaurant in France—not starting one from scratch. That said, I was sure that André would be able to help me in at least two important ways: the day-to-day operations of running a restaurant in France and, most importantly, securing a bank loan.

In the meantime, so what if my business partner couldn't help me set up the business? No biggie. I could always go to the French Chamber of Commerce. The office was located in a huge building near Les Halles. The moment I stepped inside, it was obvious that the chamber was in the middle of a huge PR campaign to change France's image as being antibusiness. Banners hung everywhere proclaiming that France was *the* best place in Europe for business start-ups.

I wondered if the PR campaign had anything to do with a recent business summit held in London where President George W. Bush had supposedly said to British prime minister Tony Blair, "The problem with the French is they don't have a word for 'entrepreneur.'" Although the quote was reported by the British press, it was never verified. But whether Bush had actually said it or not didn't matter. With the quote out there spreading like wildfire, the damage to France's reputation had already been done.

One of the ways the chamber hoped to improve France's reputation was through a program called the Young Entrepreneur. *C'est moi*, I thought as I signed up for the YE club. As a member, I received a really cool card, which served absolutely no purpose whatsoever, except that it was a really cool card.

In all fairness, the chamber did help me in two important ways. First, they took the figures from my business plan and put them into a standardized French document, which gave my company legitimacy. I could also use the document when applying for a loan from a French bank. Second, the chamber introduced me to a woman who was perfect for solving my catch-22 *à la française*. She knew the inside fast track for obtaining my commercial visa while simultaneously setting up the SAS. After months on said fast track, I finally had both. I was now ready to check off the last item on my to-do list.

While applying for my visa, I had begun scouting out potential locations for Breakfast in America. As any restaurant owner will tell you, nothing is more important than the location. Based on my market research, I focused on three target neighborhoods, places that were very near and dear to my heart: the Latin Quarter, which was full of students, tourists, and my favorite cinemas; the Marais, which was the historic district where I'd stayed in that drafty youth hostel as a student, and which had now become a hip, trendy gay neighborhood; and rue Cler, which was a lovely pedestrian street with an open-air market not far from where I'd had my first aha moment about how I belonged in France.

Unfortunately, instead of focusing on these areas, the real estate agents I met with sent me all over the city on what essentially amounted to a wild-goose chase. Each location I visited was either too big or too expensive, or the configuration wasn't right for a diner, or it was in a terrible location. It was time for a different strategy. I decided to scope out my favorite neighborhoods on my own, to see if any restaurants were giving off that "on their last legs" vibe, where the owners were clearly ready to move on, either because they were ready to retire or because they were so burned out they'd lost the will to continue. Some telltale signs include: the place hasn't been kept up in years, or it closes early, or it runs out of food halfway through service.

That was the kind of place I was looking for. And that's *exactly* how I found my perfect location! I was strolling through the Marais when I saw a restaurant space that fit my requirements to a tee. Not only had it not been renovated in years, the elderly owner looked ready to cash in his chips at any minute.

I couldn't have asked for a better spot, located right on one of the Grands Boulevards, boulevard des Filles du Calvaire, and directly across from a metro stop. As for my target demographic—the youth crowd—there were lots of schools and clubs nearby. It was also within walking distance of the Picasso Museum, which was a huge draw for American tourists.

I crossed my fingers as I entered the restaurant to ask the elderly owner, Jackie, if his place was available. It was! Even better, Jackie hadn't had a chance to advertise it with a real estate agency yet, which meant that I could save 10 to 15 percent on agency fees.

Over the next couple of weeks, Jackie and I met to hash out the details. A former featherweight boxing champion, Jackie was much more spry than he'd first let on. (I soon learned that the young woman working behind the counter wasn't an employee but his lover.) The two of us ended up sparring over everything, starting with the terms of the lease. In the end, not only did I manage to get a great deal on the rent, but I also got Jackie to agree to add a *condition suspensive* (condition precedent) into the *promesse de vente* (sales agreement). According to the *condition suspensive*, if I didn't get a bank loan—for any reason—Jackie would have to give me back my down payment in its entirety.

"You're good," Jackie said, shaking my hand after we agreed on the deal. "You sure you never boxed before?"

"Yep," I smiled. "But I have had my fair share of fights."

After my negotiations with Jackie, it was on to the next step: Le Crédit Lyonnais (LCL), where I still had my personal bank account from my *Robin Hood* days. I met with a nerdy, high-strung banker, Monsieur Légère. I showed him my updated business plan, which now included André, the future location, and a revised budget.

"Hmm, Breakfast in America *daïneur...*" Monsieur Légère said as he studied my business plan. "So you serve only dinner then?" Before I had a chance to respond, he said, "That is good. It will keep employee costs down."

Unfortunately, one cost that didn't go down was the budget for BIA. That's because the price for Jackie's space was more expensive than I'd planned on. On the plus side, however, I was able to make up the difference, thanks to an amazing stroke of luck: France had just switched over to the euro, and as was the case when I was a UConn student, the exchange rate was working in my favor again—which meant my $100,000 was now worth €120,000! That gave me all the more reason to hurry up and raise the other $65,000 I needed, before the exchange rate had a chance to go down. But before I headed back to America, I needed to know if Monsieur Légère thought I had a good chance of getting approved for the loan.

"I will need to check with the loan guarantor," he said. "But in my opinion, Monsieur Carlson, you may leave here with *l'esprit tranquille*." (Peace of mind.)

I breathed a sigh of relief; I could now put a hold on the location. As Monsieur Légère prepared a certified check for €21,300, which was 10 percent of the cost for the key money (the cost to take over a lease in France). I looked at the balance in my account. Even with the great exchange rate, I only had a couple thousand euros left. There was no more room for error.

After signing the *promesse de vente* and giving Jackie his check for the deposit, I called Jérôme to celebrate. He met me at Jackie's restaurant for a drink. By pure coincidence, there was a huge demonstration taking place that day on the boulevard right in front of the future BIA. Tens of thousands of Parisians were protesting against Jean-Marie Le Pen, the racist leader of the extreme right-wing party, le Front National. Turns out, while the French were on Easter vacation, Monsieur Le Pen had unexpectedly slipped through the first round of presidential voting.

Watching the throngs of potential BIA customers passing by, Jérôme and I saw a great opportunity for a little self-promotion. Before you knew it, we were standing beside the protesters, chanting, "Forget Le Pen! We want pancakes!" We repeated the slogan over and over, until many of the protesters were smiling and chanting along with us.

"We want pancakes! We want pancakes!"

It was an amazing moment, one of the greatest yet for Breakfast in America. And it had also been an amazing trip! Although it had taken a few months, I had accomplished everything I set out to do—and then some. I could hardly wait for my triumphant return to LA. How could anyone in their right mind refuse to invest in BIA now?

The French jazz duo, the Aldeberts,
performing at BIA's investor party.

Chapter 8

SHOW ME (MORE) MONEY!

"If opportunity doesn't knock, build a door."

—Milton Berle

I HAD THREE MONTHS TO COME UP WITH $65,000 OR RISK LOSING the restaurant location. With no job, no savings, and a mountain of debt, I was desperate. But what better way to raise money than with a big investor party? Fortunately, my friends Ericson and Rana graciously offered to let me use their spacious Venice Beach home, which was perfect for hosting a party for thirty to forty potential investors.

I went all out for the big sell—Hollywood style. My friends from Disney's marketing department made me high-quality, poster-sized photos of the Breakfast in America location for free. They also got me a great deal on BIA swag, including mugs, baseball caps, and, for the big investors, Dickies mechanic shirts with our company logo embroidered on them.

For entertainment, I arranged for live music by a husband-and-wife French jazz duo called the Aldeberts. The Aldeberts had once been part of a famous vocalese jazz group in Paris during the swinging sixties. Now getting up in years, they had moved to California with the hope of making a big comeback. That never happened, but man, did they swing!

Last but not least, using the credit-card shuffle, I flew André over from Paris to wow the crowd with his cooking. But while Rana and I ran around getting everything ready, I noticed that André barely lifted a finger. Even worse, in perfect prima-donna fashion, he decided that he no longer wanted to barbecue ribs for the party, as planned.

"I did not come all this way to cook," said the world-renowned chef.

Well, yes, actually, you did, I thought. *That's one of the reasons I paid for your ticket.* That and to give legitimacy to BIA, to sell it to the crowd, reassuring them that, as a successful French restaurateur himself, he knew from experience that BIA would work. But, of course, I didn't say any of these things out loud, because I was afraid of losing him as a partner. Instead I said, "Pleeease, André? For our guests. No one can make ribs like you!"

Truth be told, I'd never actually tasted André's ribs. In fact, I didn't even know if he knew how to make them. But my gentle stroking of André's ego worked. He went into the kitchen and started preparing ribs for the party.

Roughly forty people RSVP'd for the event. Learning from my past mistakes, I made sure to be clear about my intentions, even going so far as to put on the invitations in bold type: "**For serious investors only. Be sure to bring your checkbook!**"

Around twenty people actually showed up. They included my Disney friend and investor Sylvain, who brought along some of his animator colleagues. There was also a megarich American woman visiting from her swanky Avenue Foch apartment in Paris. And finally, an actual Hollywood celebrity, one of the stars of the classic TV series *McHale's Navy*.

Of course, one of the dangers of having a crazy idea is that it can attract a lot of crazy people. Such was the case with Bella, a friend of my sister's. Not only did Bella end up bringing an entourage of Hollywood desperados (including the *McHale's Navy* actor and his hangers-on), but unbeknownst to me, she had a completely different vision for BIA than I did. Arriving early, before the other guests, Bella took me aside and said, "Okay, so this is what I'm going to say in my announcement."

Announcement? Excuse me, but when did we agree on you making an announcement?

Bella explained that she couldn't wait to tell the crowd about her amazing plans for Breakfast in America. For her, BIA wasn't just an American diner in Paris. No, at night, it would transform into a risqué revue club *à la* Dada-era Berlin, where her gay friends could perform in drag. In fact, Bella had already worked out the first production number. Dressed as the Statue of Liberty, her drag queen would make a dramatic entrance through the diner floor via the dumbwaiter. Lady Liberty would start off the show acting innocent and pure, singing "God Bless America." Suddenly, the music would switch over to "American Woman," with its loud, throbbing beat. Lady Liberty would then strip off her robe and toss her torch into the crowd.

"Uh, Bella," I said. "You do realize that Breakfast in America is a pancake joint, right? I mean, I know I said I was open to having live music from time to time, but I was thinking more like solo acoustic guitar. Not the West Hollywood Gay Pride Parade."

From Bella's reaction, I might as well have killed her cat. She became extremely upset, giving me the evilest evil eye I'd ever seen. For the rest of the party, I was on edge, afraid that she would burst into a tantrum, ruining everything. But thankfully, Bella restrained herself; she and her *McHale's Navy* entourage spent the rest of the afternoon standing in the corner by themselves, sulking the whole time.

With that crisis averted, as far as parties go, this one was definitely a success. André's ribs turned out to be scrumptious, and the Aldeberts' swinging jazz music really cooked. But as far as *investor* parties go...

The Avenue Foch woman said she thought my idea was great, and as an expat living in Paris, she couldn't wait to go to BIA and have some pancakes. But when it came to the subject of investing, she said she would have to talk with her husband, a real estate magnate, first. We agreed to meet when I got back to Paris.

In the end, for all the hard work and expense I put into the party, only one person ended up investing that day: Bruce, a French animator who Sylvain had brought along with him. As Bruce wrote out a check for $5,000, other guests came over and said they wanted to invest too—but on one condition.

"Will you take a thousand?" they asked. "Five's too much."

Incroyable. I now found myself going from the original minimum investment of $50,000—to groveling for a mere $1,000.

"Okay, sure," I said, willing to take anything at that point. *Just hurry up and pull out your checkbook—before you change your mind,* I thought. Of course, except for Bruce, everyone had left their checkbooks at home.

As the crowd thinned out, I noticed someone watching quietly from the sidelines. It was Dorothy, a wealthy high-society woman in her seventies who famously grew reefer on the roof of her home—hence her nickname, "Pot-Smoking Grandma."

"Let's talk," she said, smiling. I didn't know whether Pot-Smoking Grandma would turn out to be my investment angel sent from on high, but one thing was certain; she *was* high.

Shortly after the party, Dorothy invited me to her fabulous three-story pink *palais* in Venice Beach for seder dinner. Noshing on gefilte fish and wearing a badly fitting yarmulke, I began to worry about the lengths to which I was willing to go to get investors. But from the moment I had met Dorothy, who was a former VIP in the music industry, she and I had become fast friends. I found her to be fascinating and fun. And I hadn't even gotten stoned with her yet.

Not to say she didn't try. If Pot-Smoking Grandma hadn't been more than thirty years my senior, I might have given in to peer pressure and taken a toke. Dorothy said she only lit up from time to time—strictly for "medicinal purposes." Or whenever her kids got on her nerves—meaning several times a day. With her white hair pulled back tight, Dorothy reminded me a lot of a really, really mellow version of my Polish grandma Mary. (If I had known that reefer had this kind of calming effect, I would have slipped some into my gram's pierogies years ago.)

During the seder dinner, Dorothy never brought up the subject of investing in BIA. I got the feeling she wanted to test my loyalty first, to see if I could be trusted. And what an adventure being tested was! One Saturday, she invited me to join her for an afternoon at the theater. Driving up the 405 North in her sleek, brand-new silver Cadillac, Dorothy flipped open the flap of her armrest and pulled out a perfectly rolled joint. She handed it to me and said, "Light it, will you, hon?"

Now, this being LA, of course, traffic was at a standstill. I could see drivers in the cars right next to me as clear as day—and vice versa.

I felt like a fish in a fishbowl. What would people think, seeing a young man like me passing a fatty to ol' grandma?

"What're you waiting for?" Dorothy snapped. "It's not gonna light itself!"

I slouched down in my seat, turned my body away from the cars in the next lane, and lit up the joint. I quickly passed it to Dorothy. She took a long, deep drag. Then—*pheeeuw*—exhaled. In no time flat, the Caddie was filled with thick, blue smoke. I turned and looked at the cars passing by. Drivers were now staring at us. I slouched deeper into my seat. Pot was still very much illegal in California. What if the cops saw me? Did that mean I'd have to wait five to ten years—with good behavior—before I'd get the chance to open BIA?

After the play, Dorothy and I went back to her place, satisfying our munchies with her homemade matzo ball soup and delicious chocolate cake. Although I was having fun hanging out with Dorothy, I was running out of time. I needed a check—and fast—but, sadly, it looked like it was never going to happen.

I chalked it up to "you win some, you lose some." To my way of thinking, if I were to list the value of my memories with Dorothy against zero investment money, I could safely say that I had ended up ahead.

As the sun began to set over the Pacific, it was time for me to say good-bye. Dorothy gave me a nice long hug, then made me promise to bring her a bottle of her favorite French perfume the next time I came back from Paris.

"I won't forget." I smiled as I made my way toward the door.

"Wait," Dorothy said. "Actually, you did forget something."

She motioned me into her office. Like a queen on her throne, Dorothy sat down behind a beautifully ornate desk, opened the top drawer, and pulled out a large checkbook.

"I must be out of my mind," she said as she wrote out a check to BIA Investments, LLC and handed it to me. "I'm glad you were willing to go down on the price."

I looked at the check. It was for $1,000. "Thank you, Dorothy," I said, genuinely surprised.

"Don't mention it," she said. "Now go make the French fat."

I nodded, folded up the check, and put it in my pocket.

The tally so far since I'd begun looking for investors stood at $41,000 with $59,000 left to go. *Mon dieu*, at this rate, I'd be Dorothy's age before I raised the rest.

Right after receiving Dorothy's check, I made an appointment with Dr. Emily. Since I no longer worked at Disney, I could only afford to see her for the most dire of situations. This was one of those situations; with less than two months to go, I had barely raised half of what I needed to secure my diner location.

Adding to my stress level, I had a big meeting coming up that had the potential to be a game changer. It was with two of my friends from USC, Scott and Gary, who had hit the Hollywood big time. They had expressed interest in possibly investing in BIA, so I did not want to blow this great opportunity.

Dr. Emily and I delved into the reasons for my anxiety—i.e., why I found it so hard to ask for anything and so on. But instead of going down our usual path of cognitive behavioral therapy, Dr. Emily offered a great piece of old-school advice.

"Before meeting with your friends," she said, "have a cocktail. It'll take the edge off."

Wiser words were never spoken.

I met Scott and Gary at a fancy Italian restaurant in West LA. With the calming effect of the Seagram's kicking in, I got down to business. I told them that for just $25,000 each, they could get their very own booth at BIA—which included a personalized plaque.

"How cool is that?" I said. "You can tell your friends you own a piece of Paris!"

Even though Scott and Gary had collaborated on a critically acclaimed film, they couldn't have been more different. Gary was the nicest and most generous trust funder I'd ever met, whereas Scott was a tough-talking kid from Boston who wasn't afraid to say exactly what was on his mind. That included his feelings about me and BIA.

"How do I know a mook like you won't lose all my money?" Scott said.

"C'mon, Scott," Gary said. "What do you care? You're rich now. You can afford it."

Scott still wasn't convinced. He grumbled something under his breath as he got up to go to the restroom. The moment Scott was out of earshot, Gary turned to me and asked, "How much for a booth again?"

"Twenty-five thousand each," I said. "But I can make an exception and let you guys share one."

Gary paused, considered my offer, then said, "Okay, but we'll do it for twenty thousand."

"Deal!"

Scott returned from the restroom. "All right, Scott," Gary said. "We're investing in Craig's restaurant. Ten thousand from me. Ten thousand from you."

"What the fuck!" Scott said. "I go to take a piss, I come back, and now I'm out ten grand!"

For some cosmic reason, after getting Scott and Gary's boost of $20,000, the rest of the money started flowing in. A couple of $5,000 investments here. A $2,500 one there. And lots of $1,000 contributions, including one from my brother—and even one from my mom in Florida. Then, right at the last minute, two more friends from USC, Jacquie and Roger, hopped on board, helping to push me right up to the edge…to $99,000. Just one thousand short of my goal.

But that was enough for me. I was done.

In the end, BIA had a total of twenty-seven investors—many more than I had anticipated having. But to me, it was the perfect number.

In preparation for my big move to Paris, I sold or donated almost all of my belongings. I then stocked up on as much authentic diner paraphernalia as I could cram into my suitcases: syrup and sugar pourers, "thank you" trays (for putting the bills on), an OPEN sign, a neon clock that had "Breakfast in America" lit up on it, and my favorite—contraband mugs.

Yes, contraband. I use this term because these were not your average, run-of-the-mill mugs. They had been salvaged from real diners and coffee shops from all across the country—with their logos still intact. Some came from obscure mom-and-pop places as far away as Maine. Others had much more familiar names, the kind of "pancake houses" and "shacks" you'd find at the end of a freeway ramp in Anywhere, U.S.A. (To avoid another fiasco à la Supertramp, I prefer *not* to mention their real names.)

Anyway, I had found the mugs buried deep in some boxes at the back of a dish warehouse in downtown LA and filled my shopping cart with as many as I could. As I stood in the checkout line, the manager eyed my cart, overflowing with trademarked mugs, and asked suspiciously, "Uh, excuse me, but what exactly are you planning to do with those mugs?"

"Oh, uh… I'm a collector," I said.

"I sure hope so," the manager said. "Because you are not

allowed to use those mugs for commercial use. If you do, you'll be in big trouble."

"I would never dare do that, sir," I said innocently as I mumbled the last part under my breath, "…in America."

Truth be told, I had big plans for those mugs once BIA opened, and I couldn't wait to try them out.

Of course, the hardest part about leaving LA was saying good-bye to all my friends, especially Fiona. Since we *still* hadn't kissed, in my mind we were just good friends who enjoyed discovering new breakfast joints together. But to Fiona, we were much more than that. I discovered this on our last night out, when she treated me to dinner at a fancy French restaurant.

I was happy to see that our waiter was a real Frenchman so I could practice *mon français* with him.

"*Oh là là!*" the waiter said, impressed. "You speak very well the French!" I blushed at his compliment, which tickled Fiona to no end. As I watched the French waiter move around the dining room, graceful and elegant and in complete control—never once breaking a sweat—I thought, *Wow, I've never seen an* American *waiter move like that.*

A few glasses of wine later, Fiona moved in real close, stared into my eyes, and then took my hand in hers. "I want to ask you a question," she said. "Promise me you won't freak out."

Okay, maybe not the best way to preface the question, I thought. But, Unfortunately, between the lovestruck look in her eyes and my hand being touched, I was definitely starting to freak out.

"I know how hard it is to start a business all by yourself," Fiona continued. Then she took a deep breath. "What would you say if I left my job, my apartment—my whole life here in LA—and came to live with you in France?"

Okay, now I was *completely* freaking out. I just sat there staring at her. Fiona deserved better than that. But I didn't know what to say. I ended up mumbling something about how nice it was for her to offer, but right now I was so broke, I could barely take care of myself.

Fiona nodded and smiled, but she was clearly devastated. "Let me ask you something," she said. "Our relationship... It wasn't just about the coffee, was it? There was something more, right?"

"Yes, of course," I said, squeezing her hand.

I meant what I said. Fiona was an amazing woman. Even after all I put her through, she still wanted to remain friends. We spoke one last time before I left for Paris. I wished her the best of luck with the novel she was writing, and she wished me the best of luck with BIA, saying that she was sure I had the passion to make it work.

Ah, passion... For my restaurant, that came easy. But for love... That was another story. *Perhaps things will be different in Paris,* I thought. I certainly hoped they would be.

In April 2002, I spent my last night in LA. Walking along the bluffs that overlooked the Santa Monica pier, I took in one last magnificent California sunset. A mix of emotions churned inside me, mirroring the ocean waves below. *Was I really going to open Breakfast in America? Would I ever return to LA? What amazing, terrifying things await me in Paris?*

Before I could let myself get carried away with anxious thoughts about the future, something caught my eye at the other end of the bluff—the silhouette of a towering old man with a cane, making his way toward me. I recognized his hobble immediately. It was Fred

G., the crazy American producer from *Robin Hood*. I couldn't believe my eyes. What were the chances of my running into Fred on my last night in LA? I was sure it had to be a good sign.

"Hey, Fred," I said. "Did you hear the news? I'm opening a diner in Paris!"

Fred's face turned beet red. "Bah!" he said, waving his cane wildly. "I had a restaurant once. Never again! It's easier to make a movie!"

And with that, Fred continued on his merry way. I watched him hobble off into the sunset, not sure what to think. First Eric from Cafe Beaujolais. And now Fred. What was it with these guys being such buzzkills?

Of course, there was no way for me to know it at the time, but I couldn't have asked for a more perfect send-off to Paris than that.

Main Course

Living My Dream

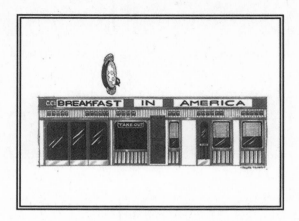

The first design plans for Breakfast in America.

Chapter 9

MY "DINER" WITH ANDRÉ

"It does not take a long time to strike a man with lightning."

——Monsieur Defarge in *A Tale of Two Cities*

ON THE LONG, TWELVE-HOUR FLIGHT TO PARIS, I COULDN'T SLEEP A wink. Part of the reason was because I was crammed into an economy seat, my knees crushed by the seat back in front of me. But the main reason was because I was too excited to sleep. Breakfast in America was on its way!

As I flipped through the channels on my video screen, I stumbled upon a French TV show about cooking and cuisine. Amazingly, the guest for this particular episode was none other than…André! He was somewhere in the countryside, being interviewed about *les plats du terroir* (regional dishes). I couldn't wait to tell André that I'd seen him on TV. I was sure it was a good omen.

At the Charles de Gaulle airport, after rolling my heavy bags up to customs, I hesitated, trying to decide if I should declare anything or not, given that my bags were stuffed with contraband diner paraphernalia, i.e., the trademarked mugs. With much trepidation, I decided to walk through the line for *rien à déclarer* (nothing to declare).

Fortunately, I did not get pulled over by a customs agent. But after taking the RER train into Paris, I nearly got a hernia lugging my massive suitcases up the long flights of stairs to the apartment of my investor and friend Rafael, who was kind enough to let me crash with him until I found a place of my own.

Bright and early the next morning, I headed over to the bank, stopping along the way to see Jackie at the restaurant. He was thrilled to hear that I had raised the rest of the money for BIA.

"*Félicitations!*" he said. Then he looked at his girlfriend, who was standing behind the counter, and nodded. As if on cue, she ran upstairs to the "dining room," which was currently being used to store tons of Jackie's crap, including piles of broken furniture, boxes of old files, and a big fat, lazy cat that, I think, was still alive.

After a moment, Jackie's girlfriend came running back down with a small paper bag and handed it to me. "*Voilà*, Monsieur Grack!" she said.

I opened it up. Inside was a T-shirt with a black-and-white photo of a young Jackie, from his championship boxing days back in the sixties, holding his fists in the air, looking as tough as his baby face could muster. The photo contrasted sharply with the elderly but still spry man sitting next to me.

"*Merci*, Jackie," I said, as I held up the T-shirt to my torso. All three of us laughed when we saw how small it was. Even if I stretched it, the T-shirt would barely reach down to my belly button.

"*Désolé*, Grack," Jackie said, smiling, "but I don't have any in American size."

"*Pas de problème*," I said, stuffing the T-shirt into my briefcase. "*Bon*," I said, standing up to leave. "On to the bank."

"*Je te dis merde!*" Jackie said. (Literally, "I say to you shit!" which actually means "Good luck!")

"*Merci!*" I hollered back as I ran out the door.

Before leaving the States, I had wired the rest of the investment money to my LCL account in France, but there was no way for me to know if it had gone through yet. Not only did transferring money take much longer than it does now, but LCL did not have online banking yet.

Sitting in Monsieur Légère's office, I waited nervously as he pulled up my account on his antiquated computer. It took forever until the numbers popped up on his screen. "*Le voilà*," Monsieur Légère said.

I looked at the screen, relieved; not only had my wire gone through, but the record exchange rate had gotten even *better*. That meant for my $65,000, I had received nearly €80,000!

"Not bad," Monsieur Légère said. "Not bad at all."

"So…" I said, smiling. "About my loan. Can I still have *l'esprit tranquille?*"

"Ah, Monsieur Carlson, you worry too much," Monsieur Légère said. "I promise you. You will have an answer soon. Before the deadline."

Of course, Monsieur Légère was referring to the *condition suspensive* that was in my agreement with Jackie. At this point, the bank had three weeks to give me a yes or no answer—in writing. If the answer was no, I would need to take the bank's letter to Jackie, who would be obligated to give my entire €21,300 deposit back. However, if the bank was late with their response, I risked losing it all.

It was during high-pressure times like these that I wished BIA were already open—I sure could have used some delicious comfort food. Luckily, I had the next best thing: André's restaurant. I went to see him before his dinner service started.

When I told André how excited I'd been to see him on TV on the airplane, he was so flattered, he sat me down on a plush banquette and began feeding me delicious Burgundy dishes, starting with a homemade *terrine de jambon* (a kind of ham pâté) followed by *bœuf bourguignon*. As I savored its rich, red-wine gravy, I was reminded of the Foire Gastronomique in Dijon.

"How is everything?" André asked.

"*Super bon!*" I said.

"Good," he said, putting on his toque. "Excuse me. I have to get back to work."

André headed into the kitchen. I sat there in the *grande salle* all alone, except for one other person: André's ex-wife, Madame Verdou. Yes, *ex*. And not only did she work at his restaurant, but she also seemed to run the show. Perched at her post next to the register by the entrance, Mme Verdou quietly observed everything—and everyone—who entered her lair. She reminded me of Madame Defarge, the cold-blooded revolutionary from Dickens's *A Tale of Two Cities*. Only she was the Coco Chanel version, dressed in an elegant outfit, with every silky, blond hair in place.

Mme Verdou always held a no. 2 pencil in her hand, constantly jotting things down in her ledger—such as payments and reservations. But with the restaurant completely empty, I wondered what other things she could be jotting down.

"Tell me, Craig," Mme Verdou said, the first French person

to ever pronounce my name correctly. "Would you be interested in working here temporarily?"

"Excuse me?"

"We have someone going on vacation for the summer. Perhaps you'd be interested in earning a little something on the side. Until your loan goes through."

Wow, color me impressed! This lady seemed to understand my situation perfectly. Not only did I need a job to rent an apartment (in France you need to have at least three payslips to demonstrate your source of income), but I could also use some more restaurant experience—especially in France. Although I'd done a two-week stint at Cafe Beaujolais when Eric went away on vacation, his French restaurant was in America, where the same rules did not apply.

"I would love to," I said to Mme Verdou. "When do I start?"

"A week from Monday," she said. "Your hours are ten a.m. to midnight, Monday through Friday, with a short *coupure* between lunch and dinner service."

Since I was pretty good at math, I quickly figured out that the job added up to a lot more than thirty-five hours a week, which is officially full-time in France. But before I had a chance to say anything, Mme Verdou said, "You will also work Saturdays. But dinner only."

"*Fantastique!*" I said.

"One last thing," Mme Verdou said. "Do you own a pressed white shirt, black slacks, and a bow tie?"

"I do not."

"Then you will need to purchase these items yourself. Along with your own pen. If you lose yours, *tant pis!* I will not replace it."

I looked behind Mme Verdou. On the counter sat a large container overflowing with pens. "Sounds good," I said. "See you next Monday!"

On my way out, I poked my head into the kitchen. André's face was beet red from snapping orders at his crew.

"*Merci* for the job, André," I said.

"Job? What job?"

André had no clue. Yep, it was clear who wore the *pantalons* in this divorce.

The job could not have come at a more opportune time. If all went well, it would take me right through to the middle of the summer, which coincided with my goal of opening Breakfast in America by July or August—the height of the tourist season.

After hunting down my penguin suit for André's restaurant, I came home to find Rafael standing in the doorway, a serious look on his face. He held a *lettre recommandée* (certified letter) in his hand.

"From LCL," he said.

"Really? Already?" In all my dealings with France, I had never seen such a quick turnaround. I ripped open the letter. Stopped reading after the first sentence: *"We regret to inform you that..."*

I stood there, stunned. *"C'est pas possible!"*

The next morning, I rushed over to LCL.

"What happened to *l'esprit tranquille*?" I asked Monsieur Légère.

"I told you from the beginning, Monsieur Carlson. It is not I who ultimately decides."

"But I don't understand. Why was I rejected?"

"I do not know. But look on the bright side, you have a rejection letter from us, which you can use to get your deposit back."

No way. Not an option. I did not want to lose the perfect location for my diner. Instead, with only two weeks to go before the deadline, I applied for loans at as many other banks as I could. Then I went to see Jackie to ask for more time.

"*Pas de problème,*" he said. "Take as long as you need."

"*Merci*, Jackie," I said. As I turned to leave, I caught a glimpse of Jackie's girlfriend watching from behind the counter. She had a very worried look on her face.

On my first day at work, I arrived early so I could fill André in on what had happened at the bank. "Can you believe it?" I said. "My own bank rejected me."

"Oh, well, what can you do?" André said. "That's why I don't like dealing with banks."

"Uh...okay," I said. *That wasn't very helpful*, I thought.

As I made my way to the employee locker room, I noticed Mme Verdou sitting on her perch, silent and stoic. As usual, she was jotting something down in her ledger with her no. 2 pencil.

After changing into my penguin suit, I began my first day of training with André's headwaiter, Bernard. A kindly and obsequious sort, Bernard came from the old-school tradition where being a headwaiter was more than just a job; it was a *métier* (profession).

Bernard turned out to be the perfect mentor for me, teaching me everything he knew about service in Paris and its multiculturalism. It turned out that André's clientele varied greatly depending on the time of day. At lunchtime, most of his customers were French businessmen and politicians, who had their own picky and particular needs. But by the evenings, the restaurant was inundated with rich Americans, Russians, and, above all, Japanese tourists. As a result, I needed to learn such important things as how to bow properly and say, "*Konnichiwa*," something I never expected to learn at a French restaurant.

Besides gaining valuable experience for BIA, I got to see another side of André that I had never seen before. Forget about him being a prima donna—this guy was a lunatic. The moment he put on his apron and toque, André transformed into a mad Mr. Hyde, treating his crew—including yours truly—like total *merde*.

One evening, an oil magnate from Texas (complete with cowboy hat) asked for some ketchup to go along with his filet mignon. I thought it was pretty *gauche* myself, but the customer is always right, right? So I went into the kitchen to grab the bottle of Heinz, which was on the shelf next to André.

"Non! Non! Non!" André screamed, grabbing the bottle out of my hand. "Are you a complete *imbécile*? This is not McDonald's! This is a restaurant *gastronomique!"*

"But the customer asked for it," I said.

"Ah, you Americans render me ill!" André grabbed a ramekin off the shelf. "It goes in here. No bottles on the outside!" André tried to pour some ketchup into the ramekin, but since it was a new bottle no ketchup immediately came out.

"I'll get this one." I smiled, being the master of ketchup retrieval, thanks to my tightwad dad. I gently tapped on the bottle's neck, slowly filling the ramekin with America's culinary gift to the world without spilling a drop. André was not impressed. He snorted, then turned to his sous-chef, Didier, and started screaming at him, calling him all versions of idiot that exist in French—of which there were many.

Watching André scream at his right-hand man like that—a guy who worked harder than anyone else—made me wonder, *Would he dare treat my staff this way?* If so, I didn't want him anywhere near them.

In the changing room at the end of our shift, I asked Bernard how he put up with André. The old *garçon* smiled and said proudly, "It is the price I must pay for being master of my ship."

On the day of the deadline for obtaining my loan, the tally from the banks was six rejections, with five more responses still to come. I had two options: hand over the bank's rejection letter to Jackie and get my deposit back. Or ask for more time. I chose the latter.

"Are you sure you're okay giving me a couple more weeks?" I asked Jackie. "Until I hear back from the other banks?"

"Yes, of course," Jackie said. "But just so you know, I've been getting a lot of other offers."

"You have?" I said, worried. "Please, Jackie, just hold on a little longer, okay? I'm so close, I can feel it."

"Okay," Jackie said, standing up and shaking my hand. "I say to you shit."

"*Merci beaucoup*," I said.

Jackie turned and went into the kitchen. The moment he was out of sight, his girlfriend came over from behind the counter. She leaned in and whispered to me, "I must tell you something: there have been *no* other offers."

"Excuse me?" I said.

"Please be careful, Monsieur Grack. Jackie may seem nice on the outside. But inside, he's a killer."

Not good. I immediately called my lawyer in France, who, unfortunately, was not Adam. (I'd met with Coudert Bros in their swanky offices on the Champs-Elysées, but I was unable to afford their swanky fees.) As it was a Friday afternoon, my French lawyer had already left for the weekend. By the time I reached him on Monday, it was too late. Blinded by my desire not to lose my dream location, I had missed the deadline by just two days.

"Is there anything I can do?" I asked my lawyer in a panic.

"Send him a *lettre recommandée* anyway," he said. "And be sure to include a copy of the bank's rejection letter. We'll have to wait and see what his next move will be after that."

Unfortunately, Jackie beat me to the punch (no pun intended). I received a *lettre recommandée* from *his* lawyer first. In it, he threatened to keep my entire €21,300 deposit, unless I came up with the remaining €200,000 needed to purchase his lease. That, of course, was impossible, since within the next few days, all of the banks—eleven in total—had rejected me.

I went to see Monsieur Légère. Given my frantic state, I'm sure that if I had been in the States, security would have dragged me away—or shot me.

"Please," I said. "I beg of you; I need to know why my loan was rejected."

Monsieur Légère looked at me with compassion, then shook his head, got up, and left his office. A minute later, he returned with the loan guarantor in tow and closed the door.

"Monsieur Carlson," the loan guarantor said in a hushed voice. "I am not authorized to tell you this, but I was told I could trust you to keep this between us."

"Yes, of course."

"Did you know that, two years ago, your partner André filed for bankruptcy protection?"

"Uh, no," I said, staring at him in shock. *Dude forgot to mention that little detail!* I thought. *Would've been nice to know when applying for a goddamn bank loan.*

The next day, I asked André if I could speak to him in private for a moment. As we stepped outside, I told him that all the banks had rejected me, but I didn't tell him why. Instead, I gave him the chance to come clean.

"Is there something I should know, André?" I asked.

"Like I said before, banks are rotten. That's why I don't like dealing with them."

"Besides that," I said, looking at him sternly.

"Oh, I don't know. Maybe a couple of years ago I might've had a little problem with *le fisc*.[3] But it was nothing. It's all worked out now."

That was it. No apology. No acknowledgment of the hell he had put me through.

"Okay, André," I said. "That's all I needed to hear."

Downstairs in the changing room, I told Bernard what had just transpired with André. Bernard did not seem surprised at all. "Did you ever stop to think why you really got this job?" he said.

"What do you mean?"

"Madame Verdou. Don't you see? It was all part of her plan. She really liked you and wanted you to see what you were getting yourself into with André."

I stood there completely numb; between the bank, Jackie's threats, and now this, I felt as if I'd been given the one-two punch several times over. That said, even before the rejections from the banks, I'd pretty much made up my mind that I didn't want to work with a lunatic like André; the bankruptcy revelation had simply sealed the deal. Still, that didn't stop me from being moved by Mme Verdou's kind gesture.

On my way out, I stopped by Mme Verdou's perch. As always, her eyes were glued to her ledger as she jotted down the night's receipts.

"I hear there's an interesting reason why I got this job," I said. "Is it true?"

Mme Verdou didn't look up. She just smiled the most delicate smile I'd ever seen.

....

3   The *fisc* is the French IRS.

"*Merci infiniment*, madame," I said, giving her my infinite thanks. "I'll never forget this."

Unfortunately, by the time I'd *un*partnered with André, it was too late. I'd lost the loan, I'd lost my dream location—and just to keep punching me when I was already down, Jackie was now threatening to sue me for damages incurred for lost time. Suddenly, I found myself on the verge of losing all of the precious investment money I'd fought so long and hard to get.

Could this be the location for the first Breakfast in America?

Chapter 10

LOCATION *NUMÉRO DEUX*

"It is impossible to live without failing at something, unless
you live so cautiously that you might as well not have
lived at all—in which case, you fail by default."

—J. K. Rowling's commencement speech at Harvard

AFTER LOSING MY DREAM LOCATION FOR BREAKFAST IN AMERICA, I was heartbroken. My friends tried to cheer me up by saying things like, "It's very common to lose your first place." And, "Don't worry, a better one will come along." "It happened for a reason." And finally, "One day, you'll be thankful it fell through."

They were right, of course. But there was no way for me to see it at the time. Jackie had smacked me upside the head so many times, I couldn't see straight. And over the next several weeks, I went extra rounds with his lawyers as I desperately tried to get at least a portion of my deposit back—without going broke.

But unlike my wonderful experience with Adam, dealing with French lawyers was a total farce. My own lawyer wouldn't even let me see any of the correspondence he was having with Jackie's lawyer. And the way both lawyers took care of everything behind closed doors, I got the distinct impression that they had already decided the outcome from the beginning. The rest was just show.

During our "negotiations," all concerned parties sat in Jackie's cluttered dining room. There was plenty of posturing, faux heated debate, and lots of *cinéma*—meaning everyone was hand-on-forehead *mélodramatique*. The legal battle seemed to stretch on forever, as both lawyers racked up as many hours of expensive legal fees as they could. By midsummer, both lawyers had come up with "the best deal possible"—I lost nearly half of my deposit, and Jackie got a nice chunk of change just for being a dishonest thug.

"It could've been a lot worse," my French friends said, which, no offense to them, I was getting a little tired of hearing.

With no location, no loan, and all of my backup plans drying up, I didn't know what to do next. To clear my head, I went for a jog in the beautiful Jardin des Plantes, an eighteenth-century botanical garden located in the Fifth arrondissement. It didn't help my mood much, since the park was filled with hungry American tourists, a painful reminder that BIA should have been open by now.

In the park, I ran into an old colleague of mine from *Robin Hood*, Claire. With her bright, dyed red hair and outrageous personality, Claire literally jumped into the air when she saw me.

"Greeeg?! What the hell are you doing here?"

"Haven't you heard? I'm opening an American restaurant in Paris!"

Claire's flaming-red hair seemed to catch on fire as she howled, "A restaurant? Are you serious? Do you know how risky that is? What if you faaail?"

Given all that I'd gone through lately, I did not need Claire's help to remember the enormous risk I'd taken with BIA. I tried to shake it off, but her words left a terrible aftertaste in my mouth. To find solace, I tried to think of the quote from that famous writer who said, "With great risk comes great failure." *Wait, that's not right.* What was that line again from all those bad Hollywood action movies? "Failure is not an option!"

Or in my particular case, having completely abandoned my life back in LA, an even better line came to mind—the one from Richard Gere in *An Officer and a Gentleman*: "I've got *nowhere* else to go!"

So true. Especially considering the most recent developments from back home.

My friend in LA who was taking care of my mail until I found a place to live in Paris had been late with just one payment on my credit cards, but it ended up causing a ripple effect; all my other credit cards quickly increased their APRs from the promotional rates of 5.5 percent to 22.9 percent. That meant that my minimum payments for all five cards jumped from $250 a month to almost $2,000!

Of course, there was no way I could pay that amount. Thus, the golden era of the credit-card shuffle came to an abrupt end. I'm not proud to admit it, but not only did I end up defaulting on my credit cards, but I also defaulted on my student loans. Shortly thereafter, frustrated collection agents passed my case on to debtor's court, and soon lawyers/mercenaries were sending me strongly worded American versions of *lettres recommandées*, threatening to take my firstborn child—and then some.

"Hey, at least you're in France," my friend back in LA said. "Don't see how they can hunt you down there."

With no choice but to keep moving forward, I pulled out my LA Rolodex to see if there was anybody left who I hadn't yet begged for help. There was: a sleazy French guy named Henri who I'd met through the French American Chamber of Commerce. I reluctantly gave him a call, hoping that he might be able to give me some good leads on finding a location and/or financing.

Henri told me about something called *le crédit brasseur*, which I'd never heard of before. I also learned from Henri that the majority of French *brasseries* were owned by people from the Auvergne region in France who were kind of like a beer mafia that gave out loans to new businesses. In order to get a *crédit brasseur*, however, you had to agree to serve the *brasseur's* beer exclusively—as well as some "softs" like Perrier and Orangina.

Of course, having been burned several times now, I wasn't ready to trust anyone. But I had no choice. This was my last resort. Henri put me in touch with a small family-owned operation called BBC Milliet located in a huge warehouse along the Seine. There I met with Serge, the no-nonsense head of the company. Surrounded by stacks of beer kegs, I filled Serge in on what had happened with Jackie.

"Tough break," Serge said. "You find another location yet?"

"No."

"*Pas de problème.*" Serge grinned. "We'll take care of you."

I gulped. It sounded a little ominous. But despite the *On the Waterfront* vibe of the enormous warehouse, I had a good feeling about Serge.

What the hell, I thought. *Let's do it!*

Conveniently, Serge had a very close relationship with a real estate agency that dealt exclusively with bars and *brasseries*. I didn't know it at the time, but nearly everyone I met at the two companies was related in some way—by blood, by marriage, or, as far as I could tell, by indentured servitude. Thus, I became the newest member of the "family."

My first meeting with the real estate agents, the Cohens, took place on July 26, which also happened to be my thirty-eighth birthday. The Cohens reminded me of a cranky old couple I used to see at Canter's Deli in LA. Monsieur Cohen was much older than his wife and always dressed in his Sunday finest. He sat quietly in the corner, letting his wife do all the talking. Madame Cohen spoke with the strongest southern French accent I'd ever heard. Her pronunciation for the word "*vin*," for instance, sounded like the lowly howl of an abandoned fawn crying out for its mother: "*VEH-IIIN*."

"Serge told me you're looking for a location," Madame Cohen said. "Boy, do I have the perfect spot for you! It's in the Quartier Latin. You know it?"

"Of course," I said. "That's always been my first choice."

"See?" She smiled. "What'd I tell you? The perfect spot!"

Madame Cohen grabbed a slip of paper and wrote down the address. Before handing it over to me, she glanced around the room, as if sharing a valuable secret, then leaned in close. "It's called Le Square," Madame Cohen whispered. "When you visit it, be very discreet. Do *not* let them know why you're there."

"Why not?"

"Just go see the place first. If it pleases you, we'll talk."

It wasn't easy finding Le Square. Nestled between a piano shop and a game store, the old café was as close to invisible as the owners could make it. Huge ficus plants blocked the windows, making it hard to see inside. And even if the plants hadn't been there, you'd still have trouble seeing anything because the place was totally dark. The only sign of life was a faint orange glow coming from the far end of the bar.

My first impression was not good.

I shoved the door open and stepped inside. Hiding behind a giant ficus beside the bar was Monsieur Marin, who had to be in his seventies. Like the name of his café, Monsieur Marin was as charmingly square as could be. His shirt was buttoned up all the way to his neck and would have been buttoned up farther if there'd been more buttons. His tall, wiry body was incapable of keeping still, and his arms constantly flailed about like those life-size inflatable puppets you see alongside American strip malls and car dealerships.

By contrast, the short and rotund Madame Marin stood as solid as a rock behind the counter. A pair of glasses hung on a chain around her neck just waiting to be raised to her eyes so she could inspect whomever walked through her door. As I stepped up to the bar, Madame examined me from head to toe.

"*Oui?*" she asked.

"*Bonjour,*" I said. "*Un café, s'il vous plaît.*"

Madame Marin looked at her husband, who jumped into action, racing over to the vintage espresso machine. As the coffee grinder spit out a dose of fresh espresso, I tried to make some small talk.

"How 'bout this heat wave, huh?"

Madame Marin was having none of it. She gave me a long, cold stare. I quickly shut up, remembering what Madame Cohen had whispered: "Be discreet!"

Once my espresso arrived, I took a sip, trying to scope the place out from the corner of my eye. The size and configuration of the room looked about right; it could easily be transformed into the interior of a diner. And the decor, if the lights had been on so you could actually see it, had a fun and funky quality to it. Ever so slowly, the filmmaker in me began to see the possibilities.

"May I see the menu?" I asked.

"No menu," Madame Marin said. "Just chips and *croque monsieurs*." (Hot ham and cheese sandwich.)

I looked toward the kitchen area where there was nothing but a toaster oven, which glowed orange with a *croque monsieur* inside. I must say, it looked delicious, the Swiss cheese on top melting into a perfect golden brown. I was tempted to order one, but since the place was empty, I figured it must be lunchtime for the Marins. Not wanting to wear out my welcome (if you could call it that), I held up the tiny espresso cup to my lips, tipped out one last drop, then placed it back on the counter.

"Where's the bathroom, please?" I asked.

"Downstairs," Madame Marin said.

As I crossed the room, I got a better look at the place. Although there was no kitchen, per se, there was a small area that could be used as one, with enough space for a flattop grill, stove, and fryer. There was also a tiny room next to it that jutted out into the courtyard of the building. *Hmm, that could be perfect for a prep area*, I thought. And best of all, there was already a small ventilation system in place, something that was very hard to get a permit for in Paris. *Not bad*, I thought.

Next, I went downstairs to the bathroom area, entering a door marked *Hommes*. Inside was a Turkish toilet, the likes of which were becoming very rare in Paris. All the better, because the toilet was nothing more than a hole in the ground with dried crap around the edges. *Yuck*.

After I finished, I pulled the chain on the tank above the hole. A huge wave of water gushed out from below, splashing all over my shoes. *Double yuck*. I quickly exited, then washed my hands—and shoes—in the sink. I noticed that on the other side of the sink was a door marked *Femmes*. I opened it and peeked inside, relieved to see a real toilet, clean and rarely used.

Back upstairs, my wet shoes sloshing, I crossed the room again, taking in one last *discreet* look at the place. For the first time, I noticed that the bar was in the perfect spot for a diner counter. All it needed was a little sprucing up. And on the other side of the room, mirrors ran the entire length of the wall, from floor to ceiling. *Hmm, might be able to do something nice with that too*, I thought.

"*Merci beaucoup!*" I said, waving at the Marins as I made my way out the door.

"*Au revoir!*" Monsieur Marin said, perking up, his arms flailing about.

Outside, I looked back at the café, smiled, and thought to myself: *Mission accomplished. I'm sure the Marins didn't suspect a thing.*

I turned around and continued walking down the sidewalk, the sound of my squeaky, wet shoes echoing down the bustling rue des Écoles.

So the potential restaurant space had passed the test. Great. But what about the neighborhood around it? I decided to take a quick stroll through *le quartier* to do some market research. The first thing I noticed was all the hotels on both sides of Le Square. Because of the English signs in their windows, I deduced that they catered to American tourists, which was a plus. Next, I made my way up the hill via rue Monge, happy to discover that it was just a short walk to rue Mouffetard, a beautiful medieval street that was popular with tourists and French students alike. Not surprising, considering there were two big *universités* nearby, the Sorbonne and Jussieu.

Making my way back down the hill, I looped around rue de la Montagne Sainte Geneviève, then turned right onto rue des Écoles. The moment I did, I stopped dead in my tracks. I couldn't believe my eyes; directly in front of me was my favorite cinema from my UConn days, the Action Écoles, the very same place where I'd seen

The 400 Blows.[4] I had no idea it was so close to Le Square—just a block and a half away.

Incroyable! It was as if my life had come full circle again. If that wasn't a sign, I don't know what was. Of course, I'd grown a little weary of signs, given my mixed track record. But this one was just too big to ignore. That, and the little voice inside me that kept screaming at the top of its lungs, *What are you, crazy? The location's great! Take it! Take it!*

I rushed back to Madame Cohen's office and said, "I'll take it!"

"Hah, I knew it!" Madame moved in close and whispered, "Were you discreet?"

"Of course," I whispered back. "Speaking of which, what's with all the secrecy?"

Madame Cohen went on to explain that after thirty-five years in business, the Marins were ready to retire. Or at least, Madame Marin was. Monsieur Marin couldn't bring himself to leave. For him, Le Square was like his baby—the only life he'd ever known. (The Marins had no children.) However, for the last two years, Madame Marin had been gently trying to push her husband out the door. Thus the ficus plants, the lights being turned off, and the short operating hours, all of which deterred customers from coming in.

"That's why I asked you to be discreet," Madame Cohen said. "If Monsieur Marin heard you talking about taking over his baby, it would have been too much for him."

What a touching, bittersweet story, I thought. But of course, it also raised an interesting dilemma. "But..." I said, "if after two years, Madame Marin still hasn't convinced her husband to retire, what makes you think she'll be able to do so now?"

"Only one way to find out," Madame Cohen said. "I'll have to talk to Madame Marin myself."

....
4   The cinema is still there today, though it has since changed its name to Le Desperado.

A couple days later, Madame Cohen called me back, sounding excited. "The Marins want to meet with you!" she said. "I think they're finally ready to sell."

"Really?" I said. "That's great!"

"Now it's just a question of whether they want to pass their baby on to you," Madame Cohen said. "Oh, and by the way, I didn't tell them you'd already stopped by, so don't mention it, okay?"

On the day of our meeting, the moment Madame Cohen and I stepped into Le Square, Madame Marin looked at me, turned to her husband, and said, "See! Told you it was him!"

"Jeez, madame," I said, "was I that obvious?"

"*Absolument!*" Madame Marin grinned mischievously.

Thus began our beautiful friendship.

The negotiations for the new location went very smoothly. The Marins didn't try to gouge me at all. They were what the French called *correctes* or *carrés*, which literally means square. But in a deeper sense, it also means fair. So I guess you could say the owners of Le Square gave me a square deal—starting with the rent.

As owners of "the walls" (the Marins lived in the apartment above the restaurant), they gave me an amazing deal—just €1,200 a month, which was a steal for that neighborhood. Next, the cost for the key money was €75,000 *less* than it had been for Jackie's place. And that included Le Square's valuable full-bar liquor IV license, which in itself was worth at least €30,000.

With all the details hashed out, I was ready to put down a deposit. But first, learning from my previous mistakes, I wanted to be 100 percent sure that I had the financing. Which meant I had to go back to the dreaded French banks. This time around, however, with André out of my business plan, I was *pre*approved for a loan right away—at two banks!

Looking again at my budget, I thought back to my research phase and how many restaurateurs had given me this sage advice: "However much you think you'll need, double it!" Of course, I couldn't do that. But just to be on the safe side, I got in touch with Serge to find out more about the infamous *crédit brasseur*.

"Sure, we can help," Serge said. "Didn't I tell you we'd take care of you?"

Sure enough, the Cohens made me an offer I couldn't refuse. With no collateral, no down payment—no nothing—they offered to give me a loan for €25,000. All that with just a good old-fashioned, old-world handshake. That and... "If you don't pay us back, we'll break your kneecaps."

Of course, they didn't actually say that. But if there'd been subtitles to our conversation, I'm pretty sure that's what the translation would've been.

The moment I put the deposit down for the location, everything started coming together really fast. I even found a tiny studio apartment a few blocks away, on rue des Boulangers, which turned out to be a lifesaver. Of course, now I could see that my friends had been right all along; how lucky I was that the first location had fallen through.

With the new location on hold, I went to the bank to finalize the loan. But instead of giving me one lump sum, the bank said they would only release funds into BIA's bank account in small installments, spread out over time, as bills for the renovations came in.

In contrast, the loan with the Cohens was much less complicated. After I signed a short contract agreeing to serve their beer and "softs" exclusively, they handed me a check for €25,000, in *my* name, not the company's.

As I held the check, Monsieur Cohen sprang to life and spoke for the first time. "Do whatever you want with it," he said. "Buy yourself some shoes. A nice shirt. Take a vacation somewhere..."

Forget that. After the meeting, I went straight to the bank and deposited the check right away—into BIA's account.

The day before the final signature on the lease, Madame Marin insisted on giving me a little tour around the neighborhood, to show me *her* Paris. Along the way, she pointed out all that had changed in the *quartier* over the years since she first moved there. For example, before the Pierre and Marie Curie University built the Jussieu campus, there used to be a huge wine market at the site. This was very fitting because, according to Madame Marin, when she and her husband first opened Le Square in the early sixties, people used to drink and dance in the streets until all hours of the night.

"Those days ended when the *bourgeois* moved in," she said. "They ruined everything."

I was surprised to learn that Madame Marin was originally from Normandy and had moved to Paris right after World War II, when she was just fourteen years old. As often happened back then, a job had been lined up for her in a *boulangerie* (a bakery), where she would work long, grueling hours in exchange for room and board. Madame described how anxious and scared she was when her father took her down to the train station to send her off. A burly, working-class man who never showed his feelings, her father loaded her onto the train without so much as a hug or a *bisou*. Instead, he made it quite clear, in no uncertain terms, that she was now on her own, with no home to come back to.

"Parents can be cruel, *n'est-ce pas?*" she said. "But I'm glad the old man did what he did. You know why? Because the world *is* cruel. And it made me tough."

That it did. But at the same time it made me wonder: *Would it be inappropriate for me to give Madame a big ol' American hug right now?*

Next, Madame and I walked past le Collège des Bernardins, a pearl of gothic architecture that once housed monks and young intellectuals from the nearby Sorbonne. But now it was just a run-down shell of a building where homeless people lived—and, if you looked closely, ghosts, Madame Marin joked.

"They're finally going to renovate it," Madame Marin said. "But being Paris, it'll take forever. They love taking their time."

Ah, yes, time… Standing there before the medieval monastery, I thought about another thing I'd always loved about Paris—how the city gives you a different notion of time. With all its ancient buildings, Paris had a wonderful way of reminding you how quickly life goes by, how we're all just passing through—while at the same time, it forces you to slow down and enjoy every precious moment while you can.

Nothing gave me this feeling more than Notre Dame, the 850-year-old cathedral, which was the culmination of Madame Marin's tour. Standing on the pont de la Tournelle bridge, Madame Marin turned to me and gestured toward the cathedral.

"Everybody talks about the statues and the gargoyles on the *front* of Notre Dame," she said. "But I think it's most beautiful from the *back*…from this very spot… Don't you?"

I nodded. It *was* magnificent. From that moment on, I was never able to look at Notre Dame the same way again.

On October 16, 2002, the Marins and I signed the final paperwork at the Cohens' office. Afterward, we went back to Le Square with the Marins' lawyer to celebrate. With a bottle of bubbly chilling in a bucket, Monsieur Marin officially handed me the keys to his place.

"To Grec," Monsieur Marin said, raising his glass of champagne.

"It's not *Grec!*" Madame Marin snapped. "It's *Crec!* He's not a Greek sandwich you know!"

During the toast, I noticed that Monsieur Marin and I were wearing the exact same outfit, a blue dress shirt and black blazer. Not only that, but I also happened to be the exact same age that Monsieur Marin was when he'd first opened his café thirty-five years earlier. (He was now seventy-three.) From the way the Marins had opened up their hearts to me, I realized then that, in a way, I was like the son they never had.

"Hey, Crec," Madame Marin said, snapping me out of my thoughts. "You never had a chance to try one of Monsieur Marin's famous *croque monsieurs*, did you?"

"No," I said wistfully. "*C'est la vie.*"

Madame Marin turned and nodded to her husband, who ran over to his toaster oven and used it one last time to make one last *croque monsieur*, just for me. As I crunched into its hot, cheesy goodness, Madame Marin said proudly, "Is that not the best *croque monsieur* you've ever tasted?"

"*Ah, oui!*" I said, causing Monsieur Marin to blush. Indeed, the simple sandwich was made all the more delicious by the happy occasion it marked and the care with which it had been made.

As the festivities wound down, the Marins began boxing up their belongings so they could take them upstairs to their apartment. Their lawyer motioned for me to join him at the bar where he lit up a smoke and emptied the last drops of champagne into my glass.

"You're a lucky man, Monsieur Carlson," he said, his voice low so the Marins couldn't hear. "You know how many people wanted this place? Hardly a week went by that somebody didn't walk through that door and make an offer—and for a lot more money."

I looked over at the Marins. This was news to me. I waited until Monsieur Marin had gone downstairs before approaching Madame Marin about the subject. "I don't understand, madame," I said. "If you had so many offers, why did you choose me?"

"*Parce que Monsieur Marin vous a trouvé gentil,*" she said. ("Because Mr. Marin found you nice.") And not only that, but the concept for BIA pleased her husband. Instead of his place being turned into yet another gyro stand or a Chinese takeout, BIA seemed closer to the spirit of his baby, his bistro.

Wow, who'da thunk it? I ended up getting the best location in the world for a great price—and from an elderly French couple no less—all because BIA was an *American* joint.

Monsieur Marin returned from the *cave* carrying a small rectangular object, which he handed over to me.

"*Voilà*, Monsieur Crec," he said. "*Un petit cadeau.*"

The object was wrapped in old newspaper and was a lot heavier than I expected. Ever so carefully, I opened it up, revealing...a cobblestone.

"It's from the revolution," Monsieur Marin said. But he didn't mean the revolution of 1789. He meant the "revolution" of May 1968, when students rioted in the streets against, among other things, capitalism, consumerism, and France's antiquated institutions. At one point, the riots got so bad that President Charles de Gaulle actually went into hiding.

Monsieur Marin pointed to the front window. "*Le pavé* came right through there, shattering the window...and then it rolled all the way over to here," he said, pointing to a spot on the floor in the back of the room.

I held up the historic cobblestone. If only it could talk, imagine the stories this chunk of rock could tell.

"*Merci beaucoup*, Monsieur Marin," I said. "I will guard it very carefully. You never know when something like this will come in handy."

At the end of the party, as we bid *adieu*, I was so overcome by the emotions of the day (not to mention the bubbly), I gave Madame Marin that big ol' American hug after all.

"*Oh là là!*" she said. "It's not like we'll never see each other again! We live upstairs, remember?"

Everyone erupted into laughter as the Marins and their lawyer left the café. After they were gone, I sat alone in the dark, empty room and took a deep breath. Now it was time for the *real* work to begin.

Transforming an old French café…   *…into an old-fashioned American diner.*

Chapter 11

COUNTDOWN TO OPENING DAY

"When you become comfortable with uncertainty,
infinite possibilities open up in your life."

—Eckhart Tolle

HAVING LONG SINCE MISSED MY GOAL OF OPENING BREAKFAST IN America for the summer tourist season, I was now on a mad dash to get the place up and running as fast as possible so I could generate some desperately needed cash flow. But before that could happen, there was a long list of things that needed to be accomplished in order to reach my new goal of opening on November 28, Thanksgiving Day—which was just *six short weeks* away.

The first thing on my list was to figure out the cheapest and most creative way to transform an old French café into a vintage American diner. Once again, Sylvain, my French friend from Disney, came to the rescue. Having studied architecture before becoming a renowned animator, Sylvain drafted design plans for me for free, coming up with ingenious ways of using elements within the existing space to save money.

On the right wall of the old café, where the full-length mirrors were, Sylvain had the clever idea of building around them so they would look like classic dining car windows. He even added blinds to enhance the illusion, just like on a movie set. Ditto for the counter/bar. By simply covering up the faux marble with authentic diner tiles, we were able to save a fortune on plumbing and masonry.

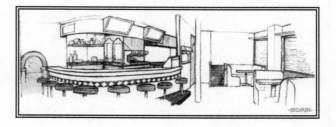

Original design sketch for Breakfast in America by Sylvain Deboissy.

Next, with Sylvain's design plans in hand, I arranged a meeting with an architect, Jean-Tho. The perfect Parisian hipster, Jean-Tho zoomed up to the diner on his vintage black Vespa with a matching black helmet, skipped over the curb and onto the sidewalk, then parked his scooter in front of the café as if he were a cowboy tethering his horse in front of a saloon.

With perfect posture that only accentuated his model-thin frame, Jean-Tho swaggered into the café. Then with one dramatic, fluid motion, he tilted his head to the side and peeled off his helmet, revealing a long, perfectly coiffed mane, which he proceeded to swoosh back and forth as if he were in a shampoo commercial. Once every silky, brown hair had settled back into place, he held out his hand, flashed a movie-star grin, and declared for the whole world to hear, "Jean-Tho! *Architecte-errr!*"

The two of us hit it off right from the start. Young and ambitious, Jean-Tho was making a name for himself as an architect and was excited by the opportunity to work on such a "one-of-a-kind" project as BIA. In fact, he confided in me how frustrated he was working in France, where ambition and risk-taking were often considered taboo. Inspired by my entrepreneurial spirit, Jean-Tho wanted to work with me so badly he was willing to lower his fee. All the better for me, since I barely had €50,000 left to pay for everything, including equipment and decor.

When Jean-Tho saw my meager budget, however, his eyes went wide. "But Greiiig-*errr!*" (Oh, when would a French person ever get my name right?) "*C'est pas possible-errr!*"

I assured Jean-Tho that, yes, indeed it was possible. In fact, I told him that between my background in film, coupled with Sylvain's inspired sketches, I could already think of a dozen creative ways to do things on the cheap.

Take the old, worn-out floor tiles, for example. They already gave the place a vintage feel. Plus the color was right, beige with small patterns of black and red. Despite Jean-Tho's objections that they were "*moche-errr*" (ugly), I convinced him to leave them as they were. Same for the ceiling. When Monsieur Marin opened Le Square back in the sixties, the drop ceiling, with its funky angles and lighting, had been radical for its time. Now, all these years later, it meshed perfectly with the quirky feeling I was going for. I was even able to salvage most of Le Square's original tables and chairs.

That said, despite the bones of the place being solid, there were still two major problems that couldn't be fixed cheaply, both of which would haunt me for years to come: the electricity and the kitchen space.

First, with its porcelain tubes and dangerously exposed wiring, the entire electrical system would have to be replaced. The kitchen space was even more of a challenge. That's because it wasn't a kitchen at all—it was just the toaster oven that Monsieur Marin had used for his world-famous *croque monsieur*. Of course, BIA would be serving much more than sandwiches, and I expected to have a lot more customers too—up to fifty people when every seat was filled. That meant we'd need a full kitchen and the expensive ventilation system that went with it. (I would have to replace the small pipe that the Marins had in place already). To complicate matters, we were dealing with a Paris-sized kitchen space, which translated to roughly seventy square feet—or the equivalent of a Beverly Hills-size walk-in shoe closet—in which we had to fit everything.

Jean-Tho and I approached the problem like a jigsaw puzzle, drawing up every conceivable configuration to fit in two burners, a flattop grill, a fryer, fridges, a freezer, a dishwasher, a kitchen sink, a prep area for cutting boards, a mandolin slicer, a meat slicer, and space for storage. After much difficulty, we finally made our little kitchen puzzle work. And what it revealed confirmed my worst fear: the original menu I had envisioned for BIA would have to change.

With Jean-Tho and his renovation crew moving full steam ahead, I had time to concentrate on this new and unexpected bump in the road. Once again, luck was on my side as someone I'd met earlier on my BIA adventure suddenly popped back into my life: Didier, the sous-chef with whom I'd worked at André's restaurant. After one too many insults from André, Didier had quit and was now running his own restaurant across town. During his breaks, he was kind enough to meet with me and offer his sage advice.

When Didier first saw my sample menu, then looked at my tiny kitchen area, he shook his head and repeated the phase that was becoming all too familiar: "*C'est pas possible!*" Not surprisingly, my original menu had been very ambitious, containing just about every delicious dish you'd find on an episode of *Diners, Drive-Ins, and Dives*. In addition to breakfast and burgers, I'd planned on serving a grand selection of comfort-food classics, which most French people wouldn't be familiar with but would be thrilled to discover (or so I hoped): meat loaf, mac 'n' cheese, barbecued ribs, patty melts, Rueben sandwiches, Philly cheesesteaks, matzo ball soup, and much more.

But given our extremely limited space, the sad reality was that BIA's menu would have to be simplified a lot, which broke my heart. But I took solace in the realization that, once BIA was up and running smoothly, I'd get a chance to try out some of the deleted items as blue-plate specials.

In the meantime, I still had to decide which items would be featured on BIA's first menu. For this, Didier had quite the novel approach: focus first on the ingredients. From there, he said, the rest would follow.

The list of ingredients for BIA was divided into two parts. The first part included all the items that were easy to find in France, like fresh fruits and vegetables that would be delivered daily from Rungis, an enormous wholesale food market that was formerly in Les Halles but was now located outside of the city. I couldn't wait to sample all their fresh produce. In France, for lots of different reasons, most fruits and vegetables are tastier than they are in the United States. It's the same with dairy products, including eggs, butter, milk, and cheese.

The second part of my ingredients list proved to be much more of a challenge. Being a diner, BIA required lots of special products, such as real bacon, breakfast sausages, maple syrup, cheddar cheese, barbecue sauce, tortilla chips, salsa, fresh burger meat (with just the right percentage of fat), veggie burgers, hamburger buns, pickles, relish, bagels, cream cheese, American-style sliced bread (both wheat and white, for toast), peanut butter, donuts, muffins, brownies, California wine, and—the biggie—American-style bottomless coffee. List in hand, I began the difficult task of hunting down as many of these "exotic" ingredients as I could find.

It was now November 6—the first day of Ramadan and just three weeks to go before opening day. At the BIA worksite, I learned that half of my crew were devout Muslims, including the electrician, Joël. Since Ramadan lasted thirty days, I was worried that the long holiday might delay our renovations. Thankfully, two of the workers, the always good-natured Sharif and Mourad, kindly put my fears to rest. They assured me that even though they might be weak from fasting every day, their hunger would only make them work harder, so they wouldn't have to think about their empty stomachs. True to their word, the dynamic duo plastered and painted their way through the diner like there was no tomorrow. They even managed to get a little ahead of schedule!

That left time for me to focus on finding all those "exotic" ingredients, which turned out to be a quest of quixotic proportions. Supplier after supplier had never heard of the products I needed. And when they did, it wasn't at all what I was looking for. The hardest thing to find was American-style bacon. Butchers would send me a big hunk of meat that kind of looked like bacon, but when we tried to cut it, our slicer almost broke from all the cartilage still intact. Other samples were closer to Canadian bacon, which wasn't bad, but my diner was not called Breakfast in Saskatchewan. In short, I desperately needed to find real, noncartilage bacon fast!

That's when fate came a-calling once again. In yet another ironic twist, it was "*Merci* to the Mouse" all over again. It turned out that Disneyland Paris had such a huge demand for American products that they had helped spawn a small but specialized network of suppliers. The most important of these was Foodex, a growing distribution company that shipped huge containers of American products from the States. Foodex was excited to work with us because they wanted to expand their client base beyond that of American hotels, bars, and amusement parks (or "parks of distraction" as the French so deliciously call them).

As for my last elusive holy grail I was finally able to find a butcher who made real American-style bacon that didn't break your teeth. Grand Boucherie Permière also became our supplier for fresh hamburger meat, delivered daily, with just the right percentage of fat to make our burgers plump and juicy.

That left just three things on my list: breakfast sausage, California wine, and bottomless American coffee. It would take almost two years for the first item to become available in France, via a British distributor. As for wine, admittedly it seemed sacrilegious to even think about offering anything other than France's very own national treasure. That's why I was more than happy to continue offering the same simple but tasty bistro wine that the Marins had served: sauvignon blanc and côtes du rhône.

When it came to American coffee, however, I had no shame! I mean, come on, what goes better with a good ol' American breakfast than a good ol' bottomless mug o' joe? Seriously, can you imagine trying to make a teeny, weeny espresso last until you've finished eating your stack of pancakes? *C'est pas possible!*

Luckily for me, getting good American-style coffee in France *was* possible, thanks to a recent development. For better or worse, Starbucks was on the verge of invading Paris, with plans of opening thirty locations in the first year alone. Enter Cafés Richard, a distributor that had been supplying excellent coffee to most of France's traditional cafés, including Le Square, for generations. Cafés Richard was very concerned that Starbucks would crush their small family business, and for some nutty reason, they thought BIA could help—so much so that Monsieur Richard himself came to see me at the diner with an interesting proposition: if I agreed to let them be our exclusive coffee supplier, they'd give us an American coffee machine *and* a fancy Italian espresso machine for free.

"Deal!" I said, saving nearly €7,000 in one, old-fashioned handshake.

There was just one problem, however: the French hated

American coffee. They called it *jus de chaussettes*, which literally means "sock juice." When I asked my French friends why they called it that, nobody could give me a definitive answer. Some said it was because American coffee tasted like the liquid that comes out of wet socks when you wring them out. Others said that American GIs used to use their socks as coffee filters during World War II, because nothing else was available.

In any case, I made it my mission to change the ugly French stereotype about America's number-one breakfast drink. I even went so far as to put *"jus de chaussette"* on the menu as the humorous translation for "American coffee."

As I met with each supplier, I was reminded of something Anthony Bourdain said in his book *Kitchen Confidential*. If you want to know the viability of your operation, just ask your suppliers. They know intuitively the first time they meet you whether your idea will work or not. If they refuse to say so directly, you'll get your answer when they demand to be paid up front, refusing to give you even a week's worth of credit.

If that's true, it must say something about BIA, because the paint hadn't even dried yet and already my suppliers were willing to give me not just a week, but a whole *month's* worth of credit! *Mon dieu*, talk about your performance anxiety. All the more reason to make sure the next thing on my list got done right—testing recipes and cooks.

The setting: a glorious Avenue Foch mansion. The cast: a Chinese man, a Texan, and a drugged-out Bostonian. The props: a spatula, a frying pan, and burning-hot oil. Sounds like the setup to an Agatha Christie murder mystery, *n'est-ce pas?*

Well, actually it was the backdrop for BIA's first *dégustation* (taste testing). With our kitchen under construction, I needed a place to test recipes and to audition short-order cooks, two of whom would be hired to man the grill on opening day, which was now just *two short weeks* away! And what a kitchen we had to work with! It was easily twice as big as BIA's future kitchen.

Of course, I'd expect nothing less from a posh Avenue Foch mansion, located just a stone's throw away from the Arc de Triomphe. The place belonged to the rich American woman who had been at my investor party back in LA. She never ended up investing in BIA, but she did ask me to dog-sit for her while she was on vacation. Needing a place for our *dégustation,* I was more than happy to oblige.

The menu that day consisted of breakfast items only. Again, given BIA's logistical constraints, I had no choice but to heed the advice of my restaurateur friends, which was to never overextend yourself, especially at the beginning.

Joining the tasting party were a half-dozen friends and investors, including Guillaume and Alex from *Robin Hood* and Diane, a fellow UConn student who was in the junior year abroad program with me. Diane was now living in Paris, and because she missed a real American breakfast almost as much as I did, she became a BIA investor.

In order to get diverse feedback, I made sure the group was split down the middle—half French, half American. This was especially important given the cultural challenges that BIA faced. For example, since the French didn't eat as much as Americans, what should our portion sizes be? I knew if I made them too big, the French would be upset, because (1) they hated wasting food, and (2) they didn't believe in *zee* doggie bag. On the other side of the scale (no pun intended), my American customers had bigger appetites and needed to feel like they were getting a bang for their buck.

Then there were the challenges of the food itself. Take eggs and omelets—the French tend to like them runny, almost to the point of being raw. Would they accept the American way of cooking them, especially scrambled eggs? And what about the separation of savory and sweet? I had learned that, for the most part, the French don't like to mix the two. My test group agreed. That's why for BIA's first brunch menu, which I called "A Taste of America," I decided to split the breakfast feast into two parts: first the savory, a choice of an egg dish served with home fries and toast, followed a choice of either a short stack of pancakes or a donut (or brownie) with a cup of yogurt.

Next, what about my ongoing concern that the French didn't really eat breakfast, except for croissants and *pains au chocolat*? The French people in my focus group, all of whom had visited the States, told me there was no need to worry. "Breakfast is the one meal you Americans do right!" they said. Guillaume was the most enthusiastic member of the bunch. With his finger on the pulse of all that was *branché* (hip), Guillaume was particularly excited that BIA would be serving breakfast *à toute heure* (all day), meaning he could order pancakes whenever he wanted—even for dinner.

Another sign that the time was right for an American diner in Paris was the newest trend to hit the city: Sunday brunch. It had become *the* thing to do—but only at select restaurants, and at an exorbitant price. It could cost up to €35 for bird-size portions that included some *viennoiseries* (pastries), a cold slab of salmon or ham, a ramekin of yogurt, and a couple pieces of fruit, all of which left you starving in the end. BIA's brunch, on the other hand, would consist of hearty portions of real American breakfast items *and* be offered at a reasonable price—just €12.50 for everything, including bottomless coffee and juice.

Last, and certainly not least, what was the group's final verdict on the recipes? I knew from the start that BIA would not do froufrou. But we *would* do fresh and tasty. I'm happy to report that, thanks in large part to all the fresh ingredients available from the Rungis market, our simple breakfast dishes went over like gangbusters—especially the pancakes, the favorite being blueberry with white-chocolate chips. (Okay, so maybe those were *my* favorite.) Also receiving top scores was our French toast made with yummy brioche bread. There was just one recipe that needed some work: our home fries. Thanks to the group's feedback, we tweaked the recipe just enough until we found the perfect mix of grilled pepper, onion, and garlic.

By the end of the *dégustation*, everyone was sprawled out all over the designer furniture, holding their stomachs, with big satisfied grins on their faces. Lying on the sofa, Guillaume, whose normally flat stomach bulged underneath his T-shirt, held up his hand and said with a burp, "And...what about...*le vrai 'amburger?*" (The real hamburger.)

"Ah, you'll have to wait for that," I said. "But not for too long, I hope."

Guillaume smiled, closed his eyes, and slowly drifted off into a blissful food coma.

Meanwhile, back at the worksite, the atmosphere contrasted sharply with that at Château Foch. Sharif and Mourad looked thin and pale, as if they might pass out at any moment from their fasting for Ramadan, which still had two weeks to go. Out of respect for the poor guys, I refrained from telling them about our delicious *dégustation* and how full I still was. Instead, I complimented them on their excellent work and, like a good coach, encouraged them to keep pushing forward!

We were now in the final stretch, just ten days away from opening. Actually, with a little luck, we might even finish a day or two ahead of schedule. It seemed too good to be true. Which, of course, it was.

Sure enough, storm clouds were brewing on the horizon, starting with Jean-Tho, *l'architecte-errr.*

I probably should've suspected from the way he swooshed his

hair that there was an *artiste* inside Jean-Tho just waiting to burst out. And when it did, *bon dieu*, look out! The first indication of trouble had actually occurred a couple of weeks earlier. Having made it very clear to Jean-Tho that I could only afford a small number of spotlights, imagine my surprise the day I came in and looked up to see dozens of holes drilled into the ceiling, with wires hanging out everywhere, waiting for extra spots to be installed.

It only got worse from there.

Before I knew it, Jean-Tho had a "new" and "inspired" vision for the place that had nothing to do with a vintage diner but everything to do with a slick, modern, colorless vanity project. Almost daily, he would come in with a whole new set of designs, insisting that I change everything, starting with the original floor tiling—something he became particularly obsessed with. His dissatisfaction then moved to the angle of the counter, which he wanted to change. And what about the custom-made booths and authentic diner upholstery that took me so long to find? Too red! And the *passe-plat* (servery), where the food was supposed to come out? "It must be removed!" he cried. The reason: "It disrupts with the fluidity of my space!"

As I desperately tried to rein in Jean-Tho's costly whims and stay on schedule, I barely heard the faint sound of something dangerous brewing from afar—something that could put my whole dream in danger: the drumbeats of war. Judging from the headlines appearing daily in the *International Herald Tribune*, George W. Bush and Dick Cheney seemed hell-bent on starting a war in Iraq. Of course, their timing couldn't have been worse, falling right in the middle of Ramadan—and coincidentally—the opening of BIA.

Naturally, Sharif and Mourad were very concerned about the situation in the Middle East. One afternoon, they took me aside and asked in hushed tones what I thought would happen. I told them not to worry. "Bush would never attack a country that hadn't attacked us," I said, not sure who I was trying to convince more, them or me.

The backlash from all the war talk was not pretty. Anti-Americanism began flaring up all over Europe, including Paris. Suddenly I had a whole new list of things to worry about. For example, did I need to rethink our sign? To minimize the risk of the diner becoming a target, should I remove the word "America" from it? Might be a little difficult, considering our name was Breakfast-in-freaking-America!

Of course, I could put whatever the hell I wanted to on our sign, but what difference would it make if we never actually opened? That's because on the Saturday before opening week, everything at BIA came to a screeching halt. I sat alone in the diner, surrounded by dangling wires. All my years of hard work had come down to just one person: Joël the electrician. Until he came in and finished his job, the rest of the crew was stuck, unable to finish theirs. The mood had been very tense since the day before, when Jean-Tho sent his crew home early because there was nothing left for them to do.

"Do not worry, Greiiig-*errr*," Jean-Tho said as he hopped onto his Vespa. "Joël will be here all this weekend to finish up." Then with a flick of his wrist, Jean-Tho bid farewell, driving his scooter off the sidewalk and calling back as he sped away:

"Ciaaa-ouuu!"

My thoughts returned to the present. I looked up at the frying-pan clock hanging on the diner wall—the first decoration I'd bought for BIA. The eggs read 3:22 p.m. Joël was still nowhere in sight, and my calls were going straight to his voice mail.

I tried to imagine where he could be. Since Joël was Moroccan and a practicing Muslim, I figured he was probably at home, unable to answer his phone because he was too weak from fasting. I refused to let my mind go down the other path...that his no-show might have something to do with the anger that was brewing throughout Europe against the United States.

At the crack of dawn on Sunday morning, I was back in the diner again, waiting. And waiting. Still no Joël. Still no rhyme or reason.

By Monday morning, I stood in the middle of the diner like a zombie, dazed and shell-shocked, as the full implications of what was in store for BIA began to sink in. Every phase of the renovations had been lined up for weeks, with each task dependent upon the other. By not showing up, Joël created a domino effect that caused the whole project to fall into complete chaos:

Sharif and Mourad: *Canceled.* With the web of electrical wires hanging out everywhere, Sharif and Mourad couldn't come in as planned to plug up the remaining holes and apply the last coat of paint.

Furniture delivery: *Canceled.* Without the restaurant space painted and clean, the custom-made booths and other furnishings couldn't be installed.

Kitchen and bar equipment delivery: *Canceled.* With no electrical outlets, none of the kitchen or bar equipment could be installed, including fridges and freezers.

Food and drink delivery: *Canceled.* With no fridges or freezers, there was no place to stock supplies.

Staff: *Canceled.* With BIA completely out of service, I had no choice but to call the two cooks I'd hired from the taste-testing, Feng and Ezra, and tell them that their first day of work—a trial run scheduled for Wednesday—was canceled. Since I was unable to offer them a new starting date, they threatened to look for other jobs. I pleaded with them to hold on for just a little longer.

Opening day: *Canceled.* With no idea when—or if—BIA

would ever open, there was just one thing I could do that helped me stay semi-sane, one thing over which I had a modicum of control. Despite Jean-Tho's vehement objections, I kept the original wall tiles behind the bar, painting more than six thousand of them by hand in red and black, to match the color of the booths and chairs. Not only did this save me a ton of money, but it also gave me something tangible to do while I desperately waited for my electrician to show up and power my dream.

Painting more than six thousand tiles by hand, one at a time.

It was now December, one week past what should have been opening day. Still no Joël. No message. No explanation. No nothing.

I tried to find another electrician, but I was told that without Joël's detailed list, it would take ages to figure out which wire went where. Making matters worse, Jean-Tho and his crew had already moved on to another project. There was no telling when they'd be available to come back and finish the job.

One thing that wasn't on hold, however, was December's rent, which was now due. Also, with the fiscal year coming to an end, my equipment and furnishing suppliers wanted to me to pay up before the thirty-first. Of course, that would be impossible until some cash started coming in. With lots of begging and pleading, I was able to convince the suppliers to split the final bill into three installments, spread out over three months, the first one due in January.

It was now make-or-break time; if BIA wasn't open by January, the company would go bankrupt.

Three weeks past our missed opening day and still no sign of Joël. But thankfully there was at least one positive sign during this difficult time—BIA's *actual* sign. It was now ready and didn't need Joël's help (or lack thereof) to be installed. However, it was only a *temporary* sign, until our request for a permit authorizing a neon DINER sign was approved. In the meantime, I was forced to use the small box that had housed Le Square's sign. But unfortunately, BIA's logo could barely fit into it, which, on the plus side, made that troublesome word "America" become so small it was barely visible.

At least we now had a diner sign—just no diner to go with it.

Friday morning, December 20. By now I had gotten so used to the daily routine of calling up my cooks and equipment people—begging them to hold on a little longer—that I barely noticed a man strolling into the diner nonchalantly, holding a toolbox.

It was Joël.

"*Bonjour, Craque!*" He smiled and waved as he made his way across the room and down into the *cave* where the electric box was, as if nothing had ever happened. I stood there with my mouth hanging wide-open, the phone dangling from my hand.

That weekend, Joël did a marathon session and finished nearly everything. Somehow I knew intuitively that I should never bring up the subject of his absence or the trouble it had caused me. If I did, I knew he'd become offended and might disappear again, this time for good. Instead, I focused my energy on the present, and in particular, how in the world was I ever going to wrangle Jean-Tho and his crew together again to finish the last of the work?

With Christmas just around the corner, the prospects for BIA opening in January looked bleak. Depending on which day a holiday falls, the French take what's called *le pont*, or "the bridge." For example, if a holiday falls on a Tuesday or a Thursday, they'll take the Monday or Friday off as well. That year, Christmas fell on a Wednesday, as did New Year's Day the following week. Did that mean the French would take two *ponts* for each holiday, meaning two whole weeks off?

As it turned out, my crew wasn't planning on taking any *pont* at all—just the holiday itself. Thank God, because I now had a brand-new goal around which I could rally the troops: getting ready in time for a special event planned for December 31. For weeks, my neighbor, Bruno, who worked at the temp agency next door, had been asking me if he could book BIA for a private New Year's Eve party with his friends. I couldn't wait to tell Bruno we just might be able to host his shindig after all! And best of all, if we were able to pull it off, it would be a boon for BIA; not only would it bring in some desperately needed cash, but it would also allow us to do a dress rehearsal before officially opening to the public the following weekend.

Having a dress rehearsal was crucial, because my cooks had never truly been vetted. I had no idea if they knew how to operate our fancy new equipment, let alone cook for a packed house. Unfortunately, Ezra wasn't available that night. But Feng was, and he assured me that, as a professionally trained cook, he'd be able to handle everything himself.

Of course, before that could happen, we still needed to get the diner ready in time. After much begging and pleading (something I was getting quite good at *en français)*, I convinced all the workers to come in over the next week and a half and finish the job in time for New Year's Eve. With the clock ticking, each day turned into an exercise of controlled chaos: the furniture people were bumping into the kitchen equipment people, who were tripping over the coffee machine installers, who were knocking over Sharif and Mourad's paint cans.

Watching my dream come together before my eyes, I felt a tremendous sense of creative fulfillment—a feeling, it occurred to me, that I'd known before—but when? It was like a déjà vu. *Ah, yes, of course*, I thought. *This was how it felt when I was directing my short films back at USC.* At that moment, I realized that putting together a restaurant was a lot like making a movie. You've got all the major components: budget, location scouting, script (as in the *theme* or *story* of the restaurant), set design, props, lighting, music, cast and crew, and of course, catering. For a brief but shining moment, as I directed each crew member in their preparation for the upcoming "scene," I felt the happiest I had in years.

On the afternoon of December 31, as the early winter darkness fell upon the city, a few straggling workers remained, including the awning people and Joël, who was still connecting the last of Jean-Tho's spotlights. With just three hours to go before guests would start arriving, I couldn't believe how much still needed to be done. First, we had to clean all the dust from the renovations, which was *everywhere*. Once that was done, we needed to stock the kitchen and bar area with glasses, plates, silverware, and drinks. Next, we still needed to hang the posters I'd hunted down of classic diner scenes from movies like *Pulp Fiction*, *When Harry Met Sally*, and *Diner*. Finally, Bruno had brought his own DJ, who needed to set up his sound system.

By 7:00 p.m., crowds began to gather outside. They tried to peek inside the diner, but couldn't see a thing because the windows were blocked out from the renovations. Little did they know that on the other side of the curtain my trusty pals from *Robin Hood* and I were in a mad frenzy to get the diner ready in time for the big night.

A few minutes before opening, I called the gang over to the counter, which was covered with a protective layer of plastic. With my buddy Jérôme filming it all, I peeled off the plastic, revealing the authentic boomerang laminate, which I'd had shipped over from the company I'd met with at the Dinerama tour. When they saw the beautiful boomerang motif, everyone erupted into applause.

I glanced over at the kitchen. Not only was the new equipment working just fine, but Feng appeared to have everything under control. He moved skillfully from one end of the tiny kitchen to the other like a lithe dancer, preparing BIA's very first meal. It smelled delicious!

Feng's menu for the evening consisted of a starter salad, followed by grilled pork chops served with a side of pasta and a medley of fresh vegetables, and ending with a dessert of choice: pecan pie, cheesecake, or brownie *à la mode*—all for the low, low price of just twenty-five euros per person, which included bottomless boxed wine (Bruno's idea). I didn't know if Feng could pull off a three-course meal for fifty people, but at this point I was operating on pure faith that everything was going to work out somehow.

Meanwhile, the murmurs from the crowd outside grew louder. I turned, looked at the gang, and nodded to see if they were ready. I took a deep breath, then stepped over to the front door. On the count of three, I tore down the paper covering the windows. Outside, Bruno and his friends whooped and hollered when they saw for the very first time, my baby, my diner, my dream—Breakfast in America!

I unlocked the door. The hungry, thirsty crowd rushed in from the cold and took their places in the warm, comfy booths.

The evening went off without a hitch. The food was delicious, the guests were happy, and except for a few of Bruno's friends who snuck in without paying, the dinner was a great financial success. Feng proved himself to be a real cook, both in the positive and negative sense: his food came out tasty, hot, and on time, but I got a glimpse of his temperamental side as well. With pots and pans piled high and the grill a filthy mess, Feng made a beeline toward the door.

"Wait a sec, Feng," I said, gesturing toward the *bordel* (mess) in the kitchen. "Aren't you forgetting something?"

"Uh-uh," he snorted. "Cooks don't clean. That's what dishies are for."

And with that, he was gone. It wouldn't be the last time Feng would leave me with the dirty work. And it would be even longer before I'd be able to afford a dishie.

As I scrubbed the pots and pans, I felt another brief but shining moment of happiness as I watched Bruno and his friends dance the night away. By 2:00 a.m. (the time restaurants are required to close in Paris), the guests began to stagger out of the diner, shaking my hand and showering me with compliments—except for one guy who offered his critique on the pork chops: "Could've used a little more salt."

"Duly noted," I said, trying not to smile too hard. Of course, he had no clue what a miracle it was that we'd managed to open at all.

After the last guest had gone, I gave a toast to the crew, thanking them for making the night such a success. I soon found myself thinking about BIA's *real* opening, which was now just three short days away. A wave of panic shot through me as I recalled a famous expression from the theater: "A good dress rehearsal means a bad opening."

Opening day!

Chapter 12

OPEN FOR BUSINESS; CLOSED FOR WAR

"Non!"

—Front-page headline of *Libération,* March 2003

6:00 A.M., SATURDAY, JANUARY 4, 2003. BREAKFAST IN AMERICA'S official opening day. That morning, I didn't roll out of bed—I sprang out. I couldn't wait to flip BIA's sign to OPEN.

After a quick shower, I got dressed and stepped outside. It was pitch-black. But also *white.* Everywhere. Paris was in the middle of its biggest snowstorm in decades. It was insanely beautiful—like a Christmas card. Naturally, I saw it as a great sign.

I arrived at the diner at 6:30, giving myself enough time to get the place ready for our 7:30 opening. The moment I stepped inside, I couldn't believe how cold it was. And drafty. That's because the facade was all glass, from floor to ceiling, with gaps between each window pane.

When the Marins first installed the facade back in the sixties, it was very *à la mode* (fashionable). But now, as I stood shivering in the empty diner, I felt like pie *à la mode*. Like a big fat scoop of ice cream.

I tried the Marin's high-tech solution for stopping the drafts—covering the gaps with scotch tape. It blocked out some of the cold. But it didn't stop the north wind from whipping in through the huge gaps at the top and bottom of the facade.

I turned on the space heaters by each booth, hoping it would be enough to warm the place up, since there was no central heating. (They weren't.) Next, I turned on the American coffee machine and excitedly got my contraband mugs ready. Of course, I had big plans for the mugs and couldn't wait to test them out on my customers.

My idea for the mugs came from an amazing cross-country road trip I'd taken to California with my friend Deb after I'd gotten accepted to USC. As we drove along Route 66 (or what's left of it), we stopped at several classic roadside diners. One place stood out in particular—a rundown concrete block on a dusty road somewhere in New Mexico. As we ate our breakfast, I noticed that every time a regular came into the diner, the waitress would grab his or her favorite mug off of a shelf that was full of a variety of mugs—all in different shapes, styles, and colors. The waitress would then bring each customer their favorite mug and serve them their morning joe in it.

I planned to do the exact same thing at BIA with my contraband mugs.

Beep. Beep. The little beeper on the coffee machine went off. BIA's first pot of coffee had been brewed! I grabbed a mug off the shelf. (I had several favorites. Today's pick was a pancake joint with a name that might evoke what a kangaroo does to get from one place to another.) I poured myself a cup, wrapped my freezing hands around the mug, and took my first glorious sip. *Ah...*

I did one last check around the room. Everything was ready.

The tables were set and the brand-new menus printed and laminated. Just one thing was missing: my cook. He was set to arrive at seven.

My eyes went over to the vintage seventies jukebox in the corner of the room. It was the last item that I'd had installed at BIA—and it didn't even cost me a cent, thanks to a company that loaned out coin-operated jukeboxes for free. All I had to do was split the coins with them. When the jukebox was delivered, however, I noticed that nearly all the music was Johnny Hallyday—the Elvis of France. When I told the jukebox guy that BIA was an American joint, he said, "Don't worry! Everybody loves Johnny!"

Everybody except me. And Americans. And possibly the rest of the planet.

"Just in case," I said, "do you have any American music?"

The jukebox man grumbled, then replaced some of Johnny's CDs with a few "American" CDs, such as Pink Floyd, Queen, and the Rolling Stones. Of course, the jukebox would only work if customers put coins into it. Until that happened, the music in the diner would have to be supplied by my iPod. I'd made several playlists, depending on the time of day and the type of clientele. Today's selection was vintage jazz.

At 7:00 a.m. on the dot, Feng came running into the diner, looking worse for the wear, as if he'd been up all night partying.

"Good morning, Feng," I said, holding up the coffeepot. "Want some?"

Feng shook his head. "*Brrr*, it's freezing in here." He ran downstairs to change and came back up in a flash. After firing up the grill, Feng held his hands over the flames.

"Hey, at least you'll be warm over there," I said.

Feng smiled, then began frying strips of real bacon and garlicky home fries on our brand-new grill. I took a whiff of the delicious aroma. It smelled like morning.

I had no idea what to expect that first day. Given all the problems with the renovations, I'd had no time (or budget) to do any real promotion. Instead, during the weeks leading up to our opening, I'd done whatever I could, such as handing out BIA business cards everywhere I went and plastering a "Coming Soon!" sign on our facade.

I think it would be safe to say that this was perhaps the softest opening of all time. But for me, that was a good thing. First, knowing the French didn't like hype, I had a hunch that they would prefer to discover BIA on their own, instead of having it rammed down their throats. I also preferred a soft opening because BIA still needed to work out the kinks. It was one thing to have fancy theories about what might or might not work, but reality was something else entirely. In other words, I still had a lot of things I needed to test out on my real-life customers, including:

Simple greetings. When a customer walked through the door, should I say "*bonjour*" or "hello"? The French famously hate it when foreigners don't try to speak their language. But, of course, we were an American joint. Would the French find a hearty "hello!" exotic or rude?

And when I spoke to them, should I use the polite form of you (*vous*) or the friendly, down-home version (*tu*)? After all, diner lingo was famous for being unpretentious. Saucy, even. Any miscalculation on my part could easily offend the French.

Business hours. American tourists get up early and eat early. Parisians do not, especially for dinner, which they rarely eat before 8:00 p.m. That's why most restaurants in France close between the hours of 3:00 p.m. and 7:00 p.m. (*la coupure*). My goal was to, eventually, keep the kitchen open all day long, with nonstop service. How would the French take to that?

In the meantime, to keep costs down, our hours (and staffing) would have to be kept to a minimum. Therefore, for the time being, food service would be from 7:30 a.m. to 3:00 p.m., Tuesday through Sunday, for breakfast only. Bar service and snacks would continue until midnight—except for Sundays, when we'd close at 4:00 p.m., after brunch. Mondays we'd close completely. Once business picked up, I intended to expand our hours as needed.

American vs. French service. In America, servers make most of their money on tips. That's why they're constantly checking on customers and catering to their every need. In France, it's much different. Not only does the concept of tips not exist, but the French don't like it when you're in their face every minute, interrupting their intense, world-changing conversations.

The same was true of bussing tables. I learned at André's restaurant never to remove a customer's plate too soon or to bring over the check until they've asked for it. Both practices are considered very rude in France; it gives the impression that you're trying to push customers out the door—as if all you care about is turning tables, *you goddamn capitalist pig, you!*

Squatters. What about customers who never leave, smoking the hours away while you've got rent and salaries (not to mention super high taxes) to pay? In my business plan, I'd broached this delicate subject as follows: "BIA may be a cool place to hang—but not for too long. Given the French propensity to sit for hours, we will gently nudge our customers to be on their way. But only during peak periods, so those waiting can be seated."

"Earth to Mr. Carlson," Feng said from the kitchen, snapping me out of my thoughts. He pointed to the frying-pan clock. The eggs read 7:29 a.m. I rushed over to the door. Right as the minute hand moved to thirty, I flipped over the authentic OPEN sign I'd brought from the States.

"BIA is now officially open for business!" I said.

Feng smiled through a thick cloud of smoking bacon. "I'm ready!" he said.

Out of consideration for my neighbors, I did not turn on the ventilation system. Not only did the motor make a lot of noise, but it also sucked in tons of cold air through the gaps in the facade. I figured I could turn on the ventilation once the room was packed with customers (along with their valuable body heat).

That was a bit of wishful thinking. I knew it would be slow on our first day, but this was ridiculous. Our first customers—a friendly couple in their thirties—didn't arrive until after 9:00 a.m.

"Hello!" I said.

The couple looked startled. "Oh my God," the wife said. "You speak English!"

"I better," I said. "Since this is an American joint."

The couple laughed, then told me that they were on vacation and had just seen our sign in the window proclaiming, "American Coffee! Free Refills!" And that's exactly what they ordered—two coffees at the counter.

"You're my very first customers," I said. "Just opened today."

"No kidding?" the husband said, checking out the room. "Wild! This place reminds me of a diner back in Jersey."

"Jersey, huh?" I searched through my mugs, grabbing a pair that had the logo of a popular coffee shop in the Northeast. "D'you guys know this place?" I set the mugs on the counter in front of them.

"Oh my God, yes!" the wife said. "We go there all the time!"

I smiled; my mug scheme seemed to be working. As I poured the couple their steaming hot coffee, I said, "Would you like to take a look at the menu?"

The couple nodded. "Oh my God, honey, look!" the wife said as she looked at the menu. "They've got pancakes!"

"No way," the husband said. "In Paris? That's awesome!"

"Oh, honey, we've got to come back here."

"Hell, yeah," the husband said. Then he grumbled, "Breakfast at our hotel totally sucks!"

"That's why we're here," I said. Then I handed them a stack of business cards. "Be sure to tell all your friends."

The wife smiled, took the cards, and shoved them into her purse. Then she held up her mug. "Can we get our coffees to go, please? We wanna beat the lines at the Louvre."

"Of course," I said.

I grabbed a pair of to-go cups and filled them with a fresh dose of java. The couple thanked me and headed out into the snowstorm with the biggest smiles on their faces. My heart filled with pride; BIA's very first customers left happier than a pigeon with a french fry.

With the snow whipping around outside, business was dead until the early afternoon. Once the storm subsided, however, a few customers strolled in, including two of Jérôme's friends—a young couple and my very first French customers! Having just returned from a vacation in New York, the couple was craving an American breakfast. And since they wanted a little bit of everything, I recommended the 2 × 2 × 2 (two pancakes, two eggs, two strips of crispy bacon). The couple ordered two of them, one with scrambled eggs, the other over easy.

"Anything to drink?" I asked.

"Two coffees, please," the man said.

"Normal or *jus de chaussettes*?" I asked, raising an eyebrow.

The couple paused, making sure they heard me right. Then they burst out laughing. "*Non, non, non,*" the man said. "*Real* coffee!"

"Okay…but you don't know what you're missing."

"Oh, I think we do," the man joked.

We all laughed. *How cool was that?* BIA's very first diner banter! Before I knew it, the couple and I were "*tu*"-ing each other like good old friends.

Ping! Feng rang the kitchen bell, indicating that the 2 × 2 × 2's were ready. I grabbed the plates and brought them over to the table.

"*Bon appétit!*" I said to the couple.

"*Merci!*"

I watched from behind the counter as the couple smothered their pancakes with 100 percent pure maple syrup, using the authentic pourers I'd brought over from America. I waited until they were well into their post-meal smoke before coming over to clear their plates.

"How was everything?" I asked.

"*Délicieux!*" the man said, blowing out a thick stream of smoke.

To be honest, the whole smoking thing was a bit of a challenge for me. I didn't smoke, but I respected the fact that, in Paris, nearly everyone did. At the same time, I wanted to make sure my non-smoking customers had clean air to breathe and weren't hacking over their hash browns. Unfortunately, there wasn't a whole lot I could do. I tried to designate an area in the back of the room as a nonsmoking section. But despite our *défense de fumer* (no smoking) sign, there was no way of stopping the pesky secondhand smoke from moseying on over there.

As the French couple snuffed out their cigarettes, I waited for them to ask for their check before bringing it over. They were clearly in no hurry. After a few more smokes, they called out, *"L'addition, s'il vous plaît?"*

As I prepared their bill, I encountered my first *petit* dilemma: What should I do for friends (and friends of friends)? I'd been warned by restaurant owners to resist giving out freebies. Not only were they costly, but they often backfired; if you gave away too much, people started expecting it all the time.

Instead, I figured something out that, in my humble opinion, was a nice compromise. I didn't remove anything from their check. But I did give them a little something to take home. In this case, a brownie and a small blueberry muffin, which I put in a doggie bag.

The couple was thrilled. Even though it was a small expense, I figured it was worth the investment. Since they were Jérôme's friends, as well as our first satisfied French customers, I hoped that they would go out and spread the word.

By midafternoon, it had gotten so slow that Feng had the grill cleaned up and was out the door by 3:00 on the dot. I stayed on until midnight, taking advantage of our full liquor license—as well as serving *limonade* which is an old-timey way of saying nonalcoholic drinks, such as coffee, tea, sodas, and juices.

Madame Marin had taught me never to underestimate the value of *limonade*. "You wouldn't think so," she said to me once, "but a *café* here…a Perrier there…it adds up quick!"

Perhaps. But it would take a lot more *limonade*—not to mention pancakes, eggs, and *especially* bacon—for BIA to survive. That's because for our first day of business, BIA took in a grand total of…€85.

I tried not to obsess about the numbers, but I couldn't help myself. Rent was €1,200 a month. The cook cost €20 an hour (once you included payroll taxes). Plus there were food costs, utilities, the bank loan, and much, much more. In other words, €85 a day just wasn't gonna cut it.

Fortunately, the next day, Sunday, we made almost three times that amount! It certainly helped that Jérôme brought along more friends. Of course, since Sunday was brunch day, I couldn't wait to try out our "Taste of America" brunch menu.

I discovered a lot of cultural differences between my American and French customers that day. For example, with my American customers, the moment I brought out their breakfasts, they reacted as if they'd just run into a long-lost friend. "Oh my God," they'd squeal at their pancakes. "I missed you soooo much!"

French customers, on the other hand, reacted as if they'd just been introduced to a *new* friend—albeit a strange and exotic one. During this courting stage, they wanted to find out as much as they could about their new acquaintance.

"What is this...bah-guelle?" (bagel), they'd ask. "And bay-cun?" (bacon.) "And how is this...pahn-cake-*errr* different from a *crêpe*?" And my favorite, "Must I really toast my own toast?"

"*Mais, bien sûr!*" I'd reply. "It's better that way. Not only do you get to make your toast as dark or light as you want, but it also comes out nice and hot, so your butter melts all over it."

"Hmph."

It took a lot of patience and hand-holding before certain French customers began to feel comfortable. And when they did, I would try to convince them to be daring and try something new...something like...I don't know, *sock juice*?

"Ahhh!" they'd shriek in horror.

Eventually, I figured out the perfect way to entice them. I'd hold up a couple of our cool American mugs and say, "Take a look at this—you get to have your *jus de chaussette* served in these! Cool, huh? Whadya say?"

Sold! After pouring their coffee, I would await their verdict, a bead of sweat rolling down my forehead. The customer would take a delicate sip, as if they were at a fancy wine tasting. Then they'd sit there in dramatic silence for what felt like forever, until finally they'd say, "*Pas mal. Pas mal de tout.*" ("Not bad. Not bad at all," which is French for, "Hey, this is pretty darn good!")

There was one other cultural difference I discovered that Sunday. French customers really appreciated the way we split the brunch menu into two parts—savory and sweet. Americans, on the other hand, couldn't care less, often asking to have their eggs, bacon, potatoes, and pancakes delivered all at once. That and… "More ketchup!"

Despite cultural differences like these, my French and American customers did agree on one thing: that our "Taste of America" menu was not only delicious, but a great value as well. I thought it was safe to say that, overall, BIA's first weekend was, "*Pas mal. Pas mal de tout.*" Pretty darn good, indeed.

BIA was closed that first Monday, but we reopened bright and early on Tuesday. However, the vibe was very different than on the weekends. First, there was our weekday cook, Ezra from Texas, with his long sideburns and even longer drawl. When he trialed for us, he didn't have working papers, but I was able to finagle a three-month visa for him, which was no easy task. The justification: since BIA was a "nontraditional" restaurant I needed an "expert" to help get it started. Ezra was no expert. But he was a decent hash slinger.

Also on weekdays, BIA had a part-time waiter named Stewart from Scotland. I had promised him a job back in November, but with all the delays in the renovations, he had to wait for BIA to open. For his patience, I gave him as many hours as I could afford, which wasn't much—just four hours a day for the lunch shift. Even then, Stewart wasn't really needed. That's because it was dead. As in doornail.

At least there were a few regulars. But not *my* regulars. The Marins' regulars—neighborhood drunks who would stumble into BIA, dazed and confused, thinking they were in their old watering hole, Le Square. Standing at the counter, these local lushes would order cheap drinks, like *pressions* (draft beer) or *ballons* (small fourteen centiliter glasses of wine). After kicking back a few, one of the lushes would inevitably take a look around the brightly lit diner—with all its flashy, red decor—then turn to me and slur, "Wherrre the hell am I? Thisss isssn't Le Sssquare."

Before I could explain, the lush's attention would be drawn to the flashy neon lights of the jukebox. *Ooh, colors!* With a cigarette dangling from his mouth, the lush would stagger over to the jukebox, leaving a long trail of cigarette ash along the way. Then he'd drop a coin into the machine, trying to stay focused long enough to push some buttons. After a moment, the screeching voice of Johnny Hallyday would start blasting out of the speakers.

I'd stare at the lush as he took a swig of his drink, a puff of his smoke. Then I'd watch as he swung his hips to the rock 'n' roll beat of the cheesy French Elvis... And I'd think, *Where the hell am I? I thought this was an* American *joint*.

Fortunately, the era of the French lush didn't last long. Shortly thereafter, the "music police" moved in—our first surprise visit from a real-life French *contrôleur*. *Contrôleurs* were power-hungry civil servants who got great pleasure out of popping into small businesses without warning and handing out big fines for the tiniest of infractions. And that's exactly what we got—a nice big fine. Or rather, the jukebox guy did, because the sticker on his machine had expired just two days earlier. Angry and frustrated, the jukebox man took his jukebox away, along with his Johnny CDs, plus his take in coins—a whopping twelve euros.

But the music *contrôleur* wasn't done yet. He promptly billed me €1,300 for the right to play my iPod in the diner. The price was based on such things as the number of seats in the restaurant, as well as the type of liquor license we had. Since mine was the best category, the fee was more expensive.

But the *contrôleur* told me there was a way I could save a few hundred euros; all I had to do was agree to play only French radio in the diner, instead of my iPod.

"*Non, merci,*" I said. I'd had enough of Johnny.

During that first month, as we worked out the kinks, I closely monitored what was working in the diner and what wasn't, especially when it came to my strategy for building up our customer base. But since I had no advertising budget, I had to come up with creative and cost-free ways to fill BIA's tables.

Once again, my experience in Disney's marketing department came in very handy. I had learned many ways to create buzz without being obvious about it, especially when it came to targeting the younger generation, who loved hearing about new places on their own via social media. I figured that if I wanted word-of-mouth to spread, it only made sense that I helped get the conversation going. And what better way to do so than by telling "The BIA Story," which I hoped would give a heart and soul to the place, distinguishing us from generic fast-food joints.

I ended up printing our story on the back of the menu.

Originally from Connecticut, BIA owner Craig Carlson first came to France as a student and instantly fell in love with the country. It was in Paris—thanks to the numerous art house cinemas—that Craig developed his love for film and decided to pursue it as a career.

After attending the prestigious USC film school in Los Angeles, Craig worked as a screenwriter and short filmmaker, then landed a job in Paris working on a TV show. During this time, the only thing Craig missed was a good ol' American breakfast in a classic diner setting... Thanks to his friends in the film industry, who came on as investors, Craig was able to bring together two of his loves under one roof—the cinema and diners.

Other strategies for bringing in customers included dropping off flyers at nearby hotels, using our website to promote early-bird specials, and finally, offering discounts at several expat places, including the American University of Paris and a dozen or so English language bookshop throughout the city.

One of my favorite moments occurred when I got a visit from the woman who ran the San Francisco Book Company, a quaint bookshop in the Sixth arrondissement. After finishing her pancakes and coffee, she exclaimed, "What I love most about BIA is when I'm here having my breakfast, I'm in America. But when I step out that door, I'm back in Paris!"

Ah, oui. The best of both worlds. I was so glad to see other people responding to the very thing that had motivated me to open BIA in the first place. And thanks to customers like her, word-of-mouth began to spread quickly. By the third weekend in January, every seat at BIA was taken! And by Saturday, January 25, BIA reached its first major milestone: we broke the one-thousand-euro mark. In just three short weeks, we went from €85 in one-day sales to €1,138!

However, our sudden surge in business also meant a major surge in problems. That's because our little diner had not been properly designed to handle big crowds. Part of the blame lay with the building itself, but the real culprits were Jean-Tho—and especially the electrician, Joël.

Right in the middle of a rush, the electricity would suddenly go out, plunging the diner into total darkness. I'd make a joke. Customers would laugh. But by the fourth or fifth power outage, nobody was laughing anymore. It took forever to figure out what the problem was. It turned out that Joël hadn't properly distributed the electricity among the dozens of appliances in the restaurant. Therefore, all it took was something as simple as three toasters being used at once and—*pop*—electricity overload.

Besides the constant blackouts, we were also inundated with frequent flash floods and tsunamis. Old buildings in Paris are notorious for having outdated plumbing, and ours was no exception. During the busiest times, when dishes were piling up and we drained the sinks upstairs, water would come gushing out of the pipes *downstairs*. Not good, considering that half of the *cave* had a dirt floor. Once the tsunami hit, the *cave* would transform into a pool of muddy quicksand.

That was just the beginning of our plumbing problems. The sewage system in the building was also not built to handle the load. Every weekend, without fail, after the thirtieth or fortieth flush, the system would back up, sending *merde* everywhere. I'd have to cordon off the stairway, then run downstairs to do *merde* control.

Imagine the scene: it's a sunny Sunday brunch. Happy customers toast their bagels, grooving to "California Dreamin'" coming from my (expensively taxed) iPod. Then *pop!* Silence. Darkness. Smoke. I run downstairs to turn the power back on, slipping and sliding through the *merde* from the overflowing toilets. Next, I open the door to the main *cave* and step inside, sinking knee deep into wet sludge. I do the breaststroke over to the main electrical power switch (which, incidentally, doesn't like getting wet). Just as I reach for the switch, another tsunami comes rushing down from upstairs—this time directly into the power box—sending sparks flying everywhere. I cower. Pray. Weep.

Coincidentally, right after one of these incidents, Jean-Tho, *l'architecte-errr*, came by BIA to pay me a surprise visit.

"Bonjour, Greiiig-*errr!*" he said, as he hobbled into BIA, banged up from a recent scooter accident. Jean-Tho did not look good. His once perfectly coiffed hair was now in snarls, his chiseled face covered with band aids and bruises. "I am here to collect on the *plus-values* for the renovations," Jean-Tho said, referring to the added costs for his work. According to his calculations, I owed him more than €5,000. "All those extra spotlights weren't cheap, you know."

A long, very awkward silence ensued. Still stinking of backed-up *merde*, I was not in a particularly good mood for dealing with the *architecte-errr*.

"Are you completely mad?" I screamed. "You and your pal, Joël, have made my life a living hell! If anything, *you* should be paying *me!*"

Jean-Tho struggled to keep his cool, running his hand through his tangled hair. He stood up and tried to flash me a grin, but the bandages on his face wouldn't let him. "Go fuck yourself!" he said, as he turned around and hobbled out of the diner.

The specter of Jean-Tho did not stop there. It continued to haunt me for months—no, *years*—to come. In addition to all the electrical and plumbing problems, the new ventilation system was a total nightmare. The motor turned out to be completely defective and had only one setting—really, really loud. As a result, a crazy French neighbor who lived on the third floor would call the police every time I turned it on. I apologized to him profusely, promising to get it fixed as soon as I could. But unfortunately, it would take months before I could save up enough money to replace the expensive system.

In the meantime, because my cooks needed to breathe, I told the crazy neighbor that I would only use the ventilation system from the late morning to the early evening. The other neighbors in the building were fine with this arrangement, but not this guy. The moment I turned on the system, he'd call the cops. Every hour, on the hour, all day long. By law, the cops were required to show up each time. I'm sure they enjoyed coming to BIA as much as I enjoyed seeing them.

One night, the crazy neighbor went too far. He came into the diner screaming at the top of his lungs. I snapped. Grabbed a broom and chased him out into the street. Madame Marin saw it all from the window of her apartment above. "Way to go!" she said, cheering me on. "You show him, Crec!"

It's hard to believe, but with all this going on, I was also starting to have my first employee problems—already! After working his third brunch, Feng demanded a raise. His reason: "A friend of mine makes over seventy euros an hour doing caricatures of tourists at Montmartre!"

Uh, okay, not the same job.

I told Feng that, since we'd just opened, he'd have to wait a little while for a raise.

"Okay," he said. "In the meantime, how about giving me some shares in the company?"

As politely as I could, I told Feng that that just wasn't going to happen. From that moment on, Feng became very passive aggressive. He refused to clean up the grill area after service, leaving me all the dirty work. Thankfully, I only had to put up with Feng for two more months. Following the advice of my accountant, I had given him a three-month temporary contract (CDD) instead of a permanent one (CDI). Now if I could just hold on until his contract ran out and somehow find a cook to replace him.

Next, my Scottish waiter, Stewart, asked me to upgrade his temporary contract to a permanent one. He said his girlfriend was putting a lot of pressure on him, because she wanted to rent an apartment together. I should have seen this as a red flag, but instead I told Stewart that I'd be happy to discuss the subject once business picked up.

During the last week of January, a tall man with curly hair entered the diner. He asked if BIA was new, because he lived nearby and had never noticed it before. Then he asked if it were possible to make a reservation for twelve people for Saturday.

"Of course," I said. "I have the perfect spot for you."

I showed the man the long booth in the back, where the non-smoking section was. It seated ten, but if he was willing to squeeze in tight, I could add another table to make room for twelve.

"Perfect," the man said.

That Saturday, the curly-haired man and his friends arrived right on time. I installed them in their booth and handed them menus. As I returned to the bar, I noticed the curly-haired man reading "The BIA Story" on the back of the menu. Then he pulled out a small notebook from his pocket and began scribbling something in it. As I watched him, a little voice inside me said that I should pay extra-close attention to the man and his friends.

After bringing them their breakfasts, I checked up on them more than usual, filling their coffee mugs, asking if they had any requests for music, and so on. For almost two hours, the curly-haired man and his friends were lost in laughter and loud conversation. As I watched them, I couldn't help but smile; for the first time, BIA was starting to feel like a real diner.

As the winter sun began to set, the curly-haired man snuck away from his friends and came over to the register to pay the bill.

"How was everything?" I asked.

"Perfect," he said, handing me his credit card. As he signed his receipt, he spoke softly. "I have a confession to make," he said. "I didn't just walk in off the street. I'm a journalist. And I want to do an article on you."

My heart started beating like crazy. *I knew it!* I tried to look calm, even though inside I was freaking out. "That's great!"

"Don't worry," he said, reading me like a book. "It'll be a good write-up."

"Really?" I said, relieved. "For what publication?"

"*Time Out*. A London magazine. Perhaps you've seen it in bars and hotels around Paris?"

"Yes, of course," I said.

What unbelievable luck! BIA had been open barely a month and already we were going to be featured in a major magazine. When the article came out two weeks later, I realized that my strategy of putting "The BIA Story" on the menu had worked after all.

> Former filmmaker Craig Carlson has transformed an old Paris café into a picture-perfect replica of an American diner, right down to the individual toasters

at each table. The grub is straight-ahead, no frills diner staples (bagels, eggs and bacon, or pancakes). Served til 3:00 p.m.

What a perfect ending to BIA's very first month in business! The *Time Out* article turned out to be a major game changer. Customers walked in carrying the magazine, asking if I was the "former filmmaker" mentioned in the article. When I said yes, they would inevitably ask what I'd done. For modesty's sake, I refrained from mentioning all the major motion pictures I'd written; instead, I proudly told them about all the films and TV shows my *investors* had made.

A lot of important changes took place that February. We expanded our hours to seven days a week and pushed our opening time from 7:30 a.m. to 8:30 a.m. It just wasn't worth opening so early for just a couple of American tourists.

The biggest change of all that month came about quite unexpectedly; customers kept asking when BIA was going to start serving hamburgers. But it wasn't our American customers who kept asking. It was our *French* customers.

"We want *un vrai 'amburger*," they said. "*Pas MacDo!*" (Not McDonald's).

Considering we still needed to build up our weekday sales, I was happy to oblige.

Right from the start, our two most popular burgers were the bacon cheeseburger and our signature burger, "The BIA Burger," which I came up with myself. It was made with cheddar cheese, grilled onions, grilled peppers, and barbecue sauce.

Completing the full diner experience, Jérôme brought in a vintage blender and began making milkshakes. They were an instant hit—selling like hotcakes (which weren't doing too badly either). Thanks to the introduction of burgers and shakes, *bouche-à-oreille* (literally, "from the mouth to the ear") spread like wildfire, and soon we were getting a lot more French customers.

Then, two weeks into the month—just as we were starting to find our legs—BIA was suddenly empty. Paris seemed to have cleared out overnight. What the hell happened? *You gotta be kidding me? Another* vacances*? In February? But we just had one at Christmas— and New Year's.* And what, pray tell, was this *vacances* for?

Winter vacation…for skiing.

Ah, *Vive la France!*

But that wasn't the only thing that happened in February. Remember those drumbeats of war? Well, I'd been so busy getting BIA ready, I hadn't had a chance to hear them. But now that the city was deserted, the drumbeats were coming through loud and clear, so much so that by the beginning of March, the sound was deafening.

France's minister of foreign affairs, Dominique de Villepin, famously gave a speech at the UN in front of U.S. Secretary of State Colin Powell, saying that France would veto any American resolution to go to war against Iraq. A few days later, the headline on the front page of the daily newspaper, *Libération*, summed it all up in one defiant word: "*Non!*"

The French rejoiced. Americans were outraged. And I was afraid that BIA would get caught in the crossfire. Fortunately, though, even though the tension caused by the rift between our two countries was as thick as Normandy *beurre,* my customers didn't seem to be holding a grudge against me or BIA. At least for now.

I'm not a religious man, but every night I went to bed praying that there would be no war. But my silent pleas went ignored.

On March 19, 2003, America invaded Iraq. Anti-Americanism

reached a boiling point throughout Europe, including in my beloved Paris. With each passing day, protests grew bigger, louder, and more frequent. It wasn't long before the inevitable happened. One afternoon, a huge group of protesters began gathering outside the Sorbonne, not far from BIA. From inside the diner, I could hear the distant roar of whistles and chants.

I looked at the cobblestone the Marins had given me, which sat on the shelf above the boomerang countertop. My gaze continued on down to the worn-out floor tiles—and then on to the exact same spot where Monsieur Marin said the cobblestone had landed after smashing through their window all those years ago.

The roar of the crowd grew louder and angrier and closer. I stepped outside. I could see them now—the outline of a huge mob making its way down rue des Écoles—directly toward BIA. I stared at them as they got closer and closer. *Is it time for another window-shattering revolution?* I thought. It had happened once before. It could certainly happen again. *Plus ça change, plus c'est la même chose.* The more things change, the more they remain the same.

*Anti-U.S.-Iraq war protesters passing
in front of BIA, March 2003.*

Chapter 13

FRENCH FRIES OR FREEDOM FRIES

"Make Cheese Not War!"

——A sign at an anti-Iraq War protest in Paris, 2003

IN FRANCE, PROTESTS ARE OFTEN REFERRED TO AS *MOUVEMENTS SOCIAUX* (social movements). This gentle-sounding term might be appropriate for demonstrations like the one I'd seen against Jean-Marie Le Pen a year earlier. But this time around, as I watched the angry mob make its way toward BIA, I was reminded more of the LA riots after the Rodney King verdict. Indeed, now was *not* a good time to start chanting, "We want pancakes!" Now was the time to lie low, to be discreet.

I looked up at our temporary sign. Luckily, it was so small that the word "America" was barely legible. Back when I first applied for a new sign, I'd cursed French bureaucracy for being so slow. But now, as the din of the angry mob got closer, I couldn't have been more grateful. I didn't need to have my windows smashed. Nor did I need to add any more cobblestones to my collection.

The protesters were so close now, I could hear what they were chanting—angry slogans against Bush and the United States. Soon, the crowd was passing directly in front of BIA. I just stood there and waved, smiling innocently and thinking to myself: *Keep going... Nothing to see here.*

The parade of people continued to march past for what felt like forever. Then, at long last, I could make out the end of the line. Just when it looked as if the danger had passed, a group of ten or so protesters stopped in front of BIA. Thirsty from all their dissent, the group asked if they could come in for a drink.

"Uh, sure." I gulped as I led the protesters inside and sat them at a big table. As I served them their *limonade*, no one seemed to notice that they were in an American joint. That is, until a female member of the group received a phone call from a fellow protester who wanted to meet up with them.

"Excuse me," she waved at me. "What's the name of this café?"

I gulped again, then said slowly, "Breakfast..."

The lady repeated into the phone, "Brrreck-fass..."

"In..."

"Een..."

"*America.*"

"A..." the woman stopped midword. There was a long, awkward silence. I raised an eyebrow and shrugged innocently, which caused the group to start laughing hysterically. The ice broken, not only did the protesters stay and finish their drinks, but they didn't smash a single thing. Instead, they let me take a picture with them. In it, half of the group was smiling at the camera; the other half was lost in passionate conversation and couldn't even be bothered to look.

I was reminded of yet another reason why I loved France: the French were able to separate politics from the personal. For them, what was most important was the *debate*—how passionate you were about your beliefs and how well you conveyed them. Not only was it okay to argue politics (or religion, for that matter), but it was highly encouraged.

Conversely, back in the States, politics were *très personnelles*. After France's *non* vote against the war, anti-French backlash exploded all across America, reaching levels of pure hysteria. Americans were dumping expensive French wine down the sewers. And Congress went so far as to actually pass legislation renaming French fries "freedom fries."

What next? I wondered. *Liberty dip sandwiches? Star-spangled toast?*

What's happening to my beloved country? I thought from afar. Had we completely lost our minds? Over the past few years, I'd often felt like I had two parents—one American, one French. But never more so than during the war.

Americans back home would ask, "Why does France hate us so much?" I tried to explain that the French didn't hate us at all. *Au contraire.* They loved us like family. They just didn't like our politics. And, just like family, they thought it was perfectly appropriate to let us know when they thought we were making a mistake.

On a personal level, though, what was most upsetting was not whether you were for or against the war in Iraq. It was that, as Americans, we weren't even allowed to have the debate. If you so much as questioned the war, you were considered a traitor. I wasn't the only one who felt this way. American expats would come into the diner, afraid to discuss the war. But eventually they would open up, relieved to see that BIA was a safe haven for them—a place where they could have the debate they so desperately needed.

Of course, during this period, the practical side of me was also very concerned. With BIA just having opened, I was worried what the backlash would be, especially with my French customers. Would the conflict end up hurting business?

At first, it was difficult to tell. Then one night, not long after the war started, a short, bespectacled Frenchwoman in her fifties entered the diner and stepped up to the bar. When I asked her what she'd like, she answered, "*Rien.*" Then she grabbed one of BIA's business cards off the counter and slowly started ripping it up into little pieces.

"*Pardon, madame,*" I said. "But you shouldn't be so harsh with your judgment. You might be surprised to learn how many Americans are against this war."

The woman still said nothing. She just glared at me as she grabbed another business card and tore it up into even smaller pieces.

Fortunately, that was about as bad as it got at BIA during the war. But that didn't mean the subject never came up again. It did. A lot. But French customers kept their criticism strictly to the man: Bush. I had the impression that many of my French customers preferred to keep the situation light—as if they wanted to make *me* feel better. For example, our friends at the piano shop next door would sometimes come in for lunch, order their *'amburgers*, and joke, "Does that come with French fries or freedom fries?"

"Only the former," I'd say with a smile.

In the end, my fears that the war would hurt business did not pan out at all. In fact, just the opposite was happening—business was starting to pick up, thanks to the press who were now coming into BIA in droves to do "man on the street" interviews with our customers about the war.

The first to come by was the BBC. Because of them, we ended up on the Associated Press loop, which meant BIA started popping up everywhere, including the *New York Post*, CNN, and a lot of international press—such as the *Bangkok News*.

Even more exciting, my hometown newspaper, the *Journal Inquirer*, did an article on BIA—*and* yours truly, pointing out that I'd once been a paperboy for them. It said, "The U.S. and

France may disagree on serious political issues, and tensions may be running high," but that doesn't stop "the locals from coming in for hamburgers!"

The biggest surprise of all happened when I was featured in the *Hollywood Reporter*, the trade paper for the film and television industry. Ironically, I had never appeared in it as a screenwriter, which is something I'd always aspired to. But judging from the headline—"Screenwriter finds solace in Paris diner"—I guess I got my wish after all.

> Lacking the success he sought in the film industry, screenwriter Craig Carlson decided to take another path: he persuaded some Hollywood friends to invest in a diner in Paris—the French culinary equivalent of a snowball's chance in hell. Since its opening, Breakfast in America has become a cultural crossroads between conflicted countries...

I was particularly proud of that last line—how BIA had become a "cultural crossroads between conflicted counties." For me, being a goodwill ambassador between the two places I loved was more fulfilling than being a screenwriter had ever been.

In a funny coincidence, not long after the *Hollywood Reporter* article came out, BIA got its first visit from a real Hollywood celebrity. Strolling in one night was Harvey Weinstein, the bigwig producer of such films as *Pulp Fiction* and *Shakespeare in Love*. I recognized him immediately, since he had produced a screenplay that was written by my friend and investor, Scott.

"Good evening, Mr. Weinstein," I said. "Welcome to Breakfast in America."

Harvey didn't say anything at first. He just stood there, looking around the diner. "I don't believe it," he finally said. "This place looks just like a diner I used to go to when I was a kid."

Not wanting to drop names or anything, I said, "I don't want to drop names or anything, but…one of the investors in this diner is writing a script for you at the moment. I'm sure you know him, Scott R—"

"Yeah, yeah, whatever," Harvey said. "You got egg creams?"

Jérôme, who was helping me behind the bar that evening, held up his vintage blender and said, "No, Mr. Weinstein. But we do have delicious milkshakes! Wanna try one?"

"Nah," Harvey said. "Gimme a root beer instead."

"No prob!" I said as I reached into the fridge, grabbed a can of A&W, and handed it to Harvey. He pulled out a wad of cash from his pocket, peeled off a twenty-euro bill, and gave it to me. I went to give him back his change.

"Nah," he said, waving his hand. "Keep it."

I didn't know how many millions Harvey was paying Scott to write his next film, but who cared? I'd just gotten a seventeen-euro tip from Monsieur *Pulp Fiction* himself!

By the middle of spring, BIA was breaking the €1,000 mark nearly every weekend! And best of all, we were finally starting to get our own regulars—not the Marins' regulars.

First, there was Mark, the Canadian hockey player who lived across the street. As the owner of his own bar, Mark would come into the diner every morning hungover. Sometimes he'd have bruises and a black eye, but I never knew if it was because of a barroom brawl or a hockey fight. Like any good regular, Mark had his favorite spot at the counter where he'd wolf down his favorite breakfast (hamsteak and eggs) and chug down gallons of American coffee.

As for our French regulars—or *les habitués*—for some reason, they included a lot of playboys. First there was Gilles, a buff underwear model whose enormous ads were plastered all over the metro. Another regular/lady killer was a handsome singer in a local rock band who would come in with groupies on each arm. Lastly, there was Nico, the winner of the French version of *American Idol* (called *Popstars* in France). Whenever he popped into the diner, I'd play his songs on BIA's iPod. Nico loved the attention, especially from all his female fans, who would ask for autographs.

Of course, for BIA to be a real diner, there had to be some weirdos too. And *those* we had in spades! First, there was the crazy old French lady who would come in every night and sit in the back booth all by herself. If it weren't for her elegant, fur-lined coat, she might have been mistaken for an SDF (*sans domicile fixe*—or homeless person). Like an old vaudeville act, she and I had the same routine every night. She'd look at the menu, then ask me in French, "What do you have that I can eat, because…" she'd scream out, "*Je n'ai pas de dents!*" ("I don't have any teeth!") Inevitably, she would end up ordering mushy scrambled eggs every time.

The biggest weirdo of all, though, was Ronald. I wasn't sure what his real name was or where he came from. Every day, he would sit outside on our sidewalk terrace for hours on end—rain or shine—reading political manifestos. Ronald never ordered anything to eat, just mugs and mugs of bottomless coffee, which would get him so buzzed, he'd start frantically highlighting long passages in his manifestos, all the while laughing maniacally.

Last but not least were the squatters from Shakespeare and Company, the famous English-language bookstore across from Notre Dame. Back then, the owner, George Whitman, would let aspiring writers crash in his bookstore for free, as long as they were writing something. BIA ended up being a second home for many of these Hemingway wannabes. And, like Ronald, they never ordered anything to eat. Instead, they spent hours drinking bottomless mugs of coffee, chain smoking, and basking in their brilliance.

Of course, every diner has its own local color. But thanks to such an eclectic mix of regulars found only in Paris, BIA was fast becoming a neighborhood hangout like no other in the world.

As our sales numbers continued to increase, I had two new priorities on which to focus my attention: repairs and hiring. For the former, I was finally able to afford to replace our Turkish toilet, as well as our faulty ventilation system. As for the plumbing and electricity, however, the problems were so vast I was never able to fix them completely. In fact, to this day, we still have leaks and the occasional power outage.

As for the hiring challenge, well... If you've ever been to France, you might have noticed that most restaurants and cafés are woefully understaffed. The reason is not what you might expect—that employees are expensive. The real reason is because of those infamous "restrictive labor laws," which leave virtually no flexibility to deal with fluctuations in business.

Consider France's infamous thirty-five-hour workweek. I'd just assumed that overtime started from the thirty-sixth hour on. Wrong. Say you've hired someone part-time at twenty hours a week. Well, for them, overtime starts on the *twenty-first* hour. Even worse, nobody is allowed to work more than 20 percent more than their contracted hours. That means if someone is on a twenty-hour contract, he or she cannot work more than twenty-four hours in one week, and four of those would be expensive overtime hours.

Crazy, *n'est-ce pas?* It gets worse. If, say, Christmas vacation is coming up and one of your employees wants to work thirty-five hours instead of their contracted twenty, you can't just let them work fifteen extra hours—even if they beg you to. Instead, you have to do an amendment to their contract, called an *avenant*. However, once you've increased an employee's hours, it's nearly impossible to decrease them afterward—even if an employee requests it.

It gets even worse. I learned that the real reason why French companies don't like to hire anyone is because they can't *fire* anyone. Unfortunately, I was about to learn that lesson the hard way.

The trouble started when my Scottish waiter, Stewart, kept bugging me for a full-time, permanent contract (CDI). With business doing better, I stayed true to my word and gave him what he asked for. Big mistake. Right after his trial-period ended, Stewart's behavior changed completely. He started coming into work unshaven and unshowered, his hair disheveled and his shirt untucked. When taking orders from customers, he would look away, completely disinterested. And when delivering their food, he would plop their plates onto the table without saying a word.

I was becoming very concerned about Stewart's erratic behavior—as were my regulars. Mark, the Canadian hockey player, took me aside one day and said, "What the hell's going on with Stewart?"

"I don't know," I said. "He's been acting like this ever since I gave him a permanent contract."

"Let me guess. I bet his trial period just ended."

"Yeah, how'd you know?"

"Because it always happens that way in France," Mark said.

"Everybody's on their best behavior until you can't fire them any-more. You know how many times I've been through this at my bar?"

I looked over at Stewart as he snorted at a customer who asked for a coffee refill. "I've got to say something to him," I said. "He's scaring the hell out of my customers."

During a lull in the lunch rush, I took Stewart aside and gave him a warning: either shape up or ship out. Stewart's pole-thin body began to shake up and down until he suddenly blew his top, threat-ening to kill me right in front of my customers. I stayed perfectly calm, exchanging a look with Mark.

At the end of his shift, I took Stewart outside and told him he was fired.

"You can't do that!" he screamed. "You just can't do that!" He charged toward me, his fists clenched. I stood my ground. After a couple minutes of a stare-down, Stewart ran off, hollering back, "You'll never get away with this!"

The next day, Stewart began stalking BIA. For hours, he would pace back and forth on the sidewalk in front of the diner, jiggling a big set of keys in his hand while glaring at customers like Ronald. The crazy revolutionary never looked up; he just sat there calmly, highlighting passages in his manifestos.

At one point, Stewart was scaring my customers so much, I had to call the cops. The minute Stewart saw the cruiser approaching, he ran away and hid behind some bushes in a small park across the street. A few seconds later, the cruiser pulled to a stop in front of the diner. Two cops got out; one female, short, and muscular; the other was a male in his forties, balding, looking like he was ready to retire yesterday.

I pointed to where Stewart had run off. "Did you just see that guy?" The cops nodded. "Well, he's been stalking my place for days, scaring all my customers."

"What do you want us to do about it?" the female cop said.

"Make him stop," I said.

"How?" the male cop said. "The sidewalk's public property."

"But there's got to be something you can do, Officer..." I looked for the name tag on his uniform. There was none. "What's your name, please?"

I don't know if it was because of my accent, or my girth, or the fact that I was standing in front of Breakfast in America, but the male cop gave me a once-over and said, "Are you American?" I nodded. "Well, this is France. Here we don't have to give out our names."

"Yeah," the female cop chimed in. "This ain't an American cop show."

"But..." I said, confused, "without your names, how am I supposed to prove you were here?"

"You can file a report at the station," the male cop said. He looked at his partner and motioned with his head toward the cruiser. End of discussion. The cops hopped into their car and sped off. The moment they were gone, Stewart reappeared in the little park across the street, his head bobbing up and down behind the bushes.

Stewart continued to stalk BIA like this for weeks—even after hours. At night, after I'd closed up, I would sometimes take the 63 bus, which passed in front of BIA. I'd look over to see Stewart pacing back and forth on the sidewalk, peering into the window of the diner as if he thought I were hiding in a booth and might come out at any second.

One morning, Mark had had enough. Covered in bruises from his most recent barroom and/or hockey brawl, he stared at Stewart hiding behind the bushes and growled, "That shithead has disrupted the tranquility of my breakfast for the last time!"

Mark threw his napkin on the counter and stormed out of the diner. Cars swerved out of his way as he made a beeline across the street to the little park. Stewart stared at him from behind the bushes. Mark moved in close and whispered something into Stewart's ear. Whatever it was put the fear of God into him. Stewart ran off like a scared chickenshit. For the longest time thereafter, Stewart would wait until Mark had left the diner before resuming his stalking duties from behind the hedges.

Being stalked was not a pleasant experience. Nor was *not* being stalked. That's because one day Stewart abruptly stopped showing up, leaving a strange, unsettling silence in his wake. I was sure *la merde* was about to hit the fan...

Between working eighteen-hours a day, seven days a week—plus worrying about Stewart all the time—I was more exhausted than I'd ever been in my life. Some nights I barely had the energy to walk the three blocks up the hill to my tiny studio apartment. Instead, I'd sleep downstairs in the *cave*, on a ratty, old mattress, and in the morning I'd shower in the staff changing room.

When my friends Todd and Tiffany came to visit the diner one day, they were shocked to see the state I was in. The two had just arrived in Paris after a whirlwind backpacking trip through Europe. Seeing the dark circles under my eyes as I picked up French fries off the diner floor, Todd said, "Remember, Craig, you're living your dream. Tell yourself that whenever you feel like you can't go on: 'I'm living my dream. I'm living my dream.'"

Sage advice. Too bad I was too exhausted to fully appreciate it.

Seeing my old friends again really boosted my morale. And since they were on a tight budget, I offered to let them stay in my tiny apartment. Only problem was, I'd been so tired the morning they arrived, I accidentally locked my keys inside. That night, all three of us ended up sleeping in the diner. (Of course, since Todd and Tiffany were BIA's very first investors, I gave them the best booth.)

Bright and early the next morning, I treated my friends to their first breakfast at BIA. They loved it. Unfortunately, they couldn't stick around for long, because they were only in Paris for the day and wanted to see the city. After bidding them *au revoir*, I stood in the diner, trying to figure out how I was ever going to get back into my apartment.

Just then, one of my French regulars, Morgan, strolled in. The moment I saw him, a lightbulb went off in my head.

"*Salut*, Morgan," I said. "Am I glad to see you! I need your help."

"Sure," Morgan said. "What do you need?"

"Well…" I smiled.

Morgan just happened to be…a professional rappeller. The next thing I knew, he was climbing onto the roof of my building, dropping a rope down to the fourth floor, and swinging through the open window of my apartment like Spider-Man. Once inside, Morgan opened the door and let me in. I thanked him and handed him a *billet* for his effort.

"*Merci*," Morgan said, stuffing the bill into his pocket as he grabbed his equipment and headed down the stairs. "See you tomorrow!"

Inside my apartment, I closed the door and let out a sigh. *What a day!* I looked at my IKEA sofa bed. It was calling out to me: *Craig… Come… Collapse onto me*. I did as I was told. As I shuffled across the room, I untied my apron and let it fall to the floor, when…*ca-chunk*. I stared at the apron. Picked it up. *You gotta be kidding me!* Inside the front pocket were…my keys. They'd been there the whole time.

At that moment, I realized that I'd better take a break soon before I killed myself. And maybe one day, I might be able to take a night off. Hell, why not a *real* vacation? *A guy can dream, can't he?*

But before I could let myself get too carried away, a *lettre recommandée* arrived in the mail, which always meant trouble.

Kimmy, waitress extraordinaire, taking an order at BIA.

Chapter 14

FRENCH LABOR PAINS

"En grève jusqu'à la retraite!" ("On strike until I retire!")

—French graffiti

OF COURSE, THE *LETTRE RECOMMANDÉE* WAS FROM STEWART. OR rather, from his girlfriend. Written in flawless French, the strongly worded letter said that Stewart was filing a lawsuit against BIA for "wrongful firing." He was also demanding several months of *future* pay (not *back* pay, mind you; after all, his contract was *forever*), as well as damages for pain and suffering. According to their calculations, Stewart and his *petite amie* felt he had suffered so much that he needed about €10,000 to feel better.

So there it was. My initiation into the world of French business was summed up in one simple equation: my *first* full-time employee + my *first* permanent French contract = my *first* experience in the

French court system. To help me through the morass, I set out to find a lawyer who specialized in fighting lawsuits. Instead, all I found were lawyers who specialized in *settling* lawsuits.

"See if Stewart will make a deal," they all said.

But I didn't want to make a deal. It wasn't just the principle of the thing; I was convinced that I had an open-and-shut case. How naive I was. I soon discovered that the entire French system was designed to be in Stewart's favor. For starters, I had to hire an expensive lawyer to defend myself, whereas Stewart had a public lawyer for free.

Next, I had the nearly impossible task of proving that I had fired Stewart because of a *faute grave* (grave fault). Considering that Stewart had gone berserk during lunch service, threatening to kill me in front of my customers, and had then stalked me for weeks, I was convinced that any logical, fair-minded person would consider such behavior to be a tad *grave*. But not in France.

"You think your case is bad?" my French lawyer said. "I know a guy who fired his groundskeeper for bludgeoning his horse to death. That's a *faute grave* if ever there was one, right? Not so. The groundskeeper sued and won."

"On what basis?" I asked incredulously.

"That his boss had caused him undue pain and suffering."

Things were not looking good for me.

The lawyer continued. "You might have had a chance if you'd let Stewart go under the lesser charge of *une faute réel et sérieuse*." (A real and serious fault.)

I had never heard of that term before. It turned out that the procedure for a real and serious fault was a real and serious pain in the ass. The process involved starting a *dossier* (case file) the moment you suspected an employee might be trouble, beginning with warnings sent by *lettres recommandées*. But there was a catch: In France, you're not allowed to let someone go for the same offense they've been given a warning about, which, of course, makes no sense. Instead, you must rack up as many different offenses as possible, until your *dossier* is nice and thick, which could take months. Or years.

How thick should the *dossier* be? The French will never give you a straight answer. "It's a question of *feeling*," they say. If you feel you have enough of a case, then you can go on to the next step, which is to summon the employee to his first (of three) one-on-one interviews. Careful, though; the summonses can't be too close together. (How close is too close? Depends. How do you *feel*?)

Once you've summoned your employee, you're about to enter the "danger zone." During these meetings, anything you say can and will be used against you, especially if the employee has brought along a public defender. You must speak vaguely and never in an accusatory manner. Usually, the best default line is, "I need time to reflect upon this difficult situation." Meaning, you need to do a second summons.

If after the second interview, you can hold out a little longer without killing yourself (or your employee, who by this point is so giddy about his future winnings, he's literally laughing in your face), then you can summon him for his third and final interview. At long last, you're allowed to say that you've made the "difficult decision" of letting him sue—I mean, letting him *go*.

"Okay, got it," I said to my lawyer. "And if I'd done everything just as you said, what would my chances have been of winning the case?"

"Let me think," the lawyer said, calculating a figure in his head. "*Statistically*…a little more than zero." And that was for the lesser charge of a "real and serious fault." It didn't take a mathematician to figure out that my chances of winning a "grave fault" were, statistically, *less* than zero.

With the court date set, I needed to whip up a detailed *dossier* in my defense, starting with eyewitness testimonials. My regulars Mark and Ronald, who were in the diner the day Stewart threatened me, were more than happy to write affidavits. Ronald was particularly enthusiastic. I was surprised to learn that he'd been secretly writing all the dates, times, and details of Stewart's erratic behavior in his manifesto.

Due to a huge backlog of cases, it took months to get my day in court. In the end, despite six eyewitness accounts, plus several (nameless) police reports, Stewart still won. The reason: the judge didn't think his threats on my life were *grave* enough.

"For it to have been *grave*," my lawyer said, "Stewart would have had to have said, 'I'm going to kill you' in three different ways, not just one."

Really? How? I'm going to kill you with a candlestick? In the library? With Colonel Mustard?

The more I thought about it, the more absurd it seemed. "What about all his crazy stalking?" I said. "Doesn't that prove I had a legitimate reason to be concerned about my safety?"

"Yeah, well…the problem is that happened *after* you fired him."

Having worked only three and a half months—most of which was part-time—Stewart was awarded almost €7,000. My French friends said that I should consider myself lucky. By having my first employee sue, I now knew how the French system worked, and hopefully the next time an employee took me to court (and won), I wouldn't have to pay him or her as much. But just to be safe, my accountant suggested that I start putting money aside, adding lawsuits to my monthly budget under "fixed costs." Only in France would "frivolous lawsuits" go under the same category as "water and electricity."

Fortunately, during this difficult period, there was a ray of sunshine that entered my life: Kimmy, a talented architect from San Francisco who was studying in Paris for a year. A petite African American in her forties, Kimmy looked half her age and had a youthful energy that was contagious. She was also chock-full of wisdom and life experience, both of which were sorely needed at BIA.

I'd first met Kimmy back when Stewart was still working at BIA. She had come into the diner with a group of French professionals who were taking English lessons at a language school run by a friend of hers. One of their class assignments was to practice English in "real-life situations"—such as an American diner.

Kimmy, who was one of the most perceptive people I'd ever met, could sense that I was having a problem with Stewart without my having to say a word. "If ever you need a waitress," she said, planting the seed, "let me know. I've got loads of experience."

As fate would have it, at the very moment that I hit my lowest point with Stewart, I ran into Kimmy at a stationery store. It was like feeling a warm sunbeam on my face after a long day of rain.

"Kimmy!" I said. "Am I glad to see you!" I cut right to the chase. "Does your offer still stand?"

"*Absolument!*" Kimmy said. I didn't even have to remind her what we'd talked about—she was *that* good.

From her first day on the job, it was as if Kimmy had always been with us. With her corn-rowed hair and earthy shawls draped across her shoulder, Kimmy brought the positive, eccentric energy that an American diner like BIA needed. She helped define our voice. And our customers adored her, especially her unique way of saying, "*D'aaacord!*" (Okeydokey!) with the most charming American accent ever.

With Kimmy in (and Stewart out), I could feel a palpable shift taking place at BIA. Thanks to her presence, even our customer base became more interesting. Soon we had important political and cultural figures, like diplomats, intellectuals, musicians, and artists all hanging out at the diner together.

The staff at BIA got better after Kimmy too. One by one, I

began building a great team, most of whom found us simply by walking through the door, résumé in hand. Our only requirements were that employees had to have some restaurant experience and speak both French and English.

The first member of the new team was Geneviève from Quebec, a fiery redhead who was very proud of her heritage. Because of her strong accent, French customers would often ask if she were Canadian. "*Non!*" she would snap back. "I'm *Québécoise!*"

Fast and efficient, Geneviève could handle an entire lunch service practically by herself, including running the food, bussing the tables, and doing all the side work. She was so good I nicknamed her Super Gen. She, in turn, called me Super-Duper Boss. Geneviève and I became very close, confiding in each other some of our most intimate secrets. For example, I learned that one of her biggest desires was to find her soul mate in Paris.

"What about you, Super-Duper Boss?" Geneviève asked me once. "Don't you want to meet that special someone?"

"Sure," I said, quickly changing the subject to something like…I don't know…my favorite love scenes in classic movies like *Casablanca.* In truth, I didn't feel very comfortable even talking about love, let alone having the courage to take the plunge.

Rounding out BIA's super-duper team were our newest cooks, Alzbeta, from the Czech Republic, and Mike, a Brit. They had been squatting at Shakespeare and Company for months and desperately needed jobs. Alzbeta and Mike became more than just cooks—they took the time to actually get to know our customers. Whenever a regular would come in for breakfast, they'd ask, "The usual?" It made our customers feel right at home.

By the end of our first year, so many amazing people became part of the BIA team, it would be impossible to name them all. But one person stood out in particular: Derrick, an unassuming Australian rules football player from Down Under. Derrick had once been in the French Foreign Legion, and like a good soldier, he was always there whenever I needed him, moving from dishie to cook to bartender with ease. He soon became my all-around wingman.

With such a strong team in place, I was able to take BIA to the next level. First, we expanded our menu to include a greater selection of burgers and breakfasts, my favorite being my signature breakfast scramble, "CC's Big Mess," made with eggs, ham, sausage, bacon, garlic potatoes, grilled onions, peppers, mushrooms, cheddar cheese, and more, all mixed together. We also added a "sandwiches, salads, and wraps" category to the menu, which included such diner classics as grilled cheese, BLTs, club sandwiches, Caesar salads, and more.

That November, we also introduced something truly special to Paris: BIA's first Traditional Thanksgiving Dinner. Americans were ecstatic. The French…not so much. They would look at their Thanksgiving feast, replete with turkey, mashed potatoes, gravy, stuffing, and cranberry sauce, and shrug. *Meh.* Compared to what most French people eat on a regular basis, it was nothing fancy. But for our American customers, it was like being back home for the holidays.

Next, to help boost lagging sales during the week, we introduced two fixed-price lunch menus (*formules*). The first was an inexpensive *formule* for students, which included a choice of a burger and fries or a 2 × 2 × 2, plus a drink. The other *formule* was for everyone else, which cost a couple more euros but included draft beer as a drink choice, as well as a free coffee at the end of the meal (either an espresso or *one* cup of sock juice—we didn't want customers squatting during the lunch rush).

The lunch *formules* not only increased our weekday sales, but for the first time since we'd opened, our French customers began to outnumber our American customers! I couldn't help but notice that the mix of clientele was starting to look exactly like the pie chart I'd made for my business plan years earlier.

Having so many French customers posed some interesting challenges, however. First, we had to teach them how to properly eat a hamburger. French customers would never grab their burger with both hands and shove it into their mouth like Americans do. Instead, they'd delicately cut each part with a knife, starting with the meat, then the bread, maybe some lettuce. Then they'd dip each tiny morsel into some ketchup before daintily inserting it into their mouth with a fork.

Another funny cultural difference was that the French didn't know what to do with the authentic sugar dispensers I'd brought over from the States. They would hold the dispenser up to the light and examine it like it was a foreign object, trying to figure out how to make it work. Sometimes they'd unscrew the top, then scoop out some sugar with a teaspoon. Other times they'd tilt the dispenser to the side while holding the flap open with their finger. I would tell them that that wasn't necessary.

"Gravity's your friend," I'd say. "Watch." Then I'd tilt the pourer without holding the flap open. "See how the sugar pours out all by itself?"

"*Ah, ouiii.*" The customer would smile at their amazing new discovery.

Another cultural challenge was what to do about tips. The concept doesn't exist in France. Of course, one of the reasons we have tips in the United States is because there's a lower minimum wage for servers in restaurants. Not so in France. There's *service compris* (service included), but that's not the same as tips; there is no percentage added on to the bill at the end. Instead, every worker in France is guaranteed a livable wage, which includes universal health care, five weeks' paid vacation, and about a thousand other perks.

Consequently, we were required by French law to put *service compris* on the menu. This upset some of our waitresses, many of whom were starving foreign students who were only legally allowed to work twenty hours a week. To help them out, I added two lines at the bottom of the menu next to *"service compris."* For the *version française*, I had to be careful how I worded it, saying, "Thanks for thinking of our friendly waitstaff!" But on the English version, I was much more up front: "Thanks for your tips!" (Translation: "Please be so kind as to leave a euro or two.")

I knew that BIA had finally arrived when we were featured in *Le Parisien*, a daily newspaper in Paris. In their article, they explained to their readers exactly what a diner was—i.e., *not* dinner. The newspaper even taught its readers how to properly pronounce the magic word *à l'américaine*. Meaning, for the first time since BIA had opened, I saw in an actual French periodical the phonetic spelling of the word—*daïneur!*

Not long after the article came out, BIA received a visit from a very special guest: Madame Marin herself. Thrilled with BIA's success, she came into the diner with her friend and ordered a hamsteak and eggs. (A woman after my own heart!) But Monsieur Marin didn't join them. Madame said it was still too hard for him to accept that Le Square was really gone.

One day, with business booming, Kimmy the Sage said, "You know what, Craig? I think it's time you had a night off!"

"Really?" I said. "Is that possible? I mean... I tried to take an *hour* off once. *Once.*"

I proceeded to tell Kimmy about the night, months earlier, when I had been so exhausted I could barely stand up. All I could think about then was collapsing onto the ratty mattress in the *cave* and taking a quick power nap. Alari, an Estonian student and BIA regular, had offered to keep an eye on the place while I caught some z's. Since the diner had been empty, I had figured it was safe to leave Alari by himself.

"If you need me for *any* reason," I'd said, "come wake me up, okay?"

Alari nodded. I locked up the register and went down to the *cave*, setting the alarm on my phone for an hour later. I was asleep before my head had hit my makeshift pillow. After my nap, I came back upstairs. At table 32, I recognized a hipster customer who came into BIA from time to time. He looked upset and motioned me over.

"Hey, man," he'd said, pointing at Alari. "Is that guy new?"

"Why? What happened?"

"I ordered a root-beer float and look what he gave me." The customer held up his glass. Inside was a melting scoop of chocolate ice cream floating on top of a glass of actual beer. *Eew.*

After apologizing profusely to the customer, I had asked Alari what had happened. "I don't know," he'd said, on the verge of tears. "The menu says 'beer.' So that's what I gave him!"

I learned two things that night: first, root beer does not exist in Estonia, and second, it was not a good idea to leave my diner alone. Ever.

"Don't worry, Craig," Kimmy said as I finished my story. "This time it'll be different."

After taking care of my staff for so long, it was nice to have one of them taking care of me. Knowing I could trust Kimmy completely, I happily took her up on her offer, taking six whole hours off! It felt strange having nothing to do…or rather, having the freedom to do whatever I wanted.

I decided to go see a movie at my favorite repertory cinema, the Action Écoles. As luck would have it, one of my favorite films was playing there—*Casablanca*. I bought *une place* (one ticket) and stepped inside the theater. As I looked around the room, I smiled and let out a sigh of contentment. For me, it felt like entering a holy sanctuary. I found a seat in the middle-middle, settling in just as the dusty, crackling 35mm print (in V.O., *version originale*, with French subtitles) began to flicker on the screen. Like a new parent on his first night out without the baby, I kept wanting to call the diner every five minutes to make sure everything was okay.

Eventually, I was able to relax, getting swept away by the romantic love story between Rick and Ilsa. That is, until one scene in the film totally freaked me out. It was the one right after Rick's place is shut down by the corrupt *gendarme*, Renault, who is "Shocked! Shocked! To find that gambling is going on!" Afterward, in the dark, empty nightclub, Rick examines his accounting ledgers with his wingman, Carl.

"How long can I afford to stay closed?" Rick asks.

"Two weeks, maybe three," Carl says.

Rick, being the noble guy he is, nods and says, "In the meantime, everybody stays on salary."

"Thank you, Herr Rick."

Wait a second! I thought. *Did I just hear that right? Two weeks—maybe three—before Rick's place goes out of business? But how is that possible? Rick's place was packed every single night!*

At that moment, I realized that even though I'd seen *Casablanca* a million times before, it wasn't until I'd opened BIA that I truly understood what the movie was about. It wasn't a love story about Rick and Ilsa. No, *Casablanca* was really about a restaurant on the verge of bankruptcy!

I could feel myself starting to panic. For the first time since I'd opened BIA, I could see with perfect clarity the enormous risk I'd taken. I felt just like the coyote in those old Warner Brothers cartoons—right after he's run off a cliff and is floating in midair, defying gravity—that is, until he looks down for the first time and sees that there's nothing underneath him. Only at that moment of awareness does the coyote fall and fall, for what feels like an eternity, until he lands with a puff of dust on the hard ground below.

That's exactly how I felt—total panic as I realized that, all this time, I'd been floating in the air without a net.

The next day at the diner, I couldn't shake the feeling from the night before. A million thoughts raced through my mind: *What if BIA got shut down like Rick's place was? How long would it be before we went bankrupt? And what if customers just stopped coming? Or if burgers and breakfasts suddenly fell out of fashion?*

I started to hyperventilate. Kimmy noticed and came over and rubbed my back. "Hey, Craig, take it easy," she said with a warm smile. "Having a night off was supposed to be *relaxing!*"

I tried to smile back, but all I could think about was how fragile life is. This message really hit home when, shortly thereafter, Jérôme called me with some very sad news: Claire, the woman Jérôme and I had worked with on *Robin Hood*—and the same woman who had freaked out when I'd told her about BIA ("What if you *fail?!*")—had collapsed while walking down the streets of Paris.

At her funeral, I was reminded once again of the old proverb: Here today, gone tomorrow. *How can we not take risks in life?* Despite how difficult the journey had been, I was so grateful I'd taken the trip. And now that all my hard work was starting to pay off, I knew in my heart that it was time for me to take the biggest risk of all.

Dessert

Love Among the Milkshakes

Sunday morning at Breakfast in America.

Chapter 15

LIFE BEGINS AT *QUARANTE* (FORTY)

"Life isn't about finding yourself. Life is about creating yourself."

—George Bernard Shaw

TODD WAS RIGHT. I REALLY WAS LIVING MY DREAM.

In just two short years, Breakfast in America had become an unequivocal success, with lines of customers down the block. The French and international press continued to have a field day with us. Hardly a month went by that we weren't featured in some newspaper, magazine, or TV show.

My favorite media hit was a popular weekly TV news magazine called *Du beau, du bon, du bien-être*, which did a segment on us called, "The Talk of the Town." The lovely hostess asked me to explain different breakfast dishes—both savory and sweet. We talked about bagels, bacon, omelets, hash browns, cookies, pecan pie, and above all, pancakes. At one point, she filmed my chef making my personal favorite—blueberry pancakes with white-chocolate chips. *Yum!*

Other shows tried to decipher exactly what it was that separated *"un vrai 'amburger"* from what you'd find at MacDo and other fast-food joints.

"Fresh ingredients, generous portions, and lots of TLC!" I said.

Milkshakes were also very popular with the press. On one program, I showed viewers how to make an Oreo milkshake. From the reaction of the reporter, it suddenly dawned on me that, for the French, diner grub—as well as my "charming" American accent—were considered *très exotique.*

Other reports focused on the cultural difference between France and America. For example, a major French TV network, M6, did a story on *"le doggie bag."* Until their report, I'd never realized that the concept of the doggie bag didn't exist in France—probably because there were never any leftovers on my plate at the end of my meals. But there were actually two very good reasons why doggie bags were a *non-non*: first, portion sizes are much smaller in France; second, it's considered *très gauche* to take leftovers home with you. According to my French friends, going out to a restaurant was considered a special occasion and should be treated as such.

No matter. Thanks to the TV report, it wasn't long before my French customers were asking for *"un doggie bag-errr"* for their left-over pancakes, home fries, and carrot cake. Unlike me, many of my French customers had trouble finishing their meals.

Another exciting development at this time was that BIA started appearing in several travel guidebooks, including Frommers, Lonely Planet, and *Paris for Dummies*, as well as the French equivalents, *Guide du Routard*, *Paris Pas Cher*, and *Le Petit Futé*. I ended up putting together a scrapbook full of press clippings. I couldn't help but think about the time André had showed me his scrapbook—and how back then the thought of BIA having one seemed like such a faraway dream. But here it was, actually happening. *Incroyable!*

Furthermore, thanks to all the press coverage, Breakfast in America—and yours truly—were starting to become famous. Sometimes when I walked down the street, people would yell out, "Hey, it's the pancake guy!" Whenever I got recognized in public like that, I always felt a little like a celebrity. Or better yet, like Marlon Brando in *The Godfather*. Call me "Don Pancaki," if you will, as I pretended to be Brando addressing his minions: "Hey, how ya doing? Nice to see ya. Here…kiss the ring."

Ah, oui, life was good! I even celebrated my fortieth birthday at the diner. Surrounded by my wonderful staff, friends, and regulars, and even a few investors, I gave a speech about how years earlier, when I first had the idea for BIA, this was exactly how I imagined my life would be when I turned forty: in Paris, at my diner, surrounded by the people I loved.

Yes, dreams do come true. My American dream…in France.

And just like the premonition I'd had back when I was doing research on diners, I realized that BIA really had become more than just a restaurant. It was now the home—and family—I'd always wanted.

Even better, BIA had become a real community. I thought about what the *Hollywood Reporter* had said about us—that BIA was a "cultural crossroads between conflicted countries." Except now, instead of being a cultural crossroads because of the war, we had become a cultural crossroads for, well…culture!

We began hosting literary nights, where actors would read passages from books by French and American authors, like Kerouac's *On the Road*. We even reenacted the famous diner scene from the film *Five Easy Pieces*, where Jack Nicholson tells the snooty waitress what she can do with her chicken salad.

Knowing I'd once been a screenwriter in Hollywood, local filmmakers would ask me to read their scripts, wanting to hear my feedback. Others would invite me to their film screenings. Still others asked if they could shoot their films in the diner. It felt so great to reconnect with that part of my life again.

Next, we started featuring live music at BIA—but no drag queens dressed as Lady Liberty coming through the dumbwaiter just yet. Instead, we had our talented waitress Laura, who performed live acoustic music à la the Indigo Girls and other folk groups. Perhaps our most popular event was when we featured a jazz quartet for La Fête de la Musique, a music festival held in Paris on the first day of summer every year. At one point, close to one hundred people crammed inside the diner and spilled out onto the street to watch the performance.

Last, but not least, during each American election cycle, members of Democrats Abroad would come into BIA, set up a table, and register expats to vote absentee. It didn't matter whether they were Republicans, Democrats, or neither. What was important was that they participated in the democratic process.

In addition to all the cultural events taking place at BIA, nothing got me more excited—or made me feel more fulfilled—than the *human* side of the business. I felt like a proud papa as I helped my staff out with their personal problems, giving them advice on life and love, while at the same time being there as a shoulder for them to cry on.

For my really exceptional staff members, I would cosign leases for their apartment rentals or give them glowing recommendations for college or future jobs. Once, one of our waitresses applied for a position at the American Embassy in Paris. Much to my surprise, the embassy called the diner to ask me for a recommendation. I raved about how amazing the waitress had been, which was true.

She got the job.

I love telling this story to my staff, the lesson being to never look down on your place of employment. You may think you're just working in a "lowly diner," but it may turn out to be an important stepping stone for your future career.

Or your future partner. That's because love was in the air at BIA! The joke became if you were looking for *l'amour*, look no further than Breakfast in America. It kind of makes sense when you think about it. Since BIA was located in the most romantic city in the world, it only followed that BIA would become the most romantic *diner* in the world. It's amazing how many of my staff members ended up meeting their future husband, wife, or significant other at BIA, often in the most serendipitous ways.

Take, for example, Alzbeta, my cook from the Czech Republic. One night, at the end of her shift, Alzbeta wanted nothing more than to join some friends at a bar across town for a drink. But she'd barely had a chance to take a sip of her beer when she got a phone call from BIA. The assistant manager, Susan, had forgotten her keys and couldn't close up. Knowing that Alzbeta had a set, Susan asked if she wouldn't mind coming back to lock up.

"But Susan," Alzbeta grumbled. "If I'm always at BIA, I'll *never* find a boyfriend!"

Alzbeta came back to BIA anyway. As the staff closed up shop, a few customers still lingered inside. Alzbeta sat at the counter sipping a beer, tired and miserable. Just then, a voice from two stools down said, "Tough night, huh?" She turned to see Jonathan, a handsome American who had come to Paris to write a novel.

It was love at first sight.

Cut to the whirlwind adventure that would become Alzbeta's new life: wedding bells in Florida, followed by two adorable kids, a master's degree from a prestigious American university, and trips to exotic places all over the world. All with a man Alzbeta happened to meet one night at BIA when she wasn't even supposed to be there.

Another grand *historie d'amour* (love story) involved Geneviève, my waitress from Quebec (*not* Canada). Ironically, her love connection turned out to be…a Canadian. (Hey, nobody's perfect.) Jason was a customer at BIA who had come to Paris to get over a bad relationship. Some mornings he would come to the diner hungover. Geneviève would nurse him back to health with a hearty breakfast and a yummy milkshake. Innocent enough—or so I thought.

A couple years later, when I attended their wedding, Jason gave a touching speech about the first time he'd met Geneviève—and what had sealed the deal for him. "I remember watching her at the diner as she made me a banana milkshake. She did it with such loving care, I thought to myself, 'Could this be the girl for me?' Any doubt I had was quickly gone when Geneviève brought me a second milkshake—for free! I knew then and there it was true love."

"*What?!* I stood up from my seat and shouted. "A *free* milkshake?"

"Thanks, Super-Duper Boss!" Geneviève said as she smiled and waved at me from the other end of the reception tent. The wedding guests erupted in laughter.

In addition to Alzbeta and Geneviève, dozens of my staff and customers would end up meeting their future significant others at BIA over the years. I had the privilege of attending a total of eight BIA weddings (including a remarriage after a divorce). And each time, I would secretly hope that there would be at least one more wedding to follow.

Yep, with all the love connections going on around me, it seemed only logical that it would be my turn next, *n'est-ce pas?* One night in my tiny apartment, as I lay alone on my IKEA sofa bed with my newly adopted tabby cat, Balzac, I thought about all the times I'd met with Dr. Emily to talk about my intimacy issues. It's hard to describe, but during our sessions back then, I'd always felt a kind of *clarity*…or *understanding*…that once BIA was up and running, I'd be ready to confront the biggest challenge of my life.

So, having turned forty and built a successful business, I knew, with the same fierce clarity as before, that it was time for me to take the plunge once and for all.

"Après l'effort, le réconfort," *a French expression,*
which means, "After the effort, comes the comfort."

Chapter 16

VIVE L'AMOUR

"Lucy, you got some 'splainin' to do!"

——Ricky Ricardo on *I Love Lucy*

I WASN'T NERVOUS ABOUT THE THOUGHT OF LOVE AT ALL. I WAS
petrified! But I figured if I could start a successful American diner in
Paris, surely I could tackle something as mundane as dating, right?

I decided to join a dating website, making it clear that I was
looking for friends only—no hookups. In my profile, I tried to come
off as witty, worldly, and debonair, writing my profile in both French
and English—open to either possibility. With my profile complete,
my heart pounded as I clicked: "Post Now." The whole experience
felt strange, like when I used to go trout fishing with my dad. Would
I get a bite? Would I be rejected?

The posting hadn't even been up for ten minutes when I heard a laser sound indicating my first message had arrived. I rushed over to my computer and opened the message. It was from my new cook at BIA, Josh. His message read: "Well, well, well... What do we have here? Lucy, you got some 'splainin' to do!"

Yes, Josh. As in my *male* cook from San Francisco. The one who, every time I stepped out of the diner, would switch the music to Madonna—and only Madonna.

Oh, did I fail to mention that the name of the site was Gaydar? Maybe that explained why, when I was at that French restaurant with Fiona years earlier, I couldn't take my eyes off that French waiter. At the time, I'd just thought it was because of his exotic *Frenchness*. But now I realized it was because of his nice derrière.

I nervously wrote back to Josh and said I would really appreciate it if he could keep this little incident between us. I was on a very personal journey right now, I said, and still trying to figure things out. Meaning, I wasn't exactly sure which way I swung. Josh answered, "*¡No problemo!*"

The next time I was in the diner, Josh and I shared a knowing smile, but that was it. He got to play as much Madonna as he wanted. And I got to keep my private life private. For the moment anyway. Of course, with BIA being one big family, my secret wouldn't last for long.

To say I was a late bloomer would be an understatement. To complicate matters, I came to the dating scene with the life experience of an adult, but with the emotional vulnerability of a teenager with abandonment issues. It didn't help that when I was growing up, I never saw anyone around me in love.

The only loving relationship I knew about back then was my

grandma Lizzy and Grandpa Noel, who my gram had married several years after my biological grandfather abandoned her and my dad during the Great Depression. Grandpa Noel was the only grandfather I ever knew, and for some reason, he preferred to sleep in a separate bedroom from my grandma Lizzy. Furthermore, if my gram so much as tried to give him a *petit bisou*, Grandpa Noel would blush like a schoolboy.

As for my own parents, other than growing up in the same small town as latchkey kids, they had absolutely nothing in common. But that didn't stop them from dating and eventually going steady. In fact, by the time they were in high school, Louise and Eddie were such an item that their pals even gave them nifty nicknames— *Lulu and Moose*. Wedding bells soon followed. Or, more accurately, wedding *brawls*. In what could be considered a not-so-subtle omen, Lulu and Moose's wedding day turned into a cross-cultural rumble. Legend has it that after my parents snuck off on their honeymoon, the drunken Carlsons and Arciszewskis polkaed the night away— right up until one side insulted the other. Before you knew it, tables, chairs, and fists were flying wildly across the reception hall.

"Ah, what a night…" both sides of the family would recall fondly for years after.

Since I'd never actually seen my parents together as a happily married couple, I asked them—separately, of course—if they'd ever been in love. Always the romantic, Fast Eddie said, "I will say this about your mother: She had a lotta class—for a Polack."

When I asked my mom if she'd ever had *le grand amour* for my dad, she struggled for some time before saying, "Well, he *was* a great dancer! I'll give him that!"

As for my Polish grandma Mary, she didn't mince words when it came to how she felt about my dad: "No good sonna bitch alcohol bastard!" In fact, she loathed my dad so much it inspired the writer in her. Virtually every week for the rest of her life, she would

would trek over to the post office and send off a poison-pen letter to him, which always started the same way: "Eddie, I want you to know Louise find good man not no good sonna bitch alcohol like you…" (Incidentally, the generic term "good man" was in reference to whoever my mom was dating that week.)

Needless to say, neither of my parents ever had the talk with me about the birds and the bees, (or as the French say, "the *flowers* and the bees"). But I did have the next best thing—my dad's letter from my twenty-first birthday. After so many years, I couldn't remember what he'd written. I decided to dig it up and see if Fast Eddie had left me any pearls of wisdom about love.

Rereading my dad's letter as an adult, I appreciated it so much more. I could see how much thought and care he had put into it. Yet, at the same time, I didn't know what I was supposed to do with lines like these: "Sexual excitement in a woman starts in her head. A man can talk a woman straight into the bedroom if he knows what to say." Okay… But what if that woman happens to be a guy? And a *French* guy at that? Did the same rules apply?

Reading further, I found this little tidbit: "A woman may feel powerless in many instances in her life… But in bed she can gain a sense of power… This kind of bonding with a man gives her a satisfaction that may be badly lacking elsewhere in her life."

Okay, now I was really confused. Which one was *me* again?

I quickly realized that my dad's advice, though well-intentioned, didn't really apply to me. He was obsessed with sex, whereas I was not looking for a *wham-bam-thank-you-monsieur* encounter. I was looking for something more. A real human connection. That said, I figured if I ended up having a little fun along the way, that would be okay too.

The year 2005 was a good one to come out. By then, France—and especially Paris—was changing in a big way. Just four years earlier, when I'd been looking for the first location for BIA, I'd noticed that bars in the Marais—the main gay *quartier* in Paris—had an underground vibe to them. Their windows were often blacked out, as if the people inside were ashamed to be seen. In fact, most gay bars didn't even have signs—just small rainbow flags stuck somewhere that was hard to find.

Even though I'd considered myself more or less straight back then (read: *confused*), I remember thinking that Paris seemed to be way less "open" than cities like New York and San Francisco. But in just a few short years, everything had changed. Windows at gay establishments were no longer blacked out; they were bright and clear, so you could actually see inside. Some places even had tables and chairs on the sidewalk, and bright neon signs proudly displaying names like Le Spyce Bar, Le Bear's Den, and Le Feeling.

Even with this exciting and new open atmosphere in Paris, I was still very uncomfortable going into places by myself. Fortunately, two of BIA's regulars, Sean and "Trust Fund" Alex, both students at the American University of Paris, let me tag along with them to clubs and bars, helping me get the lay of the land.

I have to admit, I was a little disappointed with my first foray into the gay scene. Knowing the long history of mainstream society's rejection of the LGBT community, I expected everyone to be a little more… I don't know, deep. Instead, most of the guys I met seemed to care only about clubbing and cruising and getting laid—not that different from Fast Eddie, when you think about it. After one too many vapid looks from skinny queens on X, I realized that the kind of guy I'd be attracted to probably wasn't a clubber. I decided to stick to the Internet, where I'd already made a few friends, but no love connections yet.

All that changed when I unexpectedly fell head over heels for a

Colombian named Luis. I was so smitten, I secretly started learning Spanish so that I could surprise him by speaking to him in his own language. Unfortunately, as quickly as I fell for him, Luis was gone— off to a job interview in Mexico, possibly never to return. *Not* good for my abandonment issues.

Of course, I was heartbroken, but at the same time I felt really, really stupid; my mature brain kept saying that I should've known better than to get all worked up over what essentially amounted to a high school crush. But at the same time, I had enough life experience to know that having your heart broken was part of the process, something everyone had to go through.

Sure enough, Luis landed the job in Mexico, and I never saw him again. On the plus side, I was able to speak decent Spanish, which helped with my next relationship, a Peruvian. Unfortunately, that didn't work out either. Once again, it looked like Spanish just wasn't going to be in my stars. *Non*, it was French all over again when I fell for Julien, a charming and handsome Frenchman. Of course, with Julien being French, naturally I would have to learn another language—Japanese.

It's a long story, but when Julien was in high school, he hated having to take Spanish as a language requirement, so he decided to teach himself Japanese instead. And not just how to speak it, but also how to write more than three thousand kanji—a very impressive accomplishment.

When Julien and I first started dating, whenever he tried to speak English, he would do so with a very strong *Japanese* accent— not a French one—which was hilarious. My friends joked that it could have been worse; I could have fallen for a German.

The first time I saw Julien's profile on Gaydar, I didn't write to him directly because I was too shy. Instead, I intentionally left a "trace" on his profile, meaning that he could see that I'd paid him a visit. I hoped that he would make the first move. Luckily, he did.

For our first date, we arranged to meet for a drink in the Marais. When Julien came out of the Hôtel de Ville metro stop, my first thought was, *Ah, he's even more handsome in person!* But to be honest, it was not love at first sight like I'd seen in the movies. And apparently, it wasn't *le coup de foudre* for Julien either.

I guess in a lot of ways, the two of us couldn't have been more different. For starters, Julien always dressed smartly, bordering on preppy. He was a bit too straitlaced for my taste. In fact, when I first met him, Julien didn't even own a pair of jeans. I, on other hand, only dressed up for special occasions—like weddings or funerals.

As for food, if Julien and I were to draw up a Venn diagram, our tastes would barely overlap. Of course, I adored French cuisine. But at the same time, I could happily survive on diner food for the rest of my life if I had to—especially breakfast. Julien, on the other hand, preferred food from pretty much anywhere else in the world *except* the United States. For him, "American cuisine" was an oxymoron—much like "jumbo shrimp" or "working vacation." In fact, when Julien first came to BIA, he had trouble finding something to order off the menu. It didn't help that back then, he was a vegetarian—but with a couple of glaring exceptions, such as *escargots* and foie gras. (I jokingly called him a "foie-getarian.")

Eventually, Julien did find one item he could order at BIA: pancakes! Of course, this made me very happy. That is, until I saw what he did with them. He ordered a side of guacamole and proceeded to smother it all over his pancakes. But he wasn't done yet. He then poured tons of pepper on top of the guacamole, until it turned jet black.

It took a few dates together before I felt comfortable enough to ask Julien why he had massacred perfectly good pancakes like that. His answer: "Pancakes are just *blinis, n'est-ce pas?*"

N'est-ce NOT!

It's a miracle that Julien and I ever fell in love.

I wish I could say that when I first started dating Julien, all my issues just disappeared and everything was hunky-dory. Not so—not even with a hunk like Julien. No, my fears never had anything to do with my sexuality; they'd always been about something much deeper.

Of course, before meeting Julien, my heart had already been broken twice. I did not want to go through that kind of pain again. So for the longest time, I told Julien that I wasn't looking for a serious relationship at all. Just friendship. *I really mean it this time,* I told myself. *Even if you are so incredibly handsome and charming... So please stop staring at me with those beautiful brown eyes... And stop cooking me delicious French meals... And stop smothering me with loving bisous... Don't you know I don't like to be touched and... Oh, be still my heart!*

Try as I might, resistance was futile. I found myself falling for Julien—hook, line, and sinker—*avec tout mon cœur* (with all my heart). So this was what real love felt like. *Pas mal. Pas mal de tout.*

As Julien and I got to know each other better, I felt as if I were in a classic French film *à la* Éric Rohmer (but *without* subtitles), sharing one unforgettable montage moment after another: picnicking on the *quais* by the Seine; riding bikes through the Bois de Boulogne; going to the cinema to see a documentary called *Darwin's Nightmare* about man's unrelenting destruction of the environment (that's when I knew we were *truly* in love!); and finally, taking a fabulous road trip through Brittany in my old '64 Chevy convertible, which I'd shipped over from LA in a huge container, just like Foodex did with our maple syrup and peanut butter.

But the best montage moment of all came when Julien took me down to Burgundy to meet his mother, Elisabeth. Racing through the French countryside on the high speed train (TGV), I was excited and nervous at the same time. Would she like me? Would she be okay with her son being with a guy? And, *quelle horreur*, an *American* guy at that?

But I had nothing to worry about. The moment I met Elisabeth, an elegantly dressed woman with raspberry-colored hair, she made me feel at ease, even letting me "*tu*" her. The three of us met for lunch at a French restaurant specializing in frog legs, which I'd never tried before. They were delicious—all tender and garlicky. By the time dessert rolled around (a yummy black cherry *clafoutis*), Elisabeth had made me feel as if I were part of the family, calling me her *gendre préféré* (her favorite son-in-law). I, in turn, began calling her my *belle-maman* (a nice way to say "mother-in-law").

After lunch, the three of us took a leisurely stroll down the medieval streets of Dijon. As we passed by beautiful half-timber buildings with exquisite fairy-tale creatures carved into their wooden facades, I slowly began to feel a *déjà vu* coming on, but I couldn't quite make sense of it.

"My mom's an amazing cook," Julien said, interrupting my thoughts. "Just wait until you try some of her *spécialités*." He turned to his mom and said, "What do you say we whip something up for Craig the next time we get together?"

"My pleasure," Elisabeth said with a generous smile.

"What's your favorite dish to make, *Belle-Maman*?" I asked.

"Oh, there are so many!" Elisabeth said excitedly. She began rattling off a list of classic Burgundy delicacies, including *escargots* with *pur beurre*, *bœuf bourguignon*, *coq au vin*, and *tarte tatin*.

Upon hearing the names of these familiar dishes, I suddenly

understood what my *déjà vu* had been about. "Oh my God!" I said. "This is where the famous Foire Gastronomique takes place, *n'est-ce pas?*"

"*Oui, oui,*" Elisabeth said. "Every year. Right here in Dijon."

At that moment, the memories of my trip to Dijon when I was an exchange student came flooding back. I told Julien and Elisabeth that I'd gone to the Foire years earlier—and that it had changed my life.

"Isn't that funny?" Julien said. "We used to go every year too, even when I was a kid. Who knows? Maybe we passed each other back then without even knowing it."

A shiver went down my spine. What were the chances that Julien would have grown up in the exact same place where I'd had my epiphany about wine and *haute cuisine* so many years earlier? If that wasn't a sign that we were meant to be together, I didn't know what was.

But before I could let myself get all New Agey, there was one *petit problème*. Long before I'd met Julien, he'd made plans to move to Taiwan for a year to study Chinese (because, you know, Japanese just wasn't challenging enough). Still, that didn't stop the two of us from moving in together. And for the first time in my life, I was in a *real* honest-to-goodness adult relationship. *Oh là là!*

What was most amazing, though, was how I didn't freak out at all! Okay, maybe I freaked out *un petit peu*. But only when I thought about Julien's imminent departure.

"Imminent?" Julien laughed as we snuggled together one night. "I'm not leaving for another year."

"Yeah, but time flies, you know."

"*Exactement, mon petit,*" Julien said, hugging me tight. "Which means I'll be back in Paris before you know it!"

I wanted to believe it. But, of course, I had a little history with people close to me suddenly disappearing and never coming back.

Instead, I smiled and said, "You're right, *chaton*. What's most important is to enjoy our time together right here, right now."

I'd never been more grateful to have such a fantastic staff at BIA, especially my newly promoted manager, Derrick. Thanks to them, I was able to have some time away from work to be with Julien. I apologized to everyone for being so distracted as of late. The reason, I confessed, was that I'd fallen in love.

"Yeah, we all kind of figured that out," Derrick said.

"Oh, *ouaiiis!*" Geneviève squealed, giving me a big hug. "That's super, Super-Duper Boss!"

"But there's just one thing," I said. "He's a guy."

My staff shrugged, unfazed. "Who cares?" Geneviève said. "You found someone to love. That's all that matters!"

I smiled. What a lucky guy I was—in every way, including the latest development at BIA. We'd just signed a lease for a second location! And with renovations coming up soon, I was excited to get back to work.

BIA #2 before...   ...and after.

Chapter 17

BIA #2 AND BEYOND

*"I think for Parisians, we want to go to
Breakfast in America because it's like we
are taking a plane to New York."*

—Thomas, a French customer of BIA, as quoted
in the *Today Show*'s food blog, *Bites*

I DID NOT FIND THE LOCATION FOR BREAKFAST IN AMERICA #2.
The location found me.

One day out of the blue, I received a phone call from a real
estate agent I'd met with back when I was looking for the first location. None of the places he'd shown me back then worked out, but
we stayed in touch anyway.

"*Bonjour*, Grag," the agent said. "*Ça va?* Listen, I was wondering, are you still planning to do more restaurants?"

"It's funny you should call," I said. "I've been thinking about the subject all week."

Talk about good timing. It was the summer of 2005, and according to BIA's business plan, BIA #2 was projected to open by 2006. But I'd been so busy, I hadn't given it much thought. That is, until the week the agent called.

"It's in a great location," he said. "In the heart of the Marais, near Saint-Paul. You know it?"

"Of course I know it!" The Saint-Paul metro stop was right around the corner from the drafty youth hostel where I had stayed as a UConn student.

"Want to set up an appointment to see it?" the agent asked.

"*Absolument!*"

When I saw the Marais location for the first time, it reminded me a lot of BIA #1. Like the Marins, the owners of this location were ready to retire after more than thirty years in business. And also like the Marins, the owners didn't have any employees, which was a major plus, because in France, whenever you take over a business space (even as a renter), you're required to keep the previous staff. It didn't matter if the place had been a shoe store and you wanted to convert it into a restaurant—you still had to keep all the employees, even if they'd never cooked or waited tables a day in their lives.

Although the space was smaller than BIA #1, it had a great layout, perfect for transforming into a diner. And I was able to get an amazing deal on the rent. But unlike the Marins, the couple at BIA #2 didn't own *les murs* (the walls), which meant I had to negotiate the rent with the landlord.

Fortunately, there was a new French law working in my favor

that prohibited the landlord from raising the rent more than a small percentage. The principle behind the law was that when owners are elderly and want to retire, a cheaper rent would make it easier for them to find a buyer. I liked this law. Because of it, my rent ended up being only €1,600 a month, which was a steal in the Marais.

Everything went so much smoother this time around, especially with investors. For my second restaurant location, I was able to raise the same amount in two weeks that had taken me over a year to raise before. And best of all, this time the banks were fighting over me to give me a loan. *Ah, so now you love me!*

After getting the keys to the second location, I was ready to start the renovations. However, I ran into a major obstacle that threatened to ruin everything—the nasty French neighbors. They did *not* want an American joint in their building. In a typical French paradox, I was required to set up a meeting with the *syndique*—or the homeowner's association of the building—in order to get approval to renovate the shop's decrepit wooden facade.

"What if they vote no?" I asked my lawyer.

"They can't. They don't have the right to refuse you."

"But what if they do?"

"Trust me. They can't."

"Then why bother having a vote?"

My lawyer gave me a Gallic shrug and said, "Got me."

More absurdity followed as my proposal came up for a vote. The residents rebelled in protest, saying they would only vote yes if I agreed to give up my sidewalk terrace—even though I had a city permit authorizing me to have one.

"They can't do that!" my lawyer said afterward.

"But they did."

"They have no right."

"But," I said, confused, "how else could I have gotten the neighbors to vote yes—even though you said that, technically, they weren't allowed to vote no?"

Another shrug.

Of course, I hated to give up my little terrace—even if it only sat four people. But I figured it would be good karma, that my new neighbors and I would start off on the right foot. You'd think I would have learned my lesson by now. What was the reward for my concession? At the end of the meeting, a wiry, low-rent lawyer who lived on the fifth floor came up to me and said, "Monsieur Carlson, you may have been victorious this time"—*I was?*—"but mark my words, I will make it my mission to shut you down! No matter how long it takes!"

Merde alors. And BIA #2 hadn't even opened yet.

With the building's approval, I could now proceed with renovations. Having learned my lesson with the crew who had worked on BIA #1, this time, I hired a new architect named Mounia. She cracked the whip and kept the crew on schedule—for the most part. Unfortunately, there was one guy who held everything up…the electrician. (*Quelle surprise!*)

Although Mounia had her own crew, including an electrician, Derrick convinced her to use a friend of his for the electrical work. Bad idea. The guy showed up to work late (and drunk) nearly every day. And during the last week of renovations, he got plastered at a neighborhood bar and ended up in a motorcycle accident. Fortunately, it wasn't serious, but it was bad enough that he was laid up in the hospital for several days. When the electrician finally came back to work, he was so bandaged up, he could barely raise his arms to connect the wires. Luckily, Derrick was there to help him finish the job.

I had to say, I was very impressed with the way Derrick took charge of the renovations from the get-go, working side by side with the pretty architect, Mounia—and flirting with her every step of the way. At first, I was concerned about all the ogling that was going on, but the attraction seemed to be mutual. It reminded me of the advice the French producer on *Robin Hood* had given me years earlier. "Kraaag" she'd said. "You need to flirt more to get what you want." Of course, in the States, such behavior could end up in a lawsuit. But in France, *l'art de draguer* (the art of flirting) was still alive and well.

As the renovations were nearing an end, I drew up a sign that read: "Coming soon! BIA #2!" Just as I was taping the sign to the wall at BIA #1, a voice behind me said, "I'd be interested to see what happens with your second BIA."

I turned to see a professor from a prestigious business school in Paris sitting at table eleven, sipping on a mug of sock juice. I recognized him immediately, since I'd been a guest speaker in his class. He reminded me a lot of Professor Windbag from USC.

"What do you mean?" I asked.

"Well," the professor said, his tone a little too cocky for my taste, "often when a small business expands, the owner ends up over-extending himself, which ultimately brings down both places."

"Don't worry, Professor," I said. "I've thought everything through."

"Hmph. We shall see."

Actually, I *had* thought everything through. One of the reasons I'd chosen the location for BIA #2 was that it wasn't that far from

BIA #1—just a ten-minute walk across the river. I figured in case of an emergency—i.e., if one place ran out of fries or an employee got sick—I could easily run over to the other location and solve the problem. Nevertheless, the professor's comment left a bad taste in my mouth. I hoped his ominous prediction would not turn out to be true.

On February 17, 2006, Breakfast in America #2 opened for business. However, because of some lingering electrical problems (*bien sûr*), we didn't get to open until the evening. As a result, there wasn't much fanfare, just a bunch of friends and BIA #1 regulars. But within a week—despite the professor's gloomy prediction—BIA #2 was already packed. Nobody, including me, could believe that we already had long lines. And by the summertime, BIA #2 was averaging more than €1,000 in sales every day, something that had taken nearly two years for BIA #1 to accomplish.

One great thing about having two BIAs was that whenever one of them had a line and a customer didn't want to wait, we would call the other BIA to see if they were busy. If they weren't, we'd hand the customer a business card and point to the map on the back. "There's no wait at the other BIA," we'd say. "It's just a short walk that way."

If the customer seemed reluctant to make the trip, we'd say, "Oh, but it's the most beautiful walk in Paris! Not only do you get to cross the Seine twice, but you also get the most beautiful view of Notre Dame ever!"

"Oh! Okay!" the customer would say, running off. It worked every time.

There was one noticeable difference between the two locations, however; I'd made the choice to keep BIA #2 100 percent smoke free, which was a very controversial decision at the time. (It would take a couple more years before the French caught up with the rest of Europe and banned smoking in restaurants and bars.) Everybody warned me that no French person would put up with it. But I had a good excuse for my decision; one of my waitresses was pregnant!

It was tough-going at first. One night a group of hungry French customers came in all excited to order nachos and *'amburgers*. The moment they sat down, all four of them grabbed a cig and went to light up.

"*Désolé*," I said. "But this diner is *non-fumeur*."

Their eyes went wide. "*Oh, non, non, non! C'est pas possible!*" They grabbed their things and ran out the door.

In the end, however, most of our customers—including French ones who smoked—were happy with my decision. In fact, once word got out that BIA #2 was smoke free, many customers, especially American families with kids, would come to BIA #2 specifically so that they could breathe while enjoying their pancakes.

Amazingly, by the third month, BIA #2 had already caught up to BIA #1 in sales. With both places running neck and neck, it was like a horse race. We had fun turning it into a healthy competition, battling to see which BIA would get more customers.

As time went on, I began to notice a lot of interesting differences between the two locations. Being in the Marais, with all its trendy attitude, BIA #2 attracted a clientele that was decidedly more *branché*. The regulars included dancers from the Moulin Rouge who would come in for carb-filled French toast and pancakes. We also seemed to be getting a lot more celebrity visits at BIA #2—both French and American—including a star from the American TV show

Lost and a famous French comedian. We even got a visit from the Grammy-winning duo Daft Punk.

Of course, there was another side to the chic Marais attitude. Snooty customers would come into BIA #2 and say things like, "I've been to New York-errr. This is *not* a real diner!"

Similarly, because BIA continued to get a lot of press coverage, customers would come in with super high expectations, which were often impossible to meet. It reminded me a lot of Hollywood. If someone said they'd just seen the "greatest film of all time," people's expectations would be so high that they would inevitably be disappointed.

I was learning a valuable lesson from all this: "Know thyself." BIA was—and always had been—a no-frills diner that served hearty portions of yummy comfort food at a reasonable price. There was no way we could compete with trendy places that served froufrou burgers costing upward of forty euros ("foie gras burger" anyone?) Nor did I *want* to compete with them.

That said, I was starting to notice an interesting trend that I never could have expected: Parisians were stealing my idea and opening up copycat diners of their own, albeit more upscale French versions. I was fine with it, as long as they didn't try to steal my customers. After all, as they say, imitation is the best form of flattery, *n'est-ce pas?*

Given how quickly trends come and go in Paris, I realized that having so much competition was as an opportunity for me to try out some new things, or rather, *old* things that I'd been dying to try out—meaning, classic diner dishes that had been on my original menu: meatloaf, mac 'n' cheese, and Philly cheesesteaks. I couldn't wait to try them out as blue-plate specials. Unfortunately, things did not go as planned.

I'd just hired a promising young cook from England named Kyle. Although he was very talented, Kyle also had a bit of an ego; he thought he was above diner grub and preferred to cook more upscale fare, just like our competition was doing.

"No problem," I said to Kyle. "We can try out some of your recipes as blue-plate specials!"

Kyle liked the idea. He came up with a list of "fancy" diner dishes that included roast beef, pork chops, and chicken *cordon bleu*. One busy night, with orders backing up, Kyle grabbed the order wheel and spun it around, looking to see if anyone had ordered any of his specials. He spun the wheel around again and again, but there wasn't a single special—just *'amburger* after *'amburger* after *'amburger*.

Kyle quit the next day.

Know thyself.

This experience was the exact opposite of the one I had with Lindsay, our wonderful new head chef at BIA #2. Lindsay had gone to one of the best culinary schools in France, and although she was way above BIA's league, she never flaunted it. Instead, she put her heart and soul into every dish she made, getting great satisfaction out of simply making customers happy.

One time, I saw a regular customer come into the diner with his young daughter. The moment Lindsay saw the little girl, she started preparing "the usual" for her—pancakes with a colorful smiley face made out of rainbow chips. As the waitress brought the dish out to the table, Lindsay snuck a peek through the kitchen porthole so she could watch the little girl's reaction. The moment the little girl saw her smiley face pancakes, she shrieked with delight. Lindsay stood there with the biggest smile on her face, glowing from the inside out.

Now, *that's* a professional. And an *artiste*.

As the business continued to grow, I began to notice a few disturbing trends that were starting to cause me some concern. First, many of our regular customers stopped coming in. They griped about the long lines, paraphrasing Yogi Berra's famous quip, "Nobody goes to BIA anymore. It's too crowded!"

Even more worrisome, BIA was becoming so popular that it was hard for us to maintain our mom-and-pop charm. Things we used to be able to do when we were small were impossible to do now—such as serving coffee in the contraband mugs I'd smuggled in from the States. That's because customers were *stealing* them! Same with our sugar pourers and syrup pourers.

The French have an expression for what BIA was going through: *La rançon du succès*. (Literally, "the ransom of success.") But, fortunately, there was also the *reward* of success; by the end of the year, both BIAs were turning such a healthy profit that I was able to distribute dividend checks to my jubilant investors for the first time ever.

With all my years of hard work *literally* paying off, I was finally ready to enjoy the fruits of my labor, especially now that I had a *chéri* with whom to share them. After all, wasn't it France that had taught me about the whole *quality of life* thing—where one didn't live to work—but worked to *live*?

In short, I was ready to take my first vacation *à la française* with Julien!

But unfortunately, just like the night I'd gone to see *Casablanca*, I was *still* finding it hard to pull myself away from my baby—or should I say, *babies*. Of course, I was well aware of all the things that could go wrong when the cat's away. (Incidentally, in France, the mice don't play—they *dance*).

But I knew I had to go, especially since it might be the last time Julien and I had a chance to take a trip together before he moved to Taiwan. I told myself not to worry, that I could leave with *l'esprit tranquille*. After all, I now had a team of more than forty employees—plus my newly promoted general manager, Derrick, who was a former soldier, standing guard. What could possibly go wrong?

In Arizona with Julien, mere hours before la merde *hit the fan.*

Chapter 18

MIDNIGHT ESPRESSO

"No vacation goes unpunished."

—Karl Hakkarainen

IT WAS THE FALL OF 2007, AND I COULDN'T BELIEVE I WAS FINALLY taking my first real *vacances* with Julien! It would be the longest chunk of time I'd ever been away from BIA—almost two whole weeks (or the equivalent of a long weekend for the French). The plan was to introduce him to my family and then explore the beautiful Southwest, including the Grand Canyon.

What I hadn't planned on was how much of a culture shock the trip would be. For years I'd been monitoring the goings-on in the States from afar via the *International Herald Tribune*, the Internet, and my visiting American customers. For instance, I first became aware of a certain fad diet when customers at BIA kept asking for "low-carb" breakfasts. Take away the pancakes, hash browns, and toast and you don't have much of an American breakfast left. But the customer is always right, *n'est-ce pas*? So I decided to print up new menus with a "low-carb" option. But it was all for naught; just as quickly as the fad appeared, it was gone.

Perhaps because there always seemed to be popular diets like that, I wasn't expecting to see the opposite once we arrived in the States: how huge Americans were getting. The most blatant example of this was when I took Julien to a *buffet américain*. There we saw a young father, well over three hundred pounds, walking with two plates stacked high with greasy fried food. Waddling behind him like a little duckling was his equally pudgy son, no more than six years old, also holding two overflowing plates.

Julien was shocked—and not just by how much the family was eating, but by how much the family was *wasting*—leaving piles of food on their plates to be thrown away. Julien could not understand why the boy's father wasn't setting a better example. After all, in France *l'éducation*—as in how to properly raise your child—is hugely important. In fact, to this day, whenever I dine with Julien and my *belle-maman*, Elisabeth, they're both slightly aghast that I still have a hard time using my silverware in the proper French way. "*Sers-toi correctement du couteau!*" they cry. ("Serve yourself correctly of the knife!")

Julien and I encountered many other instances of culture shock on our road trip across the Southwest—but in a good way. Perhaps because I was seeing my country through Julien's eyes, I really appreciated how friendly and upbeat Americans are. I've always been one to defend the French when people say they're rude—especially since most people who say that have never actually been to France, or if they have, it was ages ago. But Parisians have evolved a lot over the years. They can actually be *très gentils*—but mainly to *tourists*, not to those of us who actually live there.

Julien and I talked about this as we observed customer service in America. Whether it was a waiter in a restaurant or a sales clerk in a Kmart (Julien bought his very first pair of blue jeans there), we couldn't help but notice how everyone in America seemed to scurry about, trying to please you. On the contrary, service workers in Paris often treat customers as nuisances who get in the way of their gab sessions.

And just try requesting something—anything—from a Parisian. Before you've had a chance to get the words out of your mouth, you're given the ol' French motto: "*C'est pas possible!*" Sometimes, for fun, I'd make up absurd questions just to see if the rule would hold. For example, I once said to a public treasury worker, "*Pardon, madame*, I noticed that my taxes are only forty-five percent. May I please pay fifty-five percent?"

"*C'est pas possible!*"

See? It's a natural reflex for the French, like nonchalance or insouciance. But in America, everything seemed possible. This made Julien and I *très, très contents*.

Crossing the border into Arizona, I was excited to show Julien a part of America I loved so much: the magnificent painted desert. With its vivid colors and otherworldly vistas, it completely took his breath away. Like most Europeans, Julien had never seen anything quite like it: vast, unspoiled nature, the likes of which don't exist in Europe anymore. The vastness of the landscape made me feel small and insignificant—the perfect setting for coming out to my family.

Actually, truth be told, I had already come out to my siblings a few weeks earlier via email; they just hadn't met my *beau* in person yet. Not surprisingly, their reactions to the news varied greatly. My brother took a while to respond. When he did, he said that he respected my choice of "lifestyle," but that as a father, he hoped I would respect his decision not to tell his kids just yet, because he wanted them to stay "innocent" for as long as possible. (Eventually, my brother came around and accepted Julien with open arms.) On the other side of the spectrum, when my sisters saw my email with a picture of Julien, their response was, "Wow! He's so handsome!"

I didn't end up telling my mom until several months later. When she heard the news, she covered her ears, ran into the next room, and exclaimed to her husband, "Hey, Richard, wasn't that great how your Giants came from behind and won the game today?"

As Julien and I drove down the mountain pass and into Sedona, where my sisters lived, I started to feel anxious. Would I regress back to the awkward child who never felt comfortable in his own skin? Based on past experience, I knew that all the years I'd spent in therapy building up my self-esteem could by wiped out in a single second by my family.

Sensing my vulnerability, Julien took my hand in his and held it tight. "I'm here, *mon petit*," he said.

I exhaled… "*Aaah*." It felt good to have Julien by my side. I felt more secure and ready to face my family than I ever had in my life.

The moment we pulled up to the chalet where we'd be staying, my sisters Cathy and Colleen came running out to greet us—or rather, they made a beeline straight for Julien.

"Oh, wow, he's even more handsome in person, don't you think, Colleen?"

"Mm-hm. I'll say."

"I'm jealous! Aren't you?"

"Oh, yeah. Mm-hm."

Well into their forties, "the girls," as my family still called them, hadn't changed a bit since the time they'd tried to speak *le français* in my dad's station wagon all those years ago. They still wore their long blond hair straight, and they still had the same endearing, but sometimes exasperating, naïveté. Trailing behind them was Bob, Cathy's husband. His balding head struggled valiantly to grow a mullet.

"Hey, what am I?" Bob snorted. "Chopped liver?"

"Oh, Bob, don't be stupid," Cathy said. "There's no comparison."

Julien hadn't even uttered a word yet and already the girls were charmed off their feet. That's why I had no problem handing him over to them. The girls couldn't wait to show him pictures they'd taken of fairies—or as they spelled them, "faeries." (This *was* Sedona after all—a New-Age mecca, with all its vortexes.) We learned that my sisters were on the verge of self-publishing a book on how to take pictures of "nature spirits," which included elves, dwarves, orbs, and, yes, faeries. By the time the girls had pulled out their fifth massive binder full of faerie photos, Julien looked like he was ready to kill me.

Ah…welcome to America, chéri!

Feeling a tinge of sympathy for the poor guy, I asked my sisters if it was okay to take a little break because I was starting to get hungry. Taking advantage of the out, Julien sprang up from the couch and offered to cook for us. In that wonderful French way, he gathered whatever was lying around in the fridge and whipped up a delicious dinner, *poulet à la sauce aux pommes* (chicken with gravy made from apples and mixed vegetables). Of course, being a "foie-getarian," Julien didn't have any himself.

As my sisters watched Julien prepare the meal, they looked so in love with him, you'd think an actual faerie had broken through the veil and landed right there in the dining room.

After the meal, Bob took leave of us to do some work in his office. Julien, the girls, and I headed outside to the Jacuzzi. As the warm bubbles soothed our tired bodies, we sipped wine and drank in the magnificent desert sunset, watching the fading light transform the rock cliffs into a vibrant palette of reds, oranges, and yellows. I could see that Julien was moved by all the beauty around us. I tilted my glass toward him, thinking, *Life doesn't get much better than this.*

I barely had time to savor the moment before Bob came running from the chalet in a panic. "Craig!" he said, holding a wireless phone in his hand. "Paris has been trying to reach you! There's been an emergency!"

Oh God, no. Please, not now. I jumped out of the Jacuzzi and grabbed the phone. It was my friend Will, from LA. He said that my manager, Derrick, had been trying to reach me for two days but couldn't get through because of bad cell phone reception in the dessert. Doing an amazing amount of detective work, Will had finally tracked me down to Sedona and Bob's chalet.

He read Derrick's message to me: "The sky is falling! Cops have raided BIA! Thrown everyone in jail! They're going to shut the place down!"

Oh my God…my worst nightmare! At first I thought it had to be a prank. Derrick sometimes had a sick sense of humor. But unfortunately, it was no prank.

Will didn't have all the details, but he did his best to paint a picture of what had happened. It turned out that the visa of my Filipino waiter, Jeff, had just expired, which technically made him an illegal alien. To make matters worse, Jeff had invited a bunch of his illegal alien friends to BIA to party the night away after hours.

Since it had been an election year that year, Nicolas Sarkozy had decided to crack down on illegal immigration as part of his campaign for the presidency. Which explains why, when the cops who were patrolling the *quartier* that night saw BIA full of Filipinos, they decided to raid the place. Sure enough, their racist hunch paid off—they caught a month's quota of "illegals" in one fell swoop; Jeff and his friends were rounded up, arrested, and hauled off to the police station in a paddy wagon.

"Shit," I said. "Shit! Shit! Shit! What the hell am I going to do?"

"I'm getting to that," Will said. "The cops said that since you're on vacation, not to worry. You can take care of the formalities when you're back."

Bless the French. If that wasn't proof that vacations were sacred, I didn't know what was. Of course, the news put a little damper on the rest of my trip. Ever the Frenchman, Julien said, "I agree with the cops, *mon petit.* We're on *vacances*, so let's enjoy it."

Uh, yeah, okay. How could I possibly enjoy myself when my whole world was falling apart? But looking at it from the French perspective, Julien did have a point. After all, what could I do? We were six thousand miles away, in the middle of the Arizona desert. The more I thought about it, the more I realized that I had two options: choose to be miserable or choose to *profiter* from the experience.

The next day, I tried to stay positive as we drove with my sisters to the Grand Canyon, but the girls were not helping my mood any; as much as I loved them, their incessant faerie talk was turning my brain into New-Age mush. Things got even nuttier when Cathy spotted a huge black condor soaring high in the sky above us.

"Colleen, look!" She pointed up excitedly. "Oh my God, it's Dad!"

"Woo-hoo! Hi, Dad!"

My sisters waved their arms wildly out the car window. I exchanged a look of embarrassment with Julien. "*Famille stoo-peed,*" I said under my breath.

Poor Julien didn't know what to think. I went on to explain to him—*en français*—that even though my father had been dead for almost ten years, my sisters believed that spirits could communicate through animals.

"*Ah, bon?*" Julien said. "*Et pourquoi pas?*" ("And why not?") He shrugged, always the good sport.

"Look!" Cathy said, pointing at the condor. "He's following us!"

"Yes, he is!"

"I think he's trying to tell us something, don't you?"

"Uh-huh! What are you trying to tell us, Dad?"

I wondered that myself. What invaluable wisdom could my

dead father bestow upon me from the "other side" via a bird? Of course, right on cue the condor let loose a huge turd that splattered onto our windshield.

Yep, I thought to myself. *That's Fast Eddie all right.*

After the longest flight of my life, Julien and I returned to Paris. The moment I stepped into BIA, my waitress, Leslie, motioned for me to join her downstairs in *la cave.* She whispered that she had some inside information to relay to me from her husband, Fabien, who happened to be a cop in the neighborhood.

"Oh, Craig," Leslie said. "Fabien says you're in deep, deep shit."

That was the insider information? Thanks, but I kind of figured that out already.

Just then, the phone rang. Leslie looked at me guiltily. "Sorry… They asked me when you'd be in. I had to tell them."

I answered the phone. Sure enough, it was the *préfecture de police* (police headquarters).

"Monsieur Carlson," a gruff voice said. "I think you know why I'm calling. Please come to the station *tout de suite.*"

Each arrondissement has its own *préfecture de police,* and mine was barely a five-minute walk away. Like most government structures in Paris, the *préfecture* stuck out like a sore thumb among the beautiful Haussmannian buildings surrounding it. It reminded me of a nightmarish *pâtisserie*—like a five-story *mille-feuille,* if it were made of cold, crumbling concrete.

Once inside the police station, I was escorted to the office of an *inspecteur*, who was once a fit cop, but was now a flabby paper pusher. For what felt like an eternity, the *inspecteur* just sat there staring at me, not saying a word. Then he leaned in close.

"First things first, Monsieur Carlson. How was your *vacances*?"

"Great! No complaints."

"You look healthy. All tan."

"*Oui, oui,*" I nodded nervously. *Can we get this over with please?*

The *inspecteur* changed his tone and got down to business, recapping the events of that fateful night. I was surprised by what upset him most. "Did you know that your liquor license only gives you the right to serve alcohol until two a.m.?" he said. "But you were still open at two forty."

"That's impossible!" I said. "We close at eleven—and we're usually locked up by midnight, twelve thirty at the latest."

I explained to him that my waiter wasn't selling alcohol; he was *stealing* it, by throwing a party after hours. The *inspecteur* tilted his head, a bit confused.

"But…where was your *responsable*?"

"*Exactement!*" I said. Where the hell had Derrick, my manager/ soldier, been? The answer: at home playing Nintendo.

The *inspecteur* squinted at me through the bottom half of his bifocals, then said gravely, "Monsieur Carlson, be careful as to how you answer my next question: How many of the other *sans-papiers*, the illegals, were working for you?"

"None!" I said. "I don't even know them!"

"Hmm… I hope so for your sake. Because they are all going to be deported!"

Merde! This was getting serious.

The *inspecteur* grabbed a file off his desk containing BIA's police record and perused it. "You are a lucky man, Monsieur Carlson. Your record is clean."

"That's great," I said, letting out a sigh of relief. Maybe things weren't going to be so bad after all.

The *inspecteur* continued. "And since I find you agreeable, I am going to give you the smallest of punishments: a fine of five hundred euros and…ten days to be closed."

Wait, wait, what? Closed for ten days! *C'est pas possible!* My worst *Casablanca* nightmare had come true. How in the world would I ever be able to pay my staff's salaries with no cash coming in? In France, workers have the right to get paid, no matter what happens to the business they work for. And my customers? What would they think?

"Do not worry, Monsieur Carlson," the *inspecteur* said. "I will not make you put up a shameful sign. You can simply tell your clients you are closed for *rénovations*."

It took me a moment to let everything sink in. Realizing that things could've been a lot worse, I said humbly: "*Merci, Monsieur l'Inspecteur*. That's very kind of you."

I stood up to leave. The *inspecteur* held up his hand.

"*Attendez*. There is one last *petite formalité*."

Just then, two cops entered and grabbed me by the arms. "Okay, *on y va*."

"Wait, where are we going?"

No response. Instead, the cops escorted me to another room, where they proceeded to take my mug shot and fingerprints. Next, they handcuffed me and marched me outside to an unmarked police car in front of the station. The cops shoved me into the backseat, then drove over to BIA. Once there, they hid my handcuffed hands behind my back, then walked me briskly through the packed diner, past customers and staff and down into *la cave*. Luckily, because the cops were wearing plain clothes, nobody had a clue what was going on, except for Leslie, who bit her lip, looking at me with concern.

Down in the cellar, the cops found what they had come for—my business license. They grabbed it then escorted me back upstairs and through the diner again. Before I knew it, we were back at the station.

Thinking we were done, I lifted up my hands to have the hand-cuffs removed. No such luck. Instead, as a kind of walk of shame, the cops paraded me through the entire police station, past stone-faced *fonctionnaires*, this time with my handcuffs clearly visible. We continued our little stroll down into the dark medieval *cave* underneath the station. With its moldy stone walls and fusty smell, it reminded me of the kind of place where Marie Antoinette must have been held prisoner during the French Revolution.

Arriving in front of an empty cell, the cops told me to go inside and remove all my clothes. Then the tough-looking one of the two proceeded to inspect my naked body. Finding nothing, he gave me back my clothes and shoes—minus the shoelaces.

Once I was dressed again, the cops escorted me to another cell, this one full of prisoners. They threw me in and closed the gate. I could feel myself starting to panic.

"Wait!" I said. "How long am I going to be in here?"

The cops shrugged: *Who knows?* All they knew was that they were hungry, and it was lunchtime. They turned and left.

"But…my rights," I said weakly.

Chuckles came from behind me. I turned to see the cell full of druggies and *clochards* (bums) staring at me. Dazed, I made my way over to a hard steel bench against a concrete wall, which was covered with a myriad of disgusting bodily fluids.

Finding a small opening on the bench, I lay down and curled up into the fetal position, slowly rocking back and forth. As I stared at my laceless shoes, I tried to recall the mantra my friend Todd had given me for when times got tough, but for some reason it just wouldn't come out right: *Is this a dream? Is this a dream? Is this a dream?*

It would be a long time before I'd ever be able to take another French *vacances* again.

Digestif

La Grande Disillusion

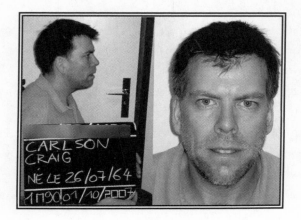

Wanted: The Pancake Guy.

Chapter 19

THE PETER PRINCIPLE

"I don't like jail, they got the wrong kind of bars in there."

—Charles Bukowski

BIA #1 is closed for renovations. We will reopen Monday, October 22. Meanwhile, BIA #2 is still open! And it's just a lovely ten-minute walk across the river Seine!

DESPITE THE CHEERY TONE OF THE SIGN POSTED ON BIA #1'S DOOR, being closed down by the cops was one of the most traumatic experiences of my life. While I was in the slammer, nobody bothered to explain to me exactly why I'd been locked up or for how long I'd be there, or if the incident would appear on my record. My waitress Leslie and her cop husband suspected that the powers that be wanted to put the fear of God into me. Well, if that was their intention, it worked.

As for my rights, I never got to have my one phone call like on an American cop show. Instead, at the end of the day, with no warning, the cops came and removed me from my cell. Then they led me to a heavily guarded area where they returned my personal effects and had me sign a bunch of forms. Before letting me go, they told me I would be getting a call from the station very soon.

"The moment you hear from us," one of the cops said, "you will have to close down your restaurant immediately. Is that clear?"

"*Oui.*" I nodded.

I thought about all the things I needed to organize beforehand, like deliveries and staff schedules. I also needed to come up with some quick renovations, anything that would make it look like we'd had a legitimate reason to be closed.

"Just a *petite question*," I asked the cop. "Can you give me an idea when I might expect that phone call?"

"Like I said," the cop snapped. "You'll hear from us soon."

All week long I waited on pins and needles for the call. It didn't come until the following Friday, at four o'clock in the afternoon, right at the end of lunch service.

"Monsieur Carlson," the anonymous voice said through the phone. "The time is now. Close your restaurant *tout de suite!*"

I hung up the phone and turned to my staff, who had been on standby for days. "Okay, everybody," I said. "Let's do it." My staff kicked into gear and began closing up shop. I stepped over to our OPEN sign and flipped it to CLOSED. (Luckily there were only a couple of customers inside having *limonade*). Then I taped the sign with the directions to BIA #2 on the window.

The cops couldn't have picked a worse time to shut us down than a Friday afternoon. When I looked at the calendar and counted out ten consecutive days, my heart sank. BIA would be closed for two full, rent-paying weekends. If the cops had picked *any* other day, the financial hit wouldn't have been as hard.

Of course, I still had to pay all my staff's salaries while the diner was closed, which meant they would end up getting what essentially amounted to *seven* weeks of paid vacation that year.

I tried to count my blessings. If BIA had been closed down for much longer, then, like Rick in *Casablanca*, I'm not sure we could have ever reopened. Another blessing was that none of our food went to waste, since we were able to take everything across the river to BIA #2. As I watched my staff rush around the diner, closing up, I vowed that I would never let something like this happen ever again.

Unfortunately, the powers that be seemed to have other ideas. I got the distinct impression that BIA had been put on a shit list, because once we finally reopened, we were getting more surprise visits from nasty government *contrôleurs* than ever, just itching to shut us down again. They included:

Inspecteur du travail (**work inspector**): He popped in to make sure we were following each and every one of the hundreds of complex—and often contradictory— French labor laws. If we weren't, I risked having to pay a huge fine…or worse.

Hygiène (**health inspector**): Besides checking to see if the restaurant was clean, the *inspecteur* also gave us reams of crippling—and often redundant—paperwork. For example, because of the *vache folle* (mad cow disease) scare at the time, we had to keep a year's worth of labels from our beef, as well as hundreds of other documents, in dozens of categories, that needed to be kept on site at all times, ready for inspection.

Sidewalk police: With tape measure in hand, these guys came by to make sure our sidewalk terrace at BIA #1 didn't go past the legal 110 centimeter limit. If customers were seated in a chair and moved it past the 110 centimeter line, the *contrôleur* would sometimes let it slide. But the moment the customer left, we had to quickly run over and move the seat back within the line.

Liquor police: Who knew there was a law going back to the dark ages requiring cafés to display mini-steins above the bar, each one indicating a different serving amount? Unfortunately, the Marins had left me with only half of the required mini-steins, having lost the others over the years. I also learned from the *contrôleur* that bars in France were required to display ten different bottles of *limonade*, so that alcoholics could see that they had an alternative to getting shit-faced.

Music police: The same guy from our jukebox days was back for another visit. Except this time, since there was no jukebox, he had to find something else to bill us for. He chose our new TV monitor, which we'd installed so that customers could watch CNN and sports games. The *contrôleur* cited us for having an undeclared TV, which resulted in a new and expensive fee.

Language police: Of all the *contrôleurs*, these guys were the worst. They came by to inspect our menu for such things as the "integrity of the French language." On their first visit, they made us add the French translation for the words bagel (*pain américain*) and tortilla chips

(*chips de maïs*), even though nearly every French person knew what those words meant.

Now, after my jail incident, the language police were back with a vengeance, and for even more absurd reasons. This time, they objected to our English translation of mushroom-swiss burger.

"You cannot call it that," the *contrôleur* said.

"Why not?" I asked.

"Because your swiss cheese is made in *France*. Not Switzerland."

I couldn't believe I was arguing with a French bureaucrat about the *English* translation of a famous kind of cheese. I explained that in America, cheese with big holes in it was called "swiss cheese," no matter where it came from.

"But, Monsieur Carlson," the *contrôleur* sneered. "You are not in America, are you?"

It would seem that Eric from Cafe Beaujolais was right when he'd said, "The French don't like it when you're successful. If you are, they'll make your life hell." *C'est vrai.* Yet despite the weekly horror show that was the "Attack of the *Contrôleurs!*" BIA's lucky streak continued, culminating in 2008 with the historic election of President Barack Obama.

Of course, it was no secret that the French despised President Bush. But the way Obamamania swept across the country surprised even me. Furthermore, for the first time in my life, I was glad that American elections were so painfully long, because for a full year, BIA became the center of a media frenzy. *NBC News*, the *New York Times*, the *Huffington Post*, and just about every TV and radio station in the country came by BIA to do a report on Obama.

On the night of the election itself, I was able to get authorization from the *préfecture* to stay open all night. The diner was so packed that crowds spilled out onto the streets, trying to catch a glimpse of CNN on our TV monitor. Because of the time difference, Obama's victory speech didn't air until the wee hours of the morning, and the last customer didn't stagger out of the diner until around 6:00 a.m.

But the fun had only just begun. That morning, the manager of BIA #2, Cameron, and I were picked up by a chauffeur and whisked away to a radio station to appear on a popular radio show starring Cauet—the Howard Stern of France. In the studio, Cameron fried bacon and whipped up pancakes for Cauet and his entourage. As we ate our hearty breakfasts live on the air, Cauet interviewed me, making off-color jokes about Obama and the United States.

"No wonder you Americans are so fat," Cauet said, wolfing down his bacon and pancakes. "Just look at what you eat every morning!"

The next day, I posted pictures of the election party on BIA's website, congratulating Obama on his historic win. I'd never felt more proud to be an American, especially when French customers would tell me they didn't think France could ever elect a black president like America had done.

But I was unpleasantly surprised when, shortly after I posted the election photos, I starting receiving hate mail from some Americans. They said that since I was a supporter of a Kenyan Muslim who had illegally taken possession of the presidency, they would never set foot in BIA. I tried to reason with them, saying that I'd always been careful not to mix business and politics. BIA was simply celebrating the democratic process, I said, not endorsing anyone.

But that didn't stop the crazies. The more I engaged with them, the more cuckoo they got. So I decided to disengage with them, even if that meant losing a few customers. But at the same time, I figured, what were the chances that Internet trolls like these would ever make a trip to France, anyway? If for some reason they did, they'd be in for a big surprise. That's because BIA's brand-new, number-one bestselling milkshake just happened to be called...the "Obama Milkshake."

At the same time as the elections were occurring, there was another historic event that shook everything up: the economic crisis of 2008. And, just as with the Iraq war, I was worried that it might hurt business. *Au contraire.* As the world's economy spun out of control, the lines at BIA got longer and longer. A lot of medium- and high-end restaurants in Paris were going out of business, but BIA seemed to be immune to the crisis as customers appreciated our reasonable prices more than ever.

Ironically, as Wall Street tanked, I ended up sending my investors their biggest dividend check yet—more than 15 percent ROI. Some of my investors said that if they'd known it was going to turn out this well, they would have invested all of their money in BIA instead of in Wall Street.

"Speaking of which," they asked, "what's going on with BIA #3?"

I was afraid my investors were going to ask me that question. According to BIA's business plan, there should have been a third diner by now. I wasn't sure how to answer them, if I should let them know that I'd been held up lately—as in *jailed.* Instead, all I said was, "Soon. Soon."

Truth be told, there was another, more personal reason why BIA #3 wasn't at the top of my list of priorities. I wanted to spend as much time as I could with Julien before he moved to Taiwan. He left that August, right before Obama's election. At the security gate at Charles de Gaulle airport, Julien and I hugged each other for as long as we could before he had to board the plane. As he took the escalator down to passport control, I smiled and waved at him until he slowly disappeared into the crowds. As tears welled up in my eyes, I realized that it had been a long time since I'd cried at an airport. But this time, it was different. This time, I wasn't the one going away. I was the one being left behind.

I didn't know how I should feel. Part of me was happy knowing that Julien was getting a chance to live *his* dream abroad, but the other part of me was convinced that I was going to lose him forever.

With Julien gone, I focused my energy on a new project—expanding both BIAs. At BIA #1, we built an enclosed sidewalk terrace, which added more than a dozen seats. With French bureaucracy being what it was, it had taken more than two years to get the approval to do it. But it was worth the wait, because we were now able to move the lines a lot faster.

At BIA #2, the situation was a little more complicated. For the second time since we'd opened, the boutique next door went out of business. I wanted to expand into that space, but before I could take it over, I needed to make sure that we'd be allowed to knock down the wall that adjoined the two places. That meant I'd have to ask for approval from the nasty French neighbors who, of course, hated our guts. When they got wind of our plans to expand, they called an emergency meeting and voted to forbid us from ever being able to tear down the wall.

Just when it looked like the deal would fall through, the boutique's ancient landlady dug up some documents dating back to the nineteenth century. The documents showed that both spaces used to be one and that the wall had been built at the turn of the century. While this clever bit of legal maneuvering didn't allow us to tear down the wall, it *did* allow us to carve out a doorway between the kitchen and the new dining room. And just like that, BIA #2 had thirty-five new seats. Combined with the original location, we had expanded the whole BIA operation by almost fifty new seats! So in a way, it was kind of like having a third BIA after all.

Every lucky streak must come to an end. Ours happened when BIA #2 got a surprise visit from an *inspecteur du travail*, who had come with some unsettling news: I could no longer do temporary contracts (CDDs) for my employees, which I'd relied on so much in the past. Instead, I was now required to do permanent contracts *only* (CDIs), just like I'd done so disastrously for Stewart. That did not bode well for BIA, especially since, after our expansion, I needed to hire a bunch of new staff.

Making matters worse, there was now a slew of new restrictive labor laws that were so complex, I had to enlist the help of a consultant from the government to help me make sense of them all. Not surprisingly, she ended up contradicting nearly everything that the *inspecteur du travail* had told me, leaving me more confused than ever.

"Ah, Monsieur Carlson," the consultant said, "you cannot listen to *inspecteurs* too much. They're just *fonctionnaires*," said the *fonctionnaire*.

Without skipping a beat, the consultant gave me a list of all the new laws I needed to learn, or else risk getting into serious trouble. Perhaps my favorite was what I nicknamed the "vacation law." It was now my responsibility to remind all my employees—in writing—to take their vacations.

"Since when does anybody in France need to be reminded to take their vacations?" I asked incredulously.

"Monsieur Carlson, you do not understand. If an employee does not take his vacation and becomes depressed, he can blame you for his unhappiness."

"Really?" I said sarcastically. "Then in that case, you've just proven that the French will never be happy."

"What do you mean?"

"Well, if I make everyone take their vacation, then it follows that everyone should be happy. But in France, everyone takes their vacations already—and they're still miserable. Ergo, the French will never be happy. So why do I need to remind them to take their damn vacations?"

"Hmm," the consultant said, nodding her head. "You do have a point."

I decided to pick the consultant's brain about some of the other problems I was having with my employees.

"I have a cook who always comes in late," I said. "But not just a few minutes late...*hours* late. I've given him warning letters, but nothing changes—even when I dock his pay."

"Wait, wait, wait," the consultant said, holding up her hand. "You can't do that!"

"Do what?"

"Dock someone's pay. It's against the law!"

Again, this was news to me. "But why should I pay someone for hours they haven't worked?"

"*Because...*" she said as if I were the most heartless person in the world. "What if he has *children*?"

"Well, if he has children, then he needs to be responsible and come to work!"

I couldn't believe what was coming out of my mouth! I was starting to sound more and more like a right-wing Republican every day, even though in the United States, I'd been registered as an independent. The *last* thing I wanted was to be seen as a mouthpiece for Fox News, but, unfortunately, France wasn't making it easy for me; I had to constantly remind myself what it was that I believed in.

So just to be clear, I believe in five weeks' paid vacation, universal health care, maternity leave (and, yes, paternity leave—but within reason), worker protections, and paid overtime (but *please*, not until an employee has worked at least thirty-five hours!).

Furthermore, I believe that being a business owner and job creator is a *privilege*, one that does not give me free rein over my employees to decide whether they receive these rights or not. No, I believe that the government—as in, the folks we freely elect to work for us—should be fighting for the little guy. But in France, just because I believe that I should have the right to fire a bad employee, I'm considered a heartless exploiter. *Absurde.*

While Julien was away in Taiwan, we Skyped each other every week. Then halfway through the year, he told me that the University of Taipei, where he was teaching French (and learning Chinese), wanted to extend his contract for a second year.

I could feel my heart pounding. "What did you tell them?" I asked.

"Nothing yet," Julien said. "I wanted to talk to you first."

I was so torn. I didn't want Julien to miss out on such a great opportunity, but at the same time, I missed him terribly and wished he were back in my arms. Before I had a chance to respond, Julien said, "Don't worry, *mon petit.* We don't have to decide until the end of the year."

Did he just say "we"? Ah, I liked the way that sounded. Maybe there was a chance I wasn't going to lose Julien after all.

As the lines outside the diners continued to grow, the situation behind the scenes was slowly starting to spin out of control.

Feeling empowered by all the new labor laws, many of my employees began to push the envelope to see what they could get away with. Forget about coming into work late; they soon figured out that they didn't have to come into work at all. All they had to do was walk into any doctor's office in the city and ask for an "*arrêt de travail*" (a work stoppage, or sick note) and, *voilà*—instant time off!

For some reason, the duration of choice by most doctors seemed to be *quinze jours*—fifteen days, or two weeks off. I couldn't believe how cavalier doctors were, handing out *quinze jours* as if they were lollipops. Worst of all, it didn't matter whether an employee was actually sick or not. All they had to do was tell the doctor that their back hurt or they were stressed (or anything else their active imaginations could come up with) and *boom*—*quinze jours*, no questions asked.

Once word got out how easy it was, employees found it difficult to resist. And why would they? No matter how many days off they took, they were guaranteed their salary, part of which was paid by social security, and the other part of which was paid by me.

I watched helplessly as giddy employees discovered they could get as many *quinze jours* as they wanted. At one point, one of my cooks had amassed so many that he ended up working only *one month* during an entire year. The rest of the time he was at home taking care of his "sore wrist."

Perhaps my favorite *quinze jours* story of all was when our newest manager at BIA #1, Ludo, went to see a doctor because he was having some sinus problems. Without doing any tests, the doctor filled out a form and handed it to him.

"*Voilà! Quinze jours!*"

Ludo hadn't gone to the doctor with the intention of taking time off and was feeling a little guilty. "Is it okay if I go back to work?" he asked.

"Sure," the doctor said. "But you are *not* allowed to go anywhere near food."

Ludo took his *quinze jours*.

Perhaps what was most upsetting to me was seeing good employees like Ludo start off with a strong work ethic, then slowly get corrupted by the French system. This happened most often with foreign employees who also happened to have a French partner. Such was the case with our newest head chef at BIA #2, Curt. Originally from Boston, Curt started off with a very positive attitude—just raring to go. But, little by little, he changed.

The first warning sign came when he asked for weekends off—*all* weekends. I reminded him that BIA was a restaurant, which meant that weekends were our lifeblood. But Curt said that his wife wanted him to stay home on weekends to be with their kid.

Fair enough. But what I should have said was, "Perhaps an office job would suit you better." Instead, I caved and said, "Okay, but on one condition: since you're the head chef, promise you'll check in on weekends from time to time."

"Of course!" he said.

Of course, he didn't.

A few months later, Curt stepped into my office and proclaimed, "I have great news! My wife and I are going to have another baby!"

"That's great!" I said. "Congratulations!"

With his family growing, Curt asked if he could get a raise. Not wanting to come off as a Scrooge I said, "Sure." How did Curt show his appreciation? Right after his baby was born, he sent me a *lettre recommandée*—in perfect French, of course. It said that according to article such and such in the worker's code, he was taking a year off—on paid paternity leave—which just happened to include his brand-new raise.

As Curt grabbed his things from the office, he said, "Don't worry, Craig. I'll be back next year, all rested up and raring to go!"

Eleven months later, right before he was supposed to come back to work, Curt sent me a text message: "I've decided to take another year off." He then cited the *update* to article such and such in the worker's code, which now gave him the right to a *second* year of paternity leave. Of course, there was absolutely nothing I could do about it. By law, I had to hold his job for him, while at the same time it was impossible to find a temporary replacement. This ended up completely disrupting the kitchen and, by extension, the whole restaurant.

As Curt's second year of paternity leave came to an end, the kitchen staff and I scrambled to get ready for his return. But it was all for naught. Mere days before he was set to start work again, Curt sent one last *lettre recommandée*, this one saying that he had decided to move on. In other words, *"Merci ...and screw you!"*

You might be wondering how in the world businesses survive in France. I was starting to wonder myself. But somehow they did. I thought about André's restaurant. How was it that we all worked upwards of fifty hours a week, but only got paid for thirty-five, and none of us complained? Same with other restaurants. They had to adhere to the same crazy French laws as I did, but somehow they managed to get through it. Why was that?

At that moment, I realized where the problem lay: Professor Windbag and those snooty brats at USC had been right—I didn't have a management plan. Or more precisely, I didn't have *good management*. After my jail incident, it became abundantly clear that my general manager just wasn't cutting it.

Derrick was the perfect example of the Peter Principle, a theory in business that states that an employee will eventually get promoted to his or her level of *in*competence. That's what had happened with Derrick. He'd been great working in the kitchen and on the floor, but he just didn't know how to manage people. Or lead them. Or motivate them. For example, one time Derrick walked into the diner right after a mad lunch rush.

"Oh my God, Derrick!" a waitress said as she wiped sweat from her brow. "You should've seen me! I just did, like, thirty milkshakes in the last half hour! All by myself!"

"What do you want me to say?" Derrick said coldly. "Thanks for doing your job?"

What caused me the most concern, however, was how Derrick let so many important things slip through the cracks. I never knew what I'd discover next, what oversight would send me back to court...or worse.

I gave Derrick every opportunity to rise to the level of his position. But month after frustrating month, nothing changed, especially his wandering hands, which were starting to become a real problem. I was getting a lot of complaints from waitresses about his behavior, which was not good, especially because France was on the verge of passing sexual harassment laws for the first time in its history.

Given the risks, I had to do something. But of course, I couldn't fire him. Nor did I want to. Fortunately, I had another option. Thanks to another new law (this one working in my favor for once), I could ask Derrick for "a divorce." President Sarkozy, a divorcé himself, had just passed a law called the *rupture conventionnelle*, which allowed employers and employees to separate ways, much like a divorce, without the risk of a lawsuit.

There was one catch, however. Both sides had to agree to the divorce. For days, I mulled over what to say to Derrick. He'd been part of the family for so long, I didn't want to hurt him. But I had no choice. The whole experience was extremely difficult, like breaking up with a girlfriend (or, in my case, a boyfriend).

As fate would have it, the day I was about to have the talk with Derrick, he was diagnosed with cancer. And to complicate matters, his treatment wasn't covered by social security, because his visa had expired—which was news to me. I offered to pay his hospital bills, which included several rounds of chemo. The total came to a very humane €9,000.

After he was out of the hospital, Derrick invited me to his wedding with his French girlfriend, who was kind enough to help him get his French citizenship. Of all the BIA weddings I'd been to, this one was by far the most bittersweet. Still weak from chemo, Derrick insisted on getting back to work. How in the world could I be so cold-blooded as to divorce my wingman now?

They say, "It's lonely at the top." That's especially true when your *chéri* is six thousand miles away. But by the end of the year, I got some great news: Julien didn't take the job in Taiwan! There were three reasons for his decision: first, he wanted to go back to the Sorbonne and finish his master's degree; second, he wanted to gain more experience in the French workforce; and third—*moi*!

Before I knew it, Julien and I were back in each other's arms. I was so proud of him. Not only had he learned to speak and write Chinese fluently, but thanks to his experience abroad, he had also landed a great job in Paris at an Asian cultural association, which allowed him to continue with his studies.

The first things Julien noticed about me when he got back were the dark circles under my eyes and the gray hairs popping up on my head. "*Oh là là, mon petit!*" he said. "What's been going on while I've been away?"

"Where do I start?" I smiled.

While Julien had been in Taiwan, I'd only touched upon the problems I was having at BIA. He was shocked to hear the whole story—how I'd been caught in a Kafkaesque nightmare of French bureaucracy, spending all my time building *dossiers* against rogue employees, even though they probably wouldn't help me in court anyway.

"Don't worry, *chaton*," I said. "I've got everything under control."

As I held Julien in my arms, I thought about what France had taught me all those years ago—the whole "quality of life" thing. That pearl of wisdom resonated with me now more than ever. And with my *chéri* back, I vowed that I would somehow find a way to pull myself back from work so that Julien and I could build a life together.

But unfortunately, the more I tried to pull myself away from BIA, the more I got dragged back in.

The turning point came when BIA reached a total of *seventy employees*—all on permanent *lifelong* contracts. With such a huge staff, Breakfast in America was in danger of losing the personal (and human) side of the business. So much had changed since the days of the Kimmys, the Genevièves, and the Alzbetas. In fact, I had trouble remembering all my employees' names.

Worst of all, the French system seemed to foster a kind of distrust between employer and employee. Despite my best efforts, the more I tried to be the nice guy, the worse things got. As problems continued to mount, I had to ask myself a difficult question: Did I have what it took to be a tough businessman? Or was I, too, a victim of the Peter Principle?

But before I had a chance to answer these questions, two professional con men inadvertently slipped through the cracks, threatening the very survival of BIA. Not to mention my *own* survival.

Government lettres recommandées *with the profile of Marianne—*
the symbol of the French Republic—which always mean trouble.

Chapter 20

ATTACK OF THE
CONTRÔLEURS—PART *DEUX*

"French people are Italian people in a bad mood."

—Jean Cocteau

FOR SAFETY'S SAKE, LET'S CALL THE CON MEN YONAS AND YAKUB.
The two had a lot in common: both were political refugees from
Ethiopia; both started off as dishwashers, one at BIA #1 and the
other at BIA #2; and both were given twenty-hour contracts, which
was supposed to minimize the risk (and expense) should they not
work out. *No such luck.*

From the beginning, I had a gut feeling that something was off
about them, especially Yonas, the mastermind of the two. He would
never smile or joke like the rest of the staff. Instead, he always kept
to himself, never looking me directly in the eye. He also took tons of

smoke breaks, stooped in the doorway of the apartment building next door to BIA, an espresso in one hand and his cell phone in the other.

None of these things in and of themselves were enough to set off any alarms. In fact, Yonas and Yakub were very hard workers, wanting to take on as many hours as they could. They also wanted to learn how to cook, which was fine by us—as long as the proper procedures were followed. They were not.

Unbeknownst to me, Yonas and Yakub had been allowed to work a ton of extra hours—way beyond what was legal. I didn't find out about it until the end of the month, when I was doing payroll. When I saw that Yonas and Yakub had worked *twice* their contracted hours, I was livid. For months, I'd warned my managers that these kinds of oversights had to stop. If we weren't careful, I said, one day someone dishonest was going to slip through the cracks and put BIA at risk.

Unfortunately, that day had arrived.

Seeing the predicament I was in, I quickly drafted up *avenants* (addendums) to their contracts, but Yonas and Yakub refused to sign them, because, as political refugees, they received generous benefits from the government, including rent subsidies and child support. And thanks to the screwy French system, if they worked full-time, they would lose most—if not all—of their benefits. Naturally, Yonas and Yakub wanted to hold on to said benefits. And they were willing to go to great lengths to do so—starting with blackmail. By refusing to sign an addendum, they were able to trap me into a double bind; I couldn't put their extra hours on their payslips without an updated contract. But at the same time, I had to figure out a way to pay them for their extra hours, or else they could report me to the labor board. Of course, all this could have been avoided if France simply allowed for greater flexibility—that is to say, if overtime actually started *after* thirty-five hours a week.

But since that's not how it works in France, my hands were

tied. I had no choice but to pay all their extra hours out of my own pocket—as in, *cash*. Big, big mistake.

Yep, I was in the *merde*. Really deep. I had to figure a way out somehow. I decided to set up an emergency meeting with Yonas at a café. There, I offered Yakub and him permanent, full-time contracts as cooks—and with a very good salary. When Yonas saw the amount I was offering, he shook his head, grabbed a pencil and a piece of paper, and wrote down two figures. The first one was the salary I'd just proposed. The second showed how much he'd make working only twenty hours a week coupled with his government benefits.

There was no comparison. Yonas would make nearly twice as much milking the system than by working full-time. I tried to make Yonas see that he was being shortsighted. Having the title of professional cook on his résumé would help him immensely in the future, I said. Not to mention all the perks he'd be eligible for, like paternity leave.

Yonas wasn't buying any of it. "You don't understand," he said, pointing to the bigger of the two numbers. "I want *that*."

But to get "that," I would have to break the law—in a major way. *Pas possible!* I did not want to end up back in the slammer.

With complete *sang-froid*, Yonas said it would be in both of our best interests to continue doing things exactly as we were. Meaning, he would work full-time, but BIA would only declare half. The rest he would receive in cold, hard cash.

I shook my head. "You know I can't do that, Yonas," I said.

"Why not?" he said. "Other restaurants do."

"Well, then, you can go work for them."

Yonas paused, took a sip of his espresso, then said in a soft tone, "Look, all I want is to be able to provide for my kid."

I could feel the pull of the nice guy inside me wanting to help. But I had to resist. "I'm sorry, Yonas," I said. "The best I can do is keep you on the schedule twenty hours a week. You'll still get your benefits. Isn't that what you want?"

Yonas shook his head. "You still don't get it, do you?" he said, pointing once again at the big number on the piece of paper, which included lots of cash. "I want *that*."

After the meeting, I immediately hired a new lawyer who was recommended to me by my accountants. Valérie was a slick, tough-as-nails ninja warrior who specialized in French labor disputes. I liked her immediately, feeling comfortable enough to tell her everything—including how I'd paid Yonas and Yakub out of my own pocket.

"Okay, not so good," she said. "But not the end of the world either. Did you get them to sign a receipt at least?"

"No," I said, frustrated at myself for not having thought of that.

"Okay," Valérie said. "Listen, whatever you do, keep them on the schedule for their contracted hours. No more, no less. We'll see what their next move is."

I did as I was told. As soon as I posted the schedules, Yonas and Yakub stopped showing up to work.

"Hmm," Valérie said. "I think they're trying to get you to fire them. But we're not going to take the bait, right?"

"Right," I said, my heart racing.

Like an intense, mind-numbing game of chess, Valérie laid out her strategy. First, I had to act as if nothing was happening and continue scheduling Yonas and Yakub for work. Next, I wasn't allowed to hire anyone to replace them, which proved to be a logistical nightmare.

"In the meantime," Valérie said, "I will send *lettres recommandées*, asking for a justification for their absence. We have to prove that they abandoned their posts."

"But isn't that obvious already?" I asked. "I mean, they haven't shown up to work for weeks."

"It's not as easy as that," Valérie said. "You should know that by now."

Unfortunately, Yonas and Yakub were already several steps ahead of us. While they were absent from work, they'd gone to see the labor board, filing an official complaint against BIA. Within a few days, we received a *lettre recommandée* from the work inspector himself. It contained a long list of grievances, all of which were lies—and all of which, unfortunately, were impossible to disprove.

For example, Yonas and Yakub said that the conditions at BIA were extremely dangerous and that we had blatantly ignored security codes, which ended up injuring them for life. How so? Our floors were too hard, they said. Standing on them destroyed their knees. Yakub, the dim-witted one of the two, went so far as to walk around with a fake limp, sometimes forgetting which leg was supposed to be injured.

When my kindly sous-chef at BIA #1, Fikru, a fellow Ethiopian, found out what Yonas and Yakub were doing, he took me aside and said that the other Ethiopian cooks had played soccer with them over the weekend, and they'd both looked fine. But when I asked the cooks if they would give testimonials, nobody wanted to get involved.

What was most hurtful, though, was the way Yonas and Yakub took every kind gesture I had made toward them and turned it against me. Remember how they wanted to cook? Well, now they were saying it was never in their contracts and that I had forced them to cook. Remember how they didn't want me to declare all their hours so that they could get their government benefits? Well, now they were saying that I had forced them to work extra hours and refused to pay them for it. Of course, being the monster that I am, I had also refused to give them full-time contracts, which they'd begged for.

"These guys are good," Valérie said. "Really good."

There was no longer any doubt; Yonas and Yakub were on the

warpath. By not showing up to work for weeks on end, they had set up the perfect trap for us. Valérie and I were forced to follow all the proper procedures (including summoning them to three interviews) before we could let them go for abandoning their posts.

Shortly thereafter, we received two more *lettres recommandées* from the government, one at BIA #1 and one at BIA #2, but both for the same thing: Yonas and Yakub had filed a double lawsuit against us, using fake schedules to justify months of back pay and damages owed to them.

"How can the government let these guys get away with this?" I said in exasperation. "It's so obvious they're lying through their teeth about *everything*!"

"*Ben, oui,*" Valérie said. "*C'est la France!*" Then after a beat, she added, "I'd be careful not to call them liars out loud. If somebody records you saying it, you could be sued for defamation of character."

So much for being able to have more time to spend with my *chéri*. It was now the winter of 2011, and I was being sucked into the *merde* more than ever. Fortunately, though, with the holidays just around the corner, I could count on one thing: *contrôleurs* went on *vacances* too, which gave me a slight respite from all the madness.

To boost my morale, Julien invited his mom to our place for Christmas. Racing up from Dijon on the TGV, Elisabeth toted a huge suitcase stuffed with a scrumptious holiday dinner, already prepared. It included *escargots* that Elisabeth had hunted down herself—as well as foie gras and *poulet aux morilles* (chicken with a creamy mushroom sauce). *Délicieux!* French comfort food at its best!

With the fireplace in our apartment aglow, the three of us raised our glasses of champagne for a toast.

"To 2012," Julien said. "I just know it's going to be our best year yet!"

"Here, here," I said. "It certainly can't be worse!"

The three of us laughed, and for one brief but shining moment, I was able to forget my troubles.

With the holidays over and Parisians back to work, I prepared myself for "Attack of the *Contrôleurs*—Part *Deux*," this time, bigger, meaner, and more horrific than ever! Sure enough, no sooner had the New Year started when I got a call from Ludo, BIA #1's manager.

"They're *heeere*."

"Which one?" I asked, trying to stay calm.

"The health department."

Oh shit. These guys were the worst. Fortunately, I knew our kitchen was spotless. But unfortunately, I'd been having a lot of problems with my head chef, Markus. In fact, I'd just sent him a warning letter about some other, non-health-related, oversights on his part.

"The *inspecteur* wants to talk to you," Ludo said.

"Okay," I said, my heart racing. "Put him on."

"Monsieur Carlson," the *inspecteur* said through the phone. "I'm afraid I'm going to have to shut you down."

Oh God, no! I thought. I'd vowed that this would never happen again.

"Why?" I asked, my eyes tearing up.

Just as I had feared, the *inspecteur* rattled off the exact same things I'd warned Markus about, such as *not* recording temperatures of the fridges and *not* keeping the labels from the beef. What upset the *inspecteur* the most, however, was that Markus had left a bottle of bleach beside the grill oil.

"For that alone, I must shut you down," the *inspecteur* said. "What if your cook grabbed the wrong bottle? *Quelle horreur!*"

The *inspecteur* went on to explain that he would not be closing us down today. That was the job of the *préfecture de police*.

"You'll be getting a call from them soon," the *inspecteur* said. "They'll give you instructions as to what to do next."

"How long will we be closed down for?" I asked.

"That depends on you," the *inspecteur* said cryptically.

As soon as I heard from the *préfecture*, I understood exactly what the *inspecteur* had meant. To punish us, the *inspecteur* had come up with a long list of renovations that we had to complete before we could reopen. They included repainting the whole restaurant, building a wall in the *cave* beside the dumbwaiter (the area where we kept the garbage bins), and a million other little things that could take weeks to finish.

And just like last time, I had to wait for orders from the *préfecture* telling us exactly when to shut down. Mercifully, this time they chose a Monday, not a Friday. As we scrambled to finish the renovations in order to reopen, I met with Markus to discuss his role in getting us shut down.

"Hey, don't blame me," he said with a shrug. "It wasn't *my* fault."

The next day, I contacted the *inspecteur*. "*Pardon, monsieur,*" I said. "But I need to confirm something with you: Is it true that you closed us down because of the actions of my head chef?"

"*Oui,*" the *inspecteur* said. "*Oh là là,* that bleach! *Quelle horreur!*"

"Would you be willing to put that down in writing?"

"*Non,*" the *inspecteur* said. "But if I'm summoned to court, I will testify." Clearly, the *inspecteur* knew what I had in mind. "Monsieur

Carlson," he continued, "let me say one last thing: If I come back and see any of the same infractions again, I will close you down for much longer. Perhaps indefinitely."

That sealed the deal for me. I summoned Markus for a second interview. He still wouldn't take any responsibility for his actions. Even worse, he clearly had no intention of changing his ways. With BIA's very survival at stake, I had no choice but to summon Markus to a third interview and let him go.

Within days, the inevitable *lettre recommandée* arrived in the mail.

Here it was—the perfect storm: three lawsuits running simultaneously; BIA #1 closed down (with no head chef); and just when I needed him most, BIA #1's manager, Ludo, suddenly disappeared. For days, I had no idea if he was dead or alive. Then out of the blue, he began sending me unsettling text messages, most of which centered around his recent breakup with his wife. Every few minutes or so, my phone would vibrate, and I'd look and see a message like this: "Loneliness has been described as social pain which frequently occurs in heavily populated cities."

After his fifth no-show week, I asked Valérie if I could finally let Ludo go—for abandoning his post and all that jazz.

"*Oui,*" Valérie said. "We can begin the *dossier.*"

"Thank God," I said, "because I can't take any more of his crazy *textos.*"

"Wait," Valérie said. "What *textos?*" After I read them to her, Valérie suddenly changed her tone. "*Oh, non, non, non!* You can't let him go. Obviously, he is *not* psychologically *apte.* If he were to jump in front of the *métro,* you'd be responsible!"

Why was I not surprised? First, I'd been responsible for my employees' happiness. And now I was responsible for their very lives.

According to Valérie, I was required to summon Ludo for an appointment with our assigned workplace doctor so that she could do a psychological evaluation of him. After I summoned Ludo to the doctor's office, he sent me a text saying: "Bless you for caring about me so much! Nobody else does ☹."

I waited in agony for the doctor's diagnosis. If it was determined that Ludo was *apte*, I would be forced to let him come back to work.

With *merde* flying all around me, I'd never been more in need of comfort food in my life. I was dying for a CC's Big Mess—our appropriately named breakfast scramble with everything in it but the kitchen sink. But I never got the chance to have my mess—not for breakfast, anyway. That's because as soon as I entered the diner, I saw one of my waitresses standing there with a very worried look on her face.

"I have a message for you," she said.

She handed me a Post-it and explained that she had just received a call from a woman in the States who was crying hysterically. The woman wouldn't leave her name, but she said that I needed to call her back right away because it was an emergency.

I looked at the phone number. The area code looked familiar. *Is that Arizona?* I thought. *Oh my God, did something happen to my sisters?*

I ran up to my office and called the number right away. The voice on the other end answered: "Student loan default department."

It turned out that the whole "emergency" was nothing more than a ruse from a debt collector who had tracked me down in Paris after all these years. *Wow, madame!* I thought. *Hats off to you!*

I'd reached my limit; I no longer wanted to go into work. And when I did go, I would rush into my office and slam the door shut. I was afraid that if one more thing went wrong, I would go completely insane. Valérie advised me *not* to communicate with any of my staff directly. Just *lettres recommandées* only. Anything else was too risky, she said, especially given my state of mind, which was becoming a tad paranoid.

Then one night, as I sat alone in my office, dazed and numb, there was a knock on my door. I stared at the door, too afraid to open it.

Reaching the breaking point; overwhelmingly long lines at BIA #2.

Chapter 21

PARIS SYNDROME

"Paris: only the strong survive."

—Chelsea Fagan[5]

"Who is it?" I asked nervously from behind my closed door.

"Sajan."

Sajan was one of our cooks at BIA #2.

"What do you want?" I asked.

....

5   Fagan discusses Paris Syndrome and its effect on travelers: "Simply put, it's a col-
    lection of physical and psychological symptoms experienced by first-time visitors
    realizing that Paris isn't, in fact, what they thought it would be. Chelsea Fagan,
    "Paris Syndrome: A First-Class Problem for a First-Class Vacation," *The Atlantic,*
    October 18, 2011, http://www.theatlantic.com/health/archive/2011/10/paris
    -syndrome-a-first-class-problem-for-a-first-class-vacation/246743/.

"Uh, nothing..." he said. "It's just... Can I talk with you for a second?"

I took a deep breath, opened the door, and reluctantly let Sajan in. I motioned for him to take a seat. He waited until I sat down first.

"What can I do for you?" I asked, trying to stay calm and professional.

"I wanted to ask...could I please be paid in cash from now on?"

"What? Why?" I said, feeling the blood rushing to my face.

Sajan looked me and started to cry. It was hard to make out what he was saying. Eventually I was able to calm him down long enough to get the full story.

It turned out that Sajan was not really Sajan at all. His identity was made up—a total fabrication. As I dug deeper, I learned that Sajan was Tamil, an ethnic group from Sri Lanka who were being massacred in a bloody civil war. Having barely escaped with his life, Sajan arrived in France only to fall victim to a scheme that took advantage of refugees like him.

The scheme was run by a kingpin in the Tamil community who would supply refugees with fake identities so they could work. In return, their pay would be wired to a special bank account from which the kingpin would take most of the money for himself, leaving only a small percentage for the worker. For the last two months, however, the kingpin had been taking *all* of Sajan's salary. The poor guy was now just one paycheck away from being homeless.

Mon dieu... I was about to collapse from it all. All I had wanted was to have pancakes in Paris. Not this. Not all this.

I had no idea what to say to Sajan. I felt tremendous compassion for him, especially since he was one of the sweetest and hardest workers BIA had ever had. But I needed to speak with my lawyer first. I told Sajan that I would get back to him as soon as possible. He nodded, wiped the tears from his eyes, and went back to work.

First thing in the morning, I called Valérie. "You have to let him go—immediately!" she said.

"What...with no warning? No interviews?"

"No," she said. "This time you have no choice. If an *inspecteur* comes in and finds a *sans-papiers* working there, not only will you be shut down right on the spot, but there's a strong chance you could end up in prison."

Been there, done that. No thank you!

When Sajan came back to work the next day, I had to give him the sad news and send him home right away. He left in tears.

That night, the thoughts of Sajan weighed heavily on my mind. That, and the trio of lawsuits. And the closure of BIA #1. And the vanishing Ludo. I lay in bed all night with my eyes wide-open, my heart pounding. A friend of mine had a great way of describing what I was going through—when you can't sleep because your mind is racing a million miles a minute with everything that can and will go wrong: "Radio KFUK: all the hits, all the time!"

Julien, who usually sleeps like a rock, couldn't sleep either. He was worried about me. "*Ça va, mon petit?*" he asked.

"*Oui, oui,*" I said, giving him a big hug and a *bisou*. "I've got you by my side. What more do I need?"

The next morning, I went into BIA #1 bright and early, determined to finally have my breakfast, without any crazy interruptions. Fikru, who had taken over the role of head chef, knew exactly what I wanted before I asked: CC's Big Mess with swiss cheese instead of cheddar, extra ham, and triple the garlic. *Yum!*

I barely had a chance to finish my last—and best—bite, when Fikru motioned for me to meet him in the *cave*. "I hope you won't be mad," he whispered, "but I was able to convince Yonas and Yakub to meet with you. Maybe we can stop all this."

I was touched by Fikru's kind gesture, telling him that I shared his desire to move on too. And even though Valérie had warned me never to talk with Yonas and Yakub without a lawyer present, I agreed to meet with them anyway—at a café near Hôtel de Ville.

Of course, Yonas and Yakub had no desire to negotiate; their goal was to *intimidate*. As usual, Yonas did all the talking. With a cigarette in one hand and a *café* in the other, he told me that he had "foot soldiers" working on the inside at BIA, ready to expose us for all the ways we were breaking the law if I wouldn't give in to his demands. Our meeting was very brief; I didn't stick around to hear more.

As I raced back to my office, I tried to dismiss what Yonas had said as a bunch of empty threats. But truth be told, I was scared as hell. It didn't help that right after our meeting, I got a strange call from someone who claimed to be a respected leader in the Parisian Ethiopian community. He wouldn't reveal his name, but he said he had gotten my number from one of my cooks (presumably Fikru). The man wanted to apologize for Yonas and Yakub, saying that they did not represent the Ethiopian community. He seemed sincere, but I wasn't sure if I could—or should—trust him.

"Is there any way you can stop them?" I asked.

"We tried," the man said. "But they wouldn't listen to us." Then after a long pause, he said, "We know that you are a good person and that you treat your employees well. I hope that this, at least, is some consolation for you."

"It is," I said. "Thank you."

After the strange phone call, I wanted nothing more than to hide in my office. But the moment I entered BIA #2, it was like a scene in a horror movie. Staff members rushed toward me as I tried to make my way across the dining room. Lucy, my assistant manager, grabbed me by the arm and told me that a band of gypsies had just raided the place, stealing customers' cell phones right off the tables in front of them. When Lucy tried to stop them, one of the gypsies bit her on the wrist.

As I passed through the kitchen door, my cook stopped me to say that we were down to our last drops of maple syrup, cranberry juice, and peanut butter because the ship containing our American supplies was stuck in customs.

In the stairway going up to my office, I passed by my dishwasher, who told me that he'd just met with his social worker and needed to talk to me about his rights. Upstairs, outside my office door, the night cook stood there with a mischievous grin on his face. "How are the lawsuits going?" he asked. He had a look in his eye as if to say, *"Hey, maybe I can get me some serious ka-ching too!"*

I ran into my office, slammed the door shut, and collapsed into my seat. I took a deep breath, trying to clear my head, but no matter how hard I tried, I couldn't get Yonas out of my mind. *Maybe he wasn't bluffing*, I thought. *Maybe there really are foot soldiers on the inside, waiting to bring BIA down.*

I thought about what had brought down the *Titanic*—not one big gash, but thousands of pinholes. *Had I reminded my staff—all seventy of them—to take their vacations? Had I ever texted my manager on his day off—even for an emergency? Were the floors at BIA really that hard? Did any of my other employees have fake identities like Sajan?*

As I felt myself heading toward a nervous breakdown, I tried to remember why I had started BIA in the first place. Wasn't it so I could live in Paris, my favorite city? And hadn't I always wanted to have a home and a family? Of course I did, but this was not how I'd imagined it. *When did my BIA family become so damn dysfunctional?*

At that moment, I couldn't help but think about my poor mom. When I was a kid, I'd always thought that she'd been dragged away to the asylum against her will—and that somehow it had been all my fault. But years later, my grandma Lizzy told me the truth—that my mom had checked *herself* into the hospital, because it was the only way she could get some R & R away from us kids.

I wanted nothing more than to do the same—to escape from my BIA family. And what better way to do so than by taking advantage of the great French social system, just like so many of my employees had?

I went to see my doctor, who, without batting an eye, gave me *quinze jours* of paid leave for "pain and suffering." And best of all, I could renew it as many times as I wanted!

Of course, it was totally absurd; there was no way I could run away from BIA like that. I had too many responsibilities, including payroll, suppliers, taxes, lawsuits, and most importantly, BIA's tenth-anniversary party, which was fast approaching.

I suddenly understood what Fred G., the producer from *Robin Hood,* had been trying to tell me all those years ago—when he said that it was easier to make a movie than to own a restaurant. Even though you may work the same long hours doing both, the difference is that eventually a movie ends. A restaurant never does. It just goes on and on and on.

That night, I was up for hours with strange heart palpitations and rashes breaking out all over my body. Julien was becoming so concerned about me that he offered to quit his job at the Asian Association so he could help me with BIA. I told him not to worry—I'd be fine.

The next morning, the two of us decided to go for a quick jog, sure that it would help relieve some of my stress.

As we made our way along the *quais* of the Seine, I thought about the mantra that Todd, my first investor, had given me years ago. But this time, I got it right, having had so many opportunities to use it since my jail incident: "Remember, Craig, you're living your dream…"

I couldn't help but smile as I repeated the mantra to myself, "I'm living my dream. I'm living my dream."

Slowly, I became aware of the warm morning sun on my shoulders. It felt good. I looked to my left and saw the magnificent Conciergerie, a former medieval palace where Marie Antoinette had been held prisoner during the revolution. And up ahead—the Louvre museum, with its "lady with the mystic smile."

Julien and I continued jogging toward the tunnel that runs underneath rue de Rivoli and Pont Neuf. The moment we entered the tunnel, I felt a wall of cold, clammy air on my skin then a strange tingling sensation moving up my legs, followed by…total darkness.

Julien stared at me in horror as my eyes rolled up into my head, and I collapsed with a thud, unconscious, onto the lovely *quais* of the Seine.

Living my dream in France.

Chapter 22

THE BIG CHILL

"As you simplify your life, the laws of the universe will be simpler."

——Henry David Thoreau,
paraphrased from *Walden*

WITH TUBES STICKING OUT OF MY ARMS, I LAY IN A HOSPITAL BED, MY French-size hospital gown bursting at the seams from my American-size girth. A no-nonsense nurse came in and plopped a lunch tray in front of me.

"*Voilà!*" she said. "*Bon appétit!*"

Just as quickly as she entered, the nurse spun around on her heels and was halfway out the door.

"Um…*excusez-moi, madame?*" I said, raising my hand weakly.

The nurse stopped in her tracks, turned, and looked back at me from the doorway, a tinge of annoyance in her voice. "*Oui?*"

"I have a *petite question*," I said, struggling to get the words out just right. "Am I...*still*...in France?"

"*Mais oui, monsieur!* Of course!" she said, as if I were the luckiest guy in the world. Then, seeing the worried look on my face, she smiled and softened her tone. "Ah, do not worry, *monsieur*. You're just disoriented from the anesthesia, that's all."

"No, it's not *that*..." I said, staring at my sad lunch tray, which consisted of a stale roll of bread, a soggy pad of butter, some generic cherry yogurt, and a Carrefour cereal bar. "It's just...since France is the *gastronomique* capital of the world, I expected the hospital food to be way better than this."

The nurse let out a deep, guttural laugh. "Hah, that's a good one, *monsieur*! Hah! I can't wait to tell the girls!" And with that she was gone, her laughter echoing down the painfully clean hallways of the cardiology ward.

I looked down at my lunch. Comfort food this was *not. But no need to worry*, I told myself. Just like in the last scene of *It's a Wonderful Life*, I was sure that once the news of my collapse got back to BIA, my staff and customers (along with some miscellaneous villagers) would come bursting through the door any minute, bearing baskets of delicious goodies...telling me how appreciated I was...and how life just couldn't go on without me.

Right on cue, the door burst open. But instead of a frantic crowd, it was Julien, all by himself. That was fine by me. I was so happy to see him.

Julien smiled and came over to the bed and put his arm around me. "How are you feeling, *mon petit?*"

"*Pas mal*," I said.

"You look so cute lying there like that." He smiled and pulled out his cell phone and started taking pictures of me as I struggled to squeeze into my bare-assed, pint-sized hospital gown. "Ha! Looks like you're gonna have to cut down on the pancakes, pancake kid!" he teased.

"Very funny, *petit con!*"

As I lay there awaiting the results of a myriad of tests, I thought about my last checkup with my doctor, the delightful Dr. Nathalie, three months earlier.

"Your blood pressure is good," she'd said. "And your sugar and cholesterol levels—all fine. But, Monsieur Carlson, do me a little favor, yes? Try to do something about *this.*" She rubbed my belly as if I were the Pillsbury Doughboy. I tried not to giggle like a fool. "Perhaps you can start by cutting back on all those…" Dr. Nathalie flashed me a devilish grin, "how do you say in English…*crêpes américaines?*"

"Okay, okay, I got it!" I grumbled. "*Entendu* already!"

When Dr. Nathalie got wind of my collapse, she insisted that I go see a cardiologist *tout de suite* because, quite frankly, she was stumped. She wanted to know exactly what had transpired on the *quais.* I ended up taking a barrage of tests, including an angiogram, which the nurse alerted me was only partially covered by social security.

"Okay," I said. "How much will I have to pay?"

"Two hundred euros," the nurse said. *Imagine that—for a full day in the hospital.* When I told the nurse how much the same procedure would cost in the States, her eyes went wide. "*Mon dieu!*"

In the end, the test results pointed toward a heart attack, but the final diagnosis was stubbornly inconclusive. The first cardiologist I met with, an aloof woman who treated me like a case from a medical textbook, wanted to put me on heart medication for the rest of my life—despite the fact that my cholesterol level and blood pressure were both fine.

I decided to get a second opinion and made a *rendez-vous* with a grizzled, old-school doctor. Unlike the first cardiologist, this doctor listened—I mean *really* listened—to my *whole* story, including the events that led up to my collapse. He then nodded calmly, took my blood pressure, and finished by giving me an EKG.

After studying the results of my tests, the doctor sat there for a moment, like a Zen master. I could see in his eyes that he was processing everything based on years of experience. This method was much more reassuring to me than any computer analysis ever could be.

The old doctor came out of his thoughts, took a deep breath, and said, "Want to know what I think, Monsieur Carlson?"

"*Bien sûr,*" I said.

"I think you simply collapsed from all the *merde* at your work," he said. "My prescription: more rest. Less stress."

I smiled. That's exactly what my gut had been saying.

After my brush with death, I took some time to do a little soul searching. I thought about how shaken up Julien had been by almost losing me. It made me realize that things had to change; otherwise, Breakfast in America—my dream—was going to kill me.

I also thought about an article my friend had sent me, which quoted *Permission to Parent*, a book by Dr. Robin Berman, a psychiatrist who focuses on healthy child development. Since my friend knew all about my childhood, she thought I'd find the article interesting. It was much more than that; it was very apropos, given all the challenges I'd been facing at BIA. Especially this line:

> Children [of narcissists] worry that if they assert
> themselves as adults, they will risk losing love. As
> a result... They want to please everybody all the
> time...in order to feel loved...

That was it. That was me. I had the "disease to please."

When I showed Julien the article, he smiled and wrapped his arms around me. "Haven't I always told you that, *chaton*," he said. "You're just too sweeet!" Julien began to smother me with *beaucoup de bisous*. As always, resistance was futile.

There was no doubt about it; it was time to clean house at BIA. In a way, it was like starting all over again. But this time, I didn't have to take on such a monumental task by myself. I had Julien by my side. He quit his job to come help me at BIA.

What a difference a Frenchman makes! Not only did Julien instinctively know how to make sense of all those crazy, illogical, contradictory French laws, but he also got great pleasure out of what he called "smashing butts!" In other words, no more *Monsieur Nice Guy*!

The first order of business: Derrick. With France finally passing sexual harassment legislation, his wandering hands were just too much of a risk. It was time for that divorce, once and for all. But before doing so, I made absolutely sure that his cancer was in full remission. It was. And just like in any good divorce, Derrick wanted a big settlement. I negotiated it down some, but in the end, knowing that he'd been with us from the beginning, I paid him what he asked for.

Next on the list: Ludo. I appealed to our workplace doctor not to declare him *apte*. I even sent her copies of his crazy text messages. "After reading these," I wrote, "I think you will agree that Monsieur Ludo is not *apte* to manage thirty employees."

Ludo was barely in the doctor's office for fifteen minutes when she gave him a big ol' *APTE* stamp, which meant I had no choice but to take him back.

Not so fast.

I called Ludo into my office and told him I wanted a divorce. During our entire conversation, I noticed that Ludo kept tilting his head downward, speaking into his shirt pocket.

"Ludo, where's your cell phone?"

"Nowhere," he said.

"May I see it, please?"

Ludo grumbled, then pulled his iPhone out of his shirt pocket. I asked him to hand it over to me. He did. Just as I suspected, the little microphone icon on his phone was on. He'd been secretly recording our conversation the whole time. I let out a sigh of relief. Yes, *relief.* Why? To paraphrase the comedian John Oliver's joke about the National Security Agency wiretapping scandal in America: "Good news! I'm *not* paranoid!"

I made Ludo shut off his phone, then proceeded to give him one very loud piece of my mind, even though in France I was technically breaking the law. I didn't give a *merde* anymore!

I got my second divorce.

Onto the lawsuits, where the strangest thing happened; when I let go of my anger and fear, it seemed to release Yonas and Yakub's death grip on me. In other words, right before our court date, they agreed to settle! Sure, it ended up costing me the equivalent of four of my Disney severance checks, but it was worth it. Their negative energy was no longer a part of BIA—or my life.

That left just one lawsuit: Markus. He surprised me by agreeing to settle as well. But then, at the last minute, he changed his mind. The reason? He caved in to the pressure from his *American* girlfriend, who wanted as much money as she could get her greedy little hands on. (Incidentally, Markus and his girlfriend—who had met at the diner—would go on to get married.) Meanwhile, Markus's case went back to the courts. It would be at least a year before we had a court date—and even longer before there'd be a verdict.

With Breakfast in America's tenth-anniversary party just a couple of months away, Julien and I were finally getting our house in order. But unlike me, Julien didn't wait for things to get out of hand. Instead, he sent off *lettres recommandées* the moment there was even the slightest hint of a problem—especially at BIA #2, which still needed a lot of housecleaning. If there was one thing Julien loved more than "smashing butts," it was building *dossiers*. *Tant mieux* (all the better), because I hated them.

Most exciting of all, though, were the wonderful changes that Julien brought to BIA. For example, there were now more diner dishes that Julien could actually eat, because he came up with a bunch of vegetarian blue-plate specials, such as buckwheat pancakes, as well as dishes for the newest rage to hit Paris—gluten free!

Finally, with Julien leading the way, I was able to move forward on a goal I'd been wanting to achieve for years, but was unable to do on my own: the creation of BIA #3, #4, and beyond! *Ah, oui,* Julien was now BIA's new *directeur de* franchising!

There was just one loose end to tie up. Using the last three years of dividends from BIA, I took care of some old business.

Credit card debt? Settled.

Student loans? See ya!

And I did it all at one low, low price. Strapped for cash after the financial crisis, the Department of Education—as well as some credit card companies—were willing to make a deal if I paid my debt in full. I was happy to take them up on their offer.

Of course, even though I had defaulted on my student loans years earlier, I'd always intended on paying them off, but the collection agent beat me to the punch. As for the credit card companies, however, they had long since given up on me. I ended up tracking *them* down, because I wanted to have a clean conscience.

I was so glad I did, because for the first time in my adult life, I was 100 percent debt free. I could feel a huge weight coming off my shoulders.

With the anniversary party right around the corner, I proudly sent my investors their biggest dividend checks yet—more than fifty percent ROI! Shortly thereafter, I received a phone call from my friend and investor Scott, the hotshot screenwriter. He said that he wouldn't be able to make the anniversary party.

"No problem," I said, knowing how far the trek was. But since I had Scott on the line, I decided to ask him a question. For years, I'd been sending his dividend check to his business manager, and I'd always wondered if he had any idea how much he'd made investing in BIA.

"Nah," he said. "No idea."

"Well, you've more than tripled your investment!" I said proudly.

"That's it? You were supposed to make me a millionaire by now," said the multimillionaire. "Instead, all you've been doing is having a ball over there in Paris—living the *dolce vita!*"

"Yeah, Scott," I said with a smile. "That's me. Living the *dolce vita.*"

BIA's tenth-anniversary boat party with investors, staff, and friends.

Chapter 23

IT *IS* A WONDERFUL LIFE

"Strange, isn't it? Each man's life touches so many other lives."

—Clarence, Angel Second Class, *It's a Wonderful Life*

ON A BITTERLY COLD APRIL DAY (SPRINGTIME IN PARIS, ANYONE?), Breakfast in America celebrated its tenth anniversary. Having survived my "near-death experience," my heart was filled with so much love, I invited nearly everyone who was—or had ever been—part of the BIA family.

It was amazing to see so many special people from different parts of my life all gathered together in one place. My wonderful staff members, both past and present, were there, as well as many people from behind the scenes who had made BIA possible: my caring accountants; my suppliers, including the folks from the beer mafia…er…beer *company*; Catpou and Flo, the extraordinary artists who created BIA's mosaics; my ninja lawyer, Valérie; and even Jean-Tho, *l'architecte-errr*.

Last, but certainly not least, were my incredible investors. I was touched by how many of them had made the long journey over from the States, excited to participate in the festivities.

Just like me, the party was divided into two parts—one French, one American. The evening began with the American part, a pre-party bash at BIA #1. There, we stuffed our faces with greasy-spoon grub—finger foods like sliders, jalapeño poppers, mozzarella sticks, onion rings, and nachos. And to wash it all down, there was bottomless Stella beer, French wine, and *limonade*.

With the diner packed to capacity, my investors Will, Jacquie, Christine, and Diane surprised me by giving heartfelt speeches about how they'd always believed in me and BIA, even though everyone (especially their accountants) had advised them not to invest in such a risky venture.

After BIA, we moved on to the French part of the party, taking a lovely stroll down to the river Seine. There, our *bateau* was waiting for us, docked across from Notre Dame. I stopped and stared at the magnificent cathedral, glowing orange from the sun setting behind it. It had never looked more beautiful.

Then I took a look at the boat. I couldn't believe my eyes. Since Julien had done most of the organizing for the party, I had no idea the boat would be so big. And luxurious! And it was just for us, to cruise down the Seine and dance the night away.

As we climbed on board, the ship's crew greeted us like royalty, handing out flutes of delicious champagne. I felt as if we had embarked on a fancy French version of *The Love Boat*, or as it was called *en français*, "*La Croisière s'amuse*," which literally means, "the cruise ship amuses itself." (Um…let's not go there, okay?)

In contrast to the greasy-spoon grub at BIA, the crew on board the boat served us fancy French delicacies, including an assortment of amuse-bouche such as caviar, salmon, foie gras, stinky cheese, and much, much more.

After much dancing and imbibing, the ship's crew called everybody up to the top deck. There, they wheeled out an enormous tenth-anniversary cake as the crowd cheered. As soon as I blew out the candles, my former waitress, Leslie, characteristically took charge and grabbed the mic from the DJ. She told me to sit down, because she had a surprise for me.

Leslie proceeded to give a speech about how she and many of BIA's international staff had come to Paris, some a little dazed and confused—others downright down and out, with only *centimes* to their name. Luckily for them, "Papa" Craig and BIA had been there to take care of them. Leslie ended her speech by saying that, since I had once worked in Hollywood, she and the staff wanted to present me with an honorary Oscar.

"For 'Best Papa'!" Leslie said. "Because you've been like a father to us!"

There was hardly a dry eye in the house. Especially mine.

But the love didn't stop there. Echoing Leslie's sentiments, Sangeeth, a former head chef at BIA #2, stepped up to tell his story. Originally from India, Sangeeth arrived in Paris penniless and alone. At BIA, he had worked his way up from dishie, to cook, and finally, to the "man in charge." Following his own version of the American dream, Sangeeth moved on to a bigger and better job (in the kitchen at a five-star hotel, no less). But he said that he would always consider the people from Breakfast in America to be more than just friends; they were family.

"It's been a feeling...I..." Sangeeth choked up, struggling to find the right words. "I speak from my heart when I say...I...I've always felt like I'm one among you."

A chorus of *ahs* emanated from the crowd. My heart was bursting with so much joy, I didn't think I could take any more.

Nevertheless, Cameron, the manager of BIA #2, took the mic and told *his* story. Originally from America, Cameron had come to France in search of the family of his estranged French father but unexpectedly found himself at BIA.

"So many of us have come from a lot of faraway places," he said. "With a lot of different kinds of dreams—some pretty big dreams—and we've all found each other here at BIA. And we've all taken care of each other. And we've all shared in each other's weddings and children and heartbreaks and everything else… Breakfast in America represents a lot to all of us," Cameron said, raising his glass to me. "Cheers, Craig!"

The crowd broke into applause. I nearly broke down into tears. Realizing how far my life had come from those days as a kid in Frenchtown—and how many lives BIA had touched—my heart filled with gratitude. And as I looked at the crowd full of beaming faces, I couldn't help but realize that I'd gotten what I'd wished for back in my hospital bed. I'd gotten my *It's a Wonderful Life* moment after all.

I knew then that everything I had ever experienced before— from Ann and Dan; to the letter getting slipped under my dorm room door; to the study abroad program; to *The 400 Blows*; to the LA riots; to the *Robin Hood* show; to my aha moment at the Pantry coffee shop; to the long and arduous journey of finding investors— and yes, even to the trifecta of agonizing lawsuits—*everything* had brought me to this moment—right here, right now.

I raised my glass to the crowd. "I love you all! Let's dance!"

In a funny footnote, not long after the party, my friend Pete told me that he had run into the producer of *Robin Hood*, Fred G., at a book signing for Fred's much-anticipated memoir on Hollywood. The elderly, semi-senile Fred didn't seem to remember Pete, who had also worked on the show. But when Pete told him about me and BIA, Fred jolted back to life, waving his cane wildly and hollering, "I told him never to do a restaurant! It's easier to do a movie!"

Perhaps. But not as wonderfully life-changing as Breakfast in America has been.

*A very special day on the pont de la Tournelle with Julien
and his mom, Elisabeth. September 17, 2015.*

Epilogue:
RECIPES FOR LIFE

SEVEN YEARS AFTER MY JAIL INCIDENT, I FINALLY GOT TO TAKE THAT French-style vacation I'd always wanted. This time, however, Julien and I were joined by his mom, Elisabeth, my *belle-maman*. She wowed my friends back in America with her delicious homemade *bœuf bourguignon* and *tarte aux escargots*, which Elisabeth made using her very own snails that she'd hunted down herself and managed to smuggle past American customs. (Long story…)

Now, back in Paris, I take a long walk around the city, rediscovering what it was that I always loved about France. Can I even count the ways? How about this one: in a nearly unheard of decision, the French court has ruled that my firing of Markus was justified. *Incroyable!*

I think about this as I head over to BIA #3, which opened its doors in October 2015, thanks to the hard work of Julien and two former cooks from BIA, who now own the franchise. I notice that parked in front of the shiny, new diner is a shiny, new delivery truck from one of our suppliers. On the side of the truck is written: "The Number One Supplier of Diners in Paris!" The word "diner" isn't even in quotes or spelled phonetically like I had to do back when I first opened BIA. Instead, the real American meaning of the word— along with a slew of French-owned diners—are now part of the Parisian landscape.

This makes me smile; turns out my crazy dream wasn't so crazy after all.

I continue my stroll down to the Seine, past the spot where I collapsed on the *quais*. Soon I find myself retracing the steps where Madame Marin, now old and frail, once gave me a tour of *her* Paris all those years ago. I walk past the "pearl of gothic architecture," le Collège des Bernardins, which had been a run-down shell of a building back when Madame Marin first showed it to me. Now, it's been completely restored to its former glory, a testament to time and patience.

Next, I stop at the same spot Madame Marin and I did on the bridge behind Notre Dame—not far from where BIA's tenth anniversary boat was docked. Madame was right, I think. Notre Dame is so much lovelier from behind. And seeing it now, its grandeur stirs my soul more than ever. I wonder if this feeling is the closest one can get to understanding the unfathomable. It makes me think of all those who passed over this bridge before me...of how short life is...how it moves on, like the Seine below, with or without us. And I think of how important it is to seize the day, to be grateful for every precious moment while we're alive.

And with each gray hair that pops up in my beard, I think about how, in addition to getting invited to my staff's weddings, I'm now getting invited to their baby showers. And like a doting grandpa, I'm filled with pride knowing that their little baby was, in some small part, created by, and even nourished by, my little diners.

But of all the Breakfast in America weddings I've been to over the years, none was more special than…my own. Yep, on September 17, 2015, Julien and I tied the knot. Although it's a bit of a logistical challenge, we now split our time between Paris and California—enjoying the best of both worlds.

Thomas Jefferson was right after all: every man *should* have two countries—his own and France. I'm fortunate to be one of those men.

Ah, oui…la vie est belle!

RECIPES FROM BREAKFAST IN AMERICA'S KITCHEN

CC's Big Mess

Ingredients

Home Fries

- 2 to 3 Charlotte potatoes
- 2 ounces onions, diced
- 2 ounces peppers, diced
- Minced garlic, to taste

The Mess

- 2 ounces mushrooms, sliced
- 2 strips bacon, cooked and chopped
- ¼ cup ham, diced
- 2 links precooked breakfast sausage, diced
- ¼ avocado, sliced
- 3 large eggs, scrambled
- 2 to 3 ounces sharp cheddar cheese, shredded
- 1 serving home fries

Preparation

To make the home fries, boil the potatoes in a pot for 15 to 20 minutes, or until a knife pierces potatoes smoothly. Drain the potatoes, then run under cold water to destarch them, let cool, and dice into bite-size pieces.

In a frying pan with oil, sauté the onions and peppers on medium heat until slightly browned. Add the potatoes to the frying pan, and cook for 2 to 3 minutes until vegetables are a crispy brown. Add salt and garlic. Remove from stove.

Place the mushrooms in a separate frying pan with oil, and sauté on medium heat until slightly browned. Add bacon, ham, sausage, and prepared home fries, and cook until hot. Shortly before the mix is done, in a separate pan, add the eggs and cook to taste. When all mixtures are finished, pile the home fries mix on a plate in a mountain shape. Next, place the eggs on top, and sprinkle cheese over the dish. Finish by adding the sliced avocado, and serve.

Yield

1 serving

Chef's suggestion: Can also be accompanied by a side of salsa or guacamole.

The Super BJA Burger

Ingredients

The Burger

- ¼ pound hamburger patty
- 1 slice cheddar cheese
- 1 sesame seed hamburger bun
- 1 large lettuce leaf
- 1 slice tomato
- 2 to 3 pickle slices
- 1 slice red onion
- 1 slice red pepper
- 2 strips bacon
- 2 to 3 tablespoons BBQ sauce

Daniel's Special BBQ Sauce

(10 to 12 servings)

- 1 cup ketchup
- ½ cup water
- ¼ cup apple cider vinegar
- 2½ tablespoons light brown sugar
- 2½ tablespoons granulated sugar
- 1 teaspoon fresh black pepper
- ½ tablespoon onion, diced
- 1 teaspoon ground mustard
- ½ tablespoon lemon juice
- ½ tablespoon Worcestershire sauce

Preparation

In a frying pan with oil, brown the red pepper ring, caramelize the onions, and cook the two strips of bacon to your liking (we suggest slightly crispy). In a separate frying pan, cook the burger to your liking. Toast the sesame seed bun. When the burger is almost finished cooking, add a cheddar slice on top. Next, place the pepper ring on top of the cheese, then add the caramelized onion in the middle of the pepper ring. Top it off with the two strips of bacon. To make the BBQ sauce, mix all ingredients in a large bowl, adding each one individually and stirring until mixed. Then, add some sauce to the burger to your liking. Place the toasted burger bun open-faced onto a large plate. Place the burger with the fixings onto the bottom half of the bun and the lettuce, tomato, and pickles on the top half. Serve with french fries or home fries.

Yield

1 serving

Chef's suggestion: Cook the burger "French-style," meaning as rare as you can handle it!

FROM BELLE MAMAN'S KITCHEN

Elisabeth's Boeuf Bourguignon

Ingredients

- 1 tablespoon butter
- 2 tablespoons olive oil
- 4 onions, peeled and diced
- 12 small mushrooms
- 4 to 5 ounces smoked lardon (similar to bacon)
- 3½ pounds beef tenderloin, cut into 1-inch morsels
- 3 cloves garlic, peeled and smashed
- 1 tablespoon flour
- 1 bottle red wine (burgundy or pinot noir)
- 1 small glass of cognac
- 2 small squares of dark chocolate (Elisabeth's secret ingredient!)
- Salt and freshly ground black pepper, to taste

Preparation

Heat the butter and olive oil in a pot. Brown the onions, mushrooms, and smoked lardon, then remove from the pot and place in a bowl. Without cleaning the pot, place the morsels of beef inside and brown on medium heat, adding the garlic cloves at the end. Next, add salt and pepper, then cover the pot and reduce heat, letting the beef simmer for five minutes. Sprinkle in the flour to prepare the roux, stirring briskly, then slowly add the bottle of red wine until the meat is thoroughly drenched. Slowly bring to a boil, then add the browned smoked lardon, onions, and mushrooms. Cover, and let simmer at very low heat for 2 hours, stirring occasionally. (The sauce should be bubbling only slightly.) Remove the pieces of meat and place on a hot serving dish to keep warm. Add the cognac into the pot with the sauce and let cook 2 minutes until boiling point. For the *coup de grâce*, add Elisabeth's secret ingredient to the sauce: 2 small squares of dark chocolate. Pour the sauce over the meat, and serve.

Yield

4 servings

Chef's suggestion: The dish should be accompanied by either white rice (steamed or boiled) or tagliatelle pasta.

Poulet à la Gaston Gérard

Ingredients

- 2 chicken breasts and 2 chicken thighs
- 1 tablespoon flour
- 1 tablespoon olive oil
- 1 teaspoon butter
- 1 cup white wine
- 7 ounces grated comté cheese
- 1 tablespoon Dijon mustard
- 3½ ounces crème fraîche (French-style fresh cream)
- Salt and freshly ground black pepper, to taste

Preparation

Dust the pieces of chicken with flour. In a pot, slowly heat the olive oil and butter until it melts, then add the chicken. Once the chicken has been lightly braised, add the white wine, salt, and pepper. Cover the pot and let simmer for 45 to 60 minutes, stirring occasionally. While the chicken is cooking, preheat the oven to 200°F. Once the chicken is browned, put into a tray and place the tray into the oven. Place the pot back onto the stove, and at low temperature, mix the grated comté cheese into the cooking juice from the chicken, letting the cheese slowly melt while stirring constantly. Once the comté cheese has melted, add the mustard and crème fraîche. Heat until the boiling point, then remove the warm chicken from the oven and pour the sauce on top. Sprinkle more

grated comté cheese on top of the chicken, then place
the tray back into the oven and bake at 350°F until the
cheese is golden brown.

Yield

4 serving

Chef's suggestion: The dish should be accompanied by steamed or boiled
white rice (8 ounces for 4 servings).

ACKNOWLEDGMENTS

When I first had the idea for *Pancakes in Paris*, I never could have imagined that writing a memoir about opening the first American diner in Paris would end up being as difficult as actually *opening* the first American diner in Paris. As I relived each and every crazy and exhausting—but ultimately rewarding—moment from my BIA adventure, I came to appreciate more than ever all the wonderful people who helped me along the way.

First, I'm very grateful for my agent, Andrea Hurst. From the moment we met at a writers' workshop in beautiful Pacific Grove, California, I knew we would be a good fit. She completely clicked with my story and understood my tragicomic tone of writing. Thanks, Andrea, for giving me a second chance.

I'm also very lucky that Andrea found the perfect publisher for me, Sourcebooks, as well as the perfect editor, Anna Michels. Working with Anna was a dream come true. Not only did she have the patience of a saint (putting up with my panic attacks as deadlines approached), but she also helped shape my story, encouraging me to focus on what was important and eliminating what was not—all while keeping me in check every time I strayed off into tangent-land. Along with the rest of the talented people at Sourcebooks, I couldn't have asked for a better team to publish my first book.

Since writing can also be a very lonely endeavor, I'm so grateful for my writer's group. They never seemed to tire of reading draft after ever-changing draft of my chapters. If they did tire of it, they never let on. I'd especially like to thank Paula Sewell, my ideal reader with the world's best sense of humor. Whenever I wrote a joke but wasn't sure if it was working, I would imagine Paula's reaction. If she laughed, the joke stayed. If not, *ba-bye*! Thanks also to Susan Lambert, who always inspired me to do my best.

I'm also fortunate to have so many dear friends who cheered me on along the way: Cecilia and Tim, Jacquie and Gregor, Will and Kelly, Greg and Kimberly, and Rod and Jeff. Thanks also to my earliest supporters: Pat Tobin, the first person to encourage me to write *Pancakes in Paris*; Paula Munier, a fellow Francophile who offered lots of helpful advice; and Iris. B. Goode, who advised me on my original business plan, which I used to raise the funds for BIA.

Which brings me to my wonderful investors, or the makers of the dream. Without their generosity and support, Breakfast in America could never have happened. Many of these individuals are mentioned in the book, but for those who aren't, I'd like to do so now: first-round investors Lionel, Aslam, Lauren, Nico, Tom, Michelle, Glenn, Nils, Susan, and Michael, as well as those who came on board for the second round: Kirt, Bill, Matthew, and Miae.

Of course, I never could have finished *Pancakes in Paris* without the support of my amazing staff at BIA, especially my manager, Brian Downie. While I was locked away in my room for weeks on end, Brian not only held down the fort, but he also went so far as to keep

ABOUT THE AUTHOR

With a background in journalism, Craig Carlson studied at the University of Southern California, where he received an MA in film production. After winning the prestigious John Huston Directing Award, Craig wrote and directed a short film, which won awards at the Chicago International Film Festival as well as the Lucille Ball Comedy Festival. In addition to being a produced screenwriter, Craig worked as a translator for *Letters: Jean Renoir*, a book on the famous French director. In 2003, Craig completely shifted gears and decided to open the first American diner in Paris. After more than a decade in business, Breakfast in America continues to serve authentic breakfasts and burgers to customers from all over the world. *Pancakes in Paris* is Craig's debut memoir.

track of the deadlines for my book, making sure not to disturb me during the busiest times. Cheers, Brian! Thanks to Cameron Finoki at BIA #2 as well.

I would be remiss if I didn't also thank all the angels in my life—the wonderful souls who made sure I stayed on the straight and narrow path when I was growing up. My family, despite having to cope with their own struggles in life, always made me feel loved. Next, the Smith family who "adopted" me into their home: Peg, Jim, Cathy, and Sandy (my sister from another mother).

I would also like to give a shout-out to my fourth-grade teacher, Mrs. Robataille, who somehow saw potential in me when I couldn't; the lady from my paper route, who gave me five dollars for every A I got in school; and Ms. Folio and Madame Bueker, both of whom were kind enough to be my faculty advisors on my high school newspaper, even though my impetuous muckraking could have cost them their jobs.

And finally, I must thank the biggest and most important angel of them all: my husband, Julien (who also happens to be a little devil too). Although he is a very private person, Julien was kind enough to let me share some of our most personal moments in the book. His patience, good humor, and unwavering moral support gave me the strength to finish the marathon that was this book. *Je t'aime fort.*